1 MON' FR~~EE~~ READING

at

www.ForgottenBooks.com

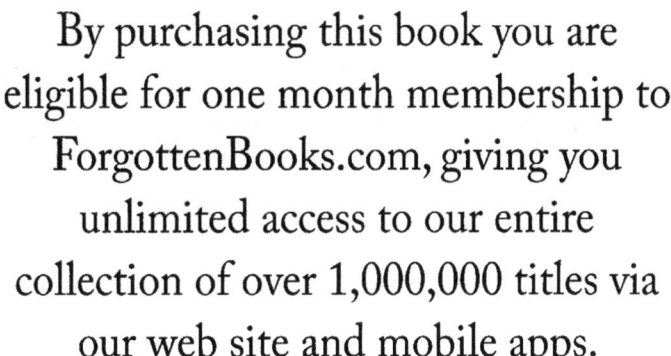

By purchasing this book you are eligible for one month membership to ForgottenBooks.com, giving you unlimited access to our entire collection of over 1,000,000 titles via our web site and mobile apps.

To claim your free month visit:

www.forgottenbooks.com/free661010

* Offer is valid for 45 days from date of purchase. Terms and conditions apply.

ISBN 978-0-331-32664-2
PIBN 10661010

THE
·Practical Bee - Master

IN WHICH WILL BE SHEWN

HOW TO MANAGE BEES

EITHER IN STRAW HIVES OR IN BOXES,

WITHOUT DESTROYING THEM,

AND WITH MORE EASE, SAFETY, AND PROFIT, THA
BY ANY METHOD HITHERTO MADE PUBLIC, VIZ.

I. To manage BEES in Straw Hives, with NEW CONSTRUCTED TOPS, at a small expence, as profitably and easily as with BOXES.

II. In BOXES of an IMPROVED and *cheap* Construction, easily to be managed, and with so little DISTURBANCE to the BEES, that all the necessary operations may be performed without any Danger.

III. To CATCH and secure the QUEEN, or to FIX her and a Swarm to any place you please.

IV. To cause BEES to quit a Hive, and to be so tractable as to suffer themselves to be HANDLED without Stinging.

V. Several Methods of Swarming BEES *Artificially.*

VI. To cause a Swarm to work in separated Glasses, without ANY HIVE; or in globular or other glasses, so that pure Virgin Honey may be taken whe in its UTMOST PERFECTION.

VII. To prevent or cause BEES t swarm.

VIII To take the Honey and yet pre serve the BEES, with *common Hives only*

IX. To unite Casts, Swarms, and Stocks

X. A Catalogue of, and Observation on, the most proper Flowers or Pastu rage for BEES.

XI. An easy and CERTAIN Metho of preserving Stocks in Winter and col Springs.

XII. Several *new* and improved Me thods of extracting the *Wax* from th Combs, two of them without eithe *Straining* or *Pressing*; and each by *single* Operation: but more perfectly and with far less Trouble and Expenc of Fuel than hitherto practiced.

TOGETHER WITH SUCH FULL AND PLAIN DIRECTIONS

That the meanest COTTAGER may attain this profitable A R
Without DIFFICULTY, and at a small EXPENCE;

INTERSPERSED WITH OCCASIONAL DISC

STRICTURES

On Mr. THOMAS WILDMAN's TREATISE ON BEES

WITH SEVERAL NEW DISCOVERIES AND IMPROVEMENTS,
THE RESULT OF LONG EXPERIENCE,

AND DEDUCED FROM ACTUAL EXPERIMENTS,

By JOHN KEYS,

BEE-MASTER.

LONDON:

Printed for the AUTHOR, and sold by him at his House in CHESHUNT-STREET
HERTFORDSHIRE; J. JOHNSON, No. 72, St. Paul's Church-Yard;

ENTERED in the

OF T

COMPANY OF S

ACCORDIN

Act of Pa

December 5

PREFACE.

THOUGH it is not the happy lot of every author to have been nursed on classic ground, yet when any publications have tended more to the benefit than to the mere amusement of the public, the candid have in general kindly thrown a veil over their imperfections in style and manner. The writer of the following pages, the fruits of his evening hours, as none other can be spared from more important avocations, thinking they may, on account of their general utility, have some claim to this indulgence, has presumed to lay them before the public. He pretends not, however, to be wholly disinterested in this publication, but acknowledges that he has some regard to his own interest, as well as to the public good.

A natural predilection in favour of these useful and entertaining insects, first introduced him to their acquaintance. But not meeting with the expected satisfaction from the rules and directions of the most generally approved authors, he was induced to

A   make

make a great variety of experiments ; in the course of which he incurred a confiderable expence, and fuffered much fmart. He thought himfelf, however, amply repaid by their refult, which was entirely to his own fatisfaction, and highly worthy, if vanity and felf-love do not deceive him, of general notice ; whether his difcoveries be really fit to be encouraged, or configned to oblivion, he now fubmits to the judgment of the impartially fkilful.

As every circumftance either unneceffary in real practice, or impracticable in itfelf, except a few which are felected for their novelty, is omitted ; a greater fcope is allowed for the defcriptions, which are particularly minute on the account of novices; who would otherwife meet with many and even infuperable difficulties.

A great number of prevailing, though deftructive, errors are here pointed out, and many new improvements and difcoveries fubftituted.

The heft methods of conducting the various operations are fo particularly and plainly defcribed, as to render the practice familiar and eafy to farmers and cottagers in general : for want of which, works of this kind have hitherto rather difcouraged than promoted a general keeping of Bees.

The author hopes, however, that this treatife will enable the country people to overcome the moft formidable obftacles,

VIZ.

viz. the little profit and often great decreafe, or even the total lofs of their Stocks, in the ufual modes of practice; or the too great expence, lofs of time, and fmart, attendant upon moft of the improved ones yet offered to the public: to which may be added the danger, infufficiency, and uncertainty of them all.

The inquifitive mind will alfo meet with fome things worthy of attention. Particular inftructions will be given how to manage boxes and glaffes of various figures, and in different arrangements, as well for entertainment as emolument. As to what is merely fpeculative on the nature of Bees, it being totally incompatible with the Author's practical plan, he refers the curious to *The Natural Hiftory of Bees,** where they will meet with a very pleafing and accurate account.

It would be entirely labour loft, fhould this method, through over refinement, be not adapted to the general ufe of the peafantry of Great Britain and Ireland. It is from them, and them alone, that any confiderable national increafe of honey and wax is to be looked for: but as very few of this great multitude have any tolerable knowledge of conducting the many neceffary operations of Bees, this branch of rural œconomy is greatly neglected. Bees,

with

---

* *Publifhed by Knapton and Vaillant, 1744.*

with proper management, are capable of multiplying prodigioufly; and it may be afferted, without any exaggeration, that there might be five thoufand times more honey and wax produced than there is at prefent, were every farmer and cottager to keep a reafonable number of Stocks; for then all the honey and wax that the vegetables of thefe kingdoms are capable of fupplying, would be as regularly collected by thefe induftrious infects, as the corn from the fields, or the fruits from the trees; and thereby prevent the neceffity thefe realms are now under, of importing great quantities of thefe very ufeful articles from foreign countries, very much to the national lofs.

It is readily acknowledged, that there is more trouble and more expence attending the method here propofed, than the old one of fuffocation; but, if the profits be trebled, or even doubled, a perfon muft pay very little regard to his own intereft, who fhould prefer the old and leaft advantageous method. What advantages would attend the keeping of poultry and pigs, if a very confiderable portion of care and expence were not beftowed upon them?

Though Bees, with little comparative trouble and expence, afford great profits, yet it is much to be apprehended that there will be no confiderable increafe of thefe beneficial infects, unlefs the patriotic and benevolent gentry in every county will

make

make a point of fetting an example, and
directing a portion of their accuftomed li-
berality to this purpofe. Ruftics are, of
all people, the laft in adopting any *new*
practices, though the *old* be ever fo evidently abfurd. No reafoning, however clear
and ftrong, is able to conquer either their
obftinacy or their prejudices. It is only
by examples of fuperior gain that they
can be roufed to deviate from their ufual
track, and induced to follow any practice
they have once either neglected or de-
fpifed.

The moft probable method of attaining
this certainly defireable object, would be to
prefent a Swarm of Bees and a couple of
new conftructed ftraw hives to poor cottagers of good characters; at the fame time
binding them, by an abfolute, promife to
manage them according to the directions, or
book, of their kind donors. This, though
at firft of fmall value, would in time prove
not only of great public utility, but would
alfo be fo very beneficial to the poor families themfelves, as, by the increafe and
produce, to afford raiment to the naked,
food to the hungry, and make the humble
habitations of many, who are now mifer-
able through extreme poverty, comfortable
and joyous: while the benign hearts of
their humane benefactors would feel fuch
tranfports of happinefs and fatisfaction, on
contemplating the change, as would amply
recompence

recompence them for the little charge and trouble it might require.

There is, it muſt be acknowledged, ſome riſque that theſe laudable intentions may be fruſtrated, and the propoſed advantages, not gained, unleſs the ſame benevolence which firſt gave the hives, would alſo condeſcend from time to time, and by caſual viſits, to inſpect their management, and obſerve whether the directions given be conformed to. Even this, perhaps, may be inſufficient for the intended purpoſe, ſhould any of theſe laborious inſect communities be conſigned to the lazy or the ſottiſh : but, Heaven forbid, that the ſweet profits of the temperate and induſtrious Bees ſhould be ſquandered abroad in riot and exceſs, while the diſtreſſed wife and children are pineing at home with want, or periſhing by the piercing ſeverity of the winter's cold!

Great, very great, are the charitable benefactions of the inhabitants of theſe kingdoms! but equally great are the inſolence and profligacy of the lower claſs of people! But, to throw out a hint, might not theſe very benefactions be made ſubſervient to a general reformation, by beſtowing them on none but the ſober, the induſtrious, and the well-behaved ? Would not this conduct, if general, excite a ſpirit of emulation among the poor to excel in virtue: as well knowing, that without this recommendation, they would certainly be deprived of all hopes of protection and encouragement ?

couragement? Here it is to be lamented, that the moft vicious are likewife the moft pufhing, and by their impudence can obtrude themfelves into notice; while the virtuous, too meek perhaps, and fubmiffive, are intimidated from afking, and muft therefore be fought out. Thus patient merit ftarves, while the mifcreant riots on what would have made a whole virtuous family grateful, comfortable, and happy! The Author's fituation in life has afforded him ample opportunities for thefe obfervations, which thofe in higher ftations are neceffarily deprived of; he therefore hopes this digreffion will be thought not altogether impertinent.

After all, perhaps, the only method of eftablifhing a proper mode of managing Bees, fo as to become univerfal and permanent, would be for fome perfon in every neighbourhood to make himfelf perfect in the art: he might then fuperintend and manage his neighbour's Bees at a moderate ftipulated price for each Stock, through the year; in a fimilar manner to thofe who go from houfe to houfe to brew, &c. Many, who through age and infirmities are rendered unfit for hard labour, might eafily acquire and practife this art to their own benefit, and that of the public.

Some, who already keep Bees, may object that the Author has inferted many well known particulars: fuch fhould confider

that

that he writes for the totally ignorant, as well as for thofe who have fome previous knowledge; that he means to inftruct in the whole art, and not in a part only. But, fhould the objector fave only one hive of Bees by the methods here pointed out, though taught by a fingle Paragraph, there furely can be no caufe of complaint; as the faving will be much more than the whole purchafe of the book.

Should this treatife merit a fecond edition, any ufeful practical information or corrections fhall be properly inferted; it being the Writer's ardent wifh that this beneficial art be brought as near perfection as poffible. Such communications addreffed to the Author, will be gratefully acknowledged.

The Writer hopes that the critics will be tender of this his only child; the child of his old age; which, though now weak, fickly, and helplefs, he flatters himfelf, may, by a little of their kind affiftance, become extenfively ufeful.

(xi)

CONTENTS.

CHAP.

THE

PRACTICAL

BEE-MASTER.

CHAPTER I.

Of the NATURE *and* QUALITIES *of the* QUEEN BEE.

1. TO have a competent knowledge of the proper management of BEES, it is firſt of all neceſſary to be well acquainted with their nature and qualities: For it muſt ſurely be deemed abſurd in any one to attempt to govern a people, without knowing any thing of their manners, cuſtoms, and propenſities.

2. Each Stock of Bees, and alſo each Swarm, is compoſed of three ſorts, or claſſes, *viz.* the Queen, (fig. 1.) the Drones, (fig. 2.) and the Working Bees, (fig. 3.)

3. The Queen is the *Common Mother* (in the ſtricteſt ſeuſe of the word) of the whole

B   Stock.

Stock.   Several modern authors however
have not only dignified her with this title,
but have also attributed to her a regal power
and polity, similar to *that* known among our
species.   Such flights of fancy may be allowed
to poets, but of the natural historian it is re-,
quired to delineate with truth and accuracy,
and without any exaggeration.

Though I have myself paid very great
attention to this point, yet I could never
observe any such instances of sovereignty ;
nor am I singular in *this* opinion, having
Monsieur Reaumur to countenance me ;
for he observes, " *If* she reigns it is over
" subjects that every moment know the
" good of their society demands what they
" perform ; and who therefore never fail
" to do it.   From this source flows their
" unparalleled attachment, tenderness, and
" respect.   They never have occasion to
" receive orders.   Both Queen and People
" invariably pursue the designs of Nature."

4. Notwithstanding the great names of
Locke and Hoadly, female government seems
to have been the *first* among men ; for we
find Eve governed Adam, and made him do
a very foul thing.   So among Bees, the
Matriarchal, was also the *first,* and is the
only one that has been admitted among them
from the beginning : However as custom
has dignified the Parent Bee with the title
of Queen, we shall distinguish her by that
appellation through the succeeding pages.

5. Her

5. Her importance among Bees is much greater than that of the greateſt monarch among the ſons of men. Without *Her* the whole ſtock or family, would be ſoon extinguiſhed. Should a natural or accidental death deprive any Stock of their Queen, confuſion, ſorrow. and neglect inevitably ſucceed. They then barely work for immediate ſubſiſtence, and for a very ſhort time ; for having no proſpect of a future race, they pine and languiſh until famine and' death put a period to their grief.

6. With reſpect to figure, the Queen, (fig. 1.) is longer and more ſlender than the Drones ; the hinder part tapering almoſt to a point ; her belly and legs are yellower than thoſe of the common Bees ; the upper part of her body is of a much darker colour, nearly approaching to a gloſſy black ; as is alſo the tapering part beyond her wings, which is divided into four joints, diſtinguiſhed by as many circles, whereas the common Bees have but three circles, and thoſe of a lighter colour ; and the nearer ſhe is to the ſeaſon of depoſiting her eggs, the more ſhining and large ſhe appears. Her wings are very ſhort in proportion to her body, hardly reaching beyond the middle, and ending about the third ring, whereas thoſe of the common Bees and Drones cover their whole body : ſo that upon the whole ſhe ſeems rather clumſy, and is not unlike a tall woman with a very ſhort cloak ; but in her deportment, ſhe is grave, ſolemn, and calm.

B 2   7. She

7. She is armed with a sting, which is neither so large nor so long as those of the Commoners ; its use, however, I cannot precisely determine ; as the roughest usage, even to pressing many of them to death in my hands, could never provoke a Queen to sting me, though they seemed to dart their stings out for that purpose. But having placed two Queens together under a glass, I observed that they stabbed each other, until death ended the combat.

8. Perhaps this unwillingness in the Queen to sting on any other occasion, may be owing to her consciousness, that on her preservation, depends the happiness and prosperity of her numerous offspring. For of her fruitfulness one may say, " that her progeny " is like the sand upon the sea shore." To bring forth young is the whole of her duty, and this important office her children know to be absolutely necessary to their mutual prosperity, and is the measure of that affectionate solicitude they bear her. To this single circumstance may all those shining qualities of royalty be reduced.

9. It might seem too fabulous to relate, had not that great and indefatigable Naturalist, Monf. Reaumur, ascertained the fact by accurate examination, that a single Queen, in the course of seven weeks, can produce ten or twelve thousand young ; and that she commonly brings forth from thirty to forty thousand in nine months. Some, however, are more prolific than others.

10. This

10. This is further confirmed by another very eminent Naturalist, Swammerdam. He difcovered in the body of a Queen Bee ready to lay, an ovarium, or egg bag, containing five thoufand one hundred vifible eggs: And if fo, there can be no difficulty in fuppofing her capable of producing fo numerous an offspring in fo fbort a time.

11. About the middle of the fpring is the height of her laying: from many circumftances it is very probable that fhe then lays about two hundred eggs a day. However prodigious this may feem to thofe not converfant with natural hiftory, feveral animals furpafs the Queen Bee in fecundity.

12. But this furprize will be greatly heightened by reflecting upon a faculty ftill more wonderful, that of appearing to be endowed with a power of keeping in her body eggs that have been impregnated feveral months before; or, (which amounts to the fame) the feed of the male, capable of vivifying the eggs at the time of their exclufion. For, though the Drones, who are the males, are feldom fuffered to remain in the hives (581) longer than the middle of Auguft, yet the Queen ftill continues to lay eggs and produce young, not only in Autumn, but alfo in the next Spring, until March or April, and in great abundance, all by virtue of the Autumnal impregnation. Nor is this faculty confined to the Queen Bee, as Wafps, Hornets, and fome other infect tribes do the fame.

13. That

13. That the Drones have any agency at all in propagation, has been elaborately difputed by the Rev. Mr. Thorly; * nor does he feem to think them of any other ufe whatever; as though Providence had made a *diftinction* without defigning it to anfwer any particular purpofe.

14. Butler, however, who wrote long before, viz. in 1623, † differs widely from him in fentiment, and feems to be not only the *firft* difcoverer of their fex, but alfo of that of the Queen. He has maintained his opinion with greater weight of argument, which later experience has fully confirmed.

15. Notwithftanding the prying eyes of fo many philofophers and naturalifts in every age, the myfteries of love remained an impenetrable fecret until the fuperior inquifitive genius of Reaumur lifted up the veil and ufhered them into day. To obtain this difcovery, he confined a Queen and a Drone in a glafs, and there had his moft fanguine wifhes compleatly fatisfied by being an eye witnefs of the nuptial confummation. His joy, however, at this fortunate difcovery was not without fome alloy, in beholding feveral fingle Drones, he had accommodated her Majefty with, die at her feet, through excefs of amorous toil. From this circumftance it fully appears, that a fmall number of males are wholly in-

            fufficient

---

* Enquiry into the Nature, &c. of Bees, 1765.
† Female Monarchy.

sufficient for the arduous task; and that a large number, generally seven or eight hundred, are required to impregnate the many thousand eggs deposited by the Queen. ·

16. But as Thorley has degraded the Drones from their office, and has represented them as unprofitable and useless, so have we an antagonist against the Queen, in Mr. Daniel Wildman, (nephew to the famous Mr. Thomas Wildman) who, in his small pamphlet, * has attempted to render her equally insignificant. ·

17. He asserts, that the opinion of the Queen being the general parent of the whole Stock, " is absolutely without foundation." He further says, " They (the common " Bees) couple together, I make no doubt, " though privily, and apart by themselves, " though they never were observed, yet they " certainly apply themselves to that business " secretly within the hives, or else abroad " where there can be no witnesses."

18. In answer to this, it may surely be urged, that as among so many millions of Bees, which many people possess, and among so many watchful eyes of naturalists and others, no such conjunction has ever been noticed, either in glass hives, or when the Bees have been abroad, it is by no means unreasonable or unwarrantable to assert, that it is highly improbable any such connections

B 4   ever

* Complete Guide for the Management of Bees, 1775.

ever take place.   We know that all other infects have no regard to what we call modesty or decency among us; therefore such delicacy in Bees, and in Bees alone, is superlatively astonishing.

19. To this it may perhaps be replied, that neither has the engendering of the Queen and Drones, ever been discovered in glass or other hives; I grant it.   The case, however, is by no means parallel.   Here is a single infect amongst a vast multitude, by whom she is constantly surrounded; whose residence likewise is always in the centre of the hive, and consequntly her person continually veiled from human eyes, except when she is depositing eggs near the extremities of the combs.

Reaumur relates, that he kept Bees in glass hives many years, but could never obtain a view of the amours of the Queen and Drones. I have placed a Swarm in seven glasses, each holding three pints, and having a common communication with each other at bottom; yet, notwithstanding the Bees were thus divided, the Queen was seen but twice the whole season; much less could any observations be made of a royal wedding.

20. But there is another insuperable objection to Mr. Daniel Wildman's principle: For although no one ever saw them engender, some *one* must have seen them deposit their eggs.   But who ever saw a working Bee with its *Tail* in a cell?   With their *Heads* they are continually seen so, in order to deposit

their

their loads; and whether alive or dead, are always found with their heads towards the bottoms of the cells. Therefore Mr. Wildman muſt grant that they lay their eggs at their mouths. I have ſeveral times held Queens in my hand who, while there, have laid their eggs, and in the ſame way as all other creatures do. Working Bees I frequently hold in my hand; and they alſo have depoſited, but never eggs, unleſs excrement may be ſo called.

21. Mr. Wildman endeavours to ſupport his doctrine by that beſt of all proofs, experiment. But it is neither one nor two, but a long ſeries of ſimilar reſults, that amount to a certainty. He declares he often repeated ſome particular experiments to determine the point; and gives us an account of one, in which, after taking out the Bees from a hive, he ſeparated from them the old Queen*, and a young one, not yet come to maturity; this laſt he ſtuck up in another hive, with a ſufficient quantity of Bees with it, and obſerved at the ſame time that there were no young Bees in the other common cells. At the end of three or four days he took the Bees out again, and obſerved *young Bees* in every cell.

22. This experiment, however, appears to me on ſeveral accounts a very doubtful one; for he could by no means be certain there
were

---

* Although he calls his Treatiſe complete, the ſecret *how*, he reſerves to himſelf.

were no young in the common cells, unlefs
he had taken out and examined each comb
feparately.   But even allowing that there
were no young in the cells before, yet how is it
poffible there could be *young Bees* at the end
of three or four days ? For it is an incontef-
table fact, that the egg itfelf is three days
in that ftate, and five or fix more under the
appearance of a maggot.   Mr. Wildman
muft therefore moft certainly be miftaken in
this ; as he is alfo when he affirms that a
Royal Bee is five or fix weeks hatching.

23. But Mr. Wildman proceeds ftill further,
and obferves that there were not only young
Bees in the old combs, but alfo in new combs,
which the Bees had built in the courfe of
four days. The young Queen moft probably,
was not in a fufficient ftate of maturity to
breed thefe ; but it does not follow that
fome other young Queen, who had eluded
his fearch, did not.   I have myfelf been frequently difappointed in fearching for the
Queen, and have been obliged to repeat the
operation two or three times before I could
find her.   Thefe experiments therefore, cannot by any means be deemed decifive, efpe-,
cially when attended with fo many improba-
bilities.   It would have been more fatisfac-
tory had this gentleman acquainted us with,
the number of combs and Bees put into the
hive, and at what feafon.

We hope he will favour us with fome
future experiments on this fubject, made
. with

with precifibn, and in the prefence of intel-
ligent perfons.

24. In the mean time, to ftrengthen the
arguments already offered in fupport of our
opinion, let us add the teftimony of Swammerdam and Reaumur. Thefe gentlemen
beheld in the ovarium of a Queen Bee, five
thoufand three hundred eggs at one time.
Now, fuppofing there had only been half
that number, what can fuch a multitude
be defigned for, if, as Mr. Wildman afferts,
the Queen only produces three or four young?
Befides, there never have been found any vef-
tiges of an *ovarium* in common Bees; therefore, as Mr. Wildman admits that by dif-
fection of a drone the fex may be afcertained,
this argument muft be allowed to be full
as applicable and conclufive when applied
to the Queen and the common Bees.

25. Although he does not admit of the
Queen being the common mother, yet in
feveral pages he acknowledges, " That with-
" out a young Queen there can be no Swarm.
" That a hive fhall be well ftocked with
" honey and Bees, and yet all fhall die in
" the winter, occafioned by the lofs of the
" Queen; for when this happens they will
" neither work nor eat." I fhall make no
comments upon this, as it coincides with the
general received opinion as to the abfolute
neceffity of a Queen to the profperity of
every Stock or Swarm. Though from him
we cannot learn from whence that neceffity
can poffibly arife.

26. I

26. I have lately met with another fingular fentiment of a foreigner refpecting the royal brood, as related to a friend of mine, viz. that by taking any common egg, and fixing it in a royal cell, it will become a young Queen ; and this (as he fuppofes) from the extraordinary fupply of food.

That nature fhould endow a multitude of creatures with fuch a peculiar conftruction of veffels, as can be ufeful only to a few in many millions, is as repugnant to obfer-vation and experience, as it is to probability. The Drones are much larger and of a different conformation to the Queen and Commons. Can this arife purely from any peculiarity in the nutriment? The refult of fuch an experiment would more likely be a drone, a heavy clumfy infect, with an obtufe anus, than a Queen, whofe body is no thicker than that of a common Bee, but which extends much longer and terminates in a point. We might as well expect that our hens would all produce cock eggs by giving them a double portion of food.

27. That the gentleman might have taken a common egg and placed it in a royal cell, and that a young Queen had been afterwards produced, I will not difpute. For there might be a Queen already in the hive unperceived by him, who might lay a royal egg in that cell, the working Bees having firft taken away the common egg. Befide, why fhould a Queen be capable of furnifh-ing feveral fupernumerary princeffes, when

in

in case of miscarriage, the commoners could so easily supply the deficiency? And doubtless these would have been furnished with that instinct or knowledge, had it been so.

28. Let this be as it will; in practice it can be of no consequence or use; as he acknowledged that a common egg must be deposited *in a royal cell.* To do this the Bees must be drove, and some combs cut out; in doing which a real royal egg may be destroyed, and the rest of the young injured. The operation itself is likewise troublesome. All which inconveniences may easily be avoided, by setting the *Queenless* Stock at night over some other. (382.)

29. Having thus attempted to establish the principles we set out with, we proceed next to treat of the generation of Bees. And, first, the Royal Nursery. This is composed of cells or nests (fig. 4, *a*, *b*.) which are of a circular form, of a considerable thickness, and in appearance rather clumsy; for one of these cells weighs as much as a hundred of the common; the royal cell, when about half made, resembles the lower part of an acorn turned upside down; (fig. 4 *a*.) but it is gradually lengthened in proportion to the growth of the inclosed embryo, until at last it is sealed or covered over at the top with wax (fig. 4. *b*). Sometimes these cells hang from the middle of a comb; but oftener from the sides, ends, or edges of the combs (fig. 4). They hang in a perpendicular direction, with the *open end* point-
ing

ing down towards the floor. The number of thefe cells are various, from two or three to ten or twelve. After the royal brood is out, they are generally taken to pieces, and the wax applied to other ufes. But if the wax be not wanted, they are permitted to remain.

30. A young Queen is capable of being fecundated four or five days after her birth; but until fhe *is,* no Swarm will rife with her; and that fometimes does not happen for fome weeks, for want of Drones. Her colour changes to a deeper hue, in proportion to her age; and the nearer fhe is to her laying-time, the more fhining and large fhe appears.

31. A Swarm has generally the fagacity to fingle out the forwardeft to lead them. Tho' it frequently happens, that fome bold virago will intrude, and hazard her life for an empire. But when fettled in a hive, fhe that is ready to lay will be enthroned, and her competitor expelled or flain.

32. The Queen begins to lay in February or fooner, if the weather proves mild, and proper flowers are in bloffom (512) and will in fome fituations, continue laying until October. I have taken Stocks often at that time with brood in them. But at what time foever the Bees carry in little balls upon their legs, it may be looked upon as a fure indication of the Queen's breeding.

33. As moft of the infect tribes exhibit transformations, which might be accounted
                                                  miraculous,

miraculous, were they not fo common, fo
the Bees undergo fimilar and equally fur-
prizing changes, which we fhall now endeavour to defcribe.

The Queen firft lays an egg, at the bottom
of thofe holes, or waxen cells, which form
the combs (fig. 4); after the egg has remained in this ftate about three days, it becomes a *maggot*; which lies in the bottom of
the cell rolled up in the form of a half moon,
and is furrounded with a clammy fubftance.
The Bees continually feed it at the mouth
during five or fix days. The embryo being
then confiderably increafed in bulk, the cell
is clofed or fealed over with a covering of
wax by the common Bees; having been
thus left about twelve days more, the young
Bee breaks through this waxen covering, and appears in its perfect form. But
a royal egg is longer in hatching than a common one.

34. There is alfo, and generally in the
middle of every hive, a comb appropriated
for the Drone brood, the cells being much
deeper than the common ones: and when
the young are fealed up, inftead of a *flat*,
they have a convex cover, which is a little
oval.

35. The duration of a Queen's life, as
alfo of the inferior Bees, feem to be about a
year. The Queen therefore that breeds *early*
in one fpring, can hardly be the fame that
breeds thro' the next and the fucceeding fummer; I the rather think fo, becaufe at times I

have

have had Stocks die or dwindle away;
for which no other reason could be assigned,
but the death of the Queen; none being
found upon examination in the hive, though
there was plenty of honey. This may, perhaps, explain why sometimes in the spring
Bees desert a plentiful hive; the Queen
being dead before any royal eggs were deposited.

CHAPTER II.

A DESCRIPTION *of the* DRONES *and* COMMON BEES.

36. THE common Bees (fig. 3). being so well known, need no other
description than that they are of no sex,
being neither male nor female. These are
generally, and indeed truly and emphatically
called the *Working Bees*.

37. The Drones, (fig. 2.) as we have before observed, are the males: they are both
larger and longer than the common Bees,
but shaped nearly like them. They are
without stings; instead of which, their tail
end contains the distinguishing characteristic
of their sex: and which mere pressure will

force

force out of their body. . They have no fangs, and are more tender than the Workers. Eight or ten hundred of thefe are found in a good Stock, whofe *fole* defignation is the fervice of the Queen.

37. The tongue of the Drones being fhorter than that of the workers, difables them from fucking honey from the flowers, and therefore they are obliged to be fuftained by the honey laid up in the hives. Except paying their court to the Queen, they do no work ; neither do they ftir out of the hive until the fun has warmed the air, and invites them by it's fplendor. The fweets of love, a plentiful and delicious table, and a fhort life, but free from care, from ficknefs, and from anxiety, is their happy lot. Confidered *only* in this point of view, who would not wifh to be a Drone ?

38. Some have thought, that the bodily heat of the Drones, is neceffary in hatching the brood : but I could never obferve them in the leaft attentive to that point. Befides, it is well known that great numbers of Bees are bred early in the fpring, long before any Drones are hatched, and when the air is much colder than when thefe appear ; as alfo long after they are expelled the hives.

39. Several authors are alfo miftaken in affirming that the brood is wholly depofited in the center of the combs. Numbers of my Stocks have yearly extended their breeding cells quite to the edges of the

C   combs,

combs, and clofe to the windows of the boxes, without fuffering any prejudice.——Thorly agrees with me in this obfervation.

40. I particularly notice this, becaufe it has been a point of confequence in the conftruction and arrangement of boxes; and thereby has occafioned more trouble and expence than otherwife would have been neceffary; but as the principle has no folid foundation; a peculiar conftruction of boxes for *that purpofe* muft be needlefs. The truth is, the Bees breed in our climate rather too faft than too flow. And they often die in backward fprings by having a great number of young mouths to feed from too fcanty a larder.

41. The age of a Bee, confidered fingly, feems to be that of a year; although a Stock, if the combs did not become too foul, might exift for centuries, that is, *by fucceffion*; juft as the human race do in populous cities; while fome are hourly taken off by age, accident, or infirmities, others are rifing into life and manhood, to repair thefe unavoidable, and even neceffary breaches of mortality.

42. Young Bees may be diftinguifhed from the old by their being of a lighter brown colour. Old Bees are more red or dark. The wings of the young are intire; but thofe of the old fhagged and torn by their unremitted labours. A Bee juft hatched has a great belly, ftuffed out with the fuftenance it took whilft a maggot. By thefe marks

may

may be diftinguifhed in a fwarm the old, the young, and the middle aged.

43. Bees have a quick and an extenfive fmell, either of honey, or honey dews; but are not difgufted with fmells that are difagreeable to us, if not within their hives. In the fpring they are often feen fipping in drains, and places wetted with urine. Tar they are fond of, and if in their reach will injure their honey with it.

44. By their acute faculty of fmelling (or perhaps by a fenfe of which we can have no idea) they diftinguifh the Bees of their own hive from any others; and know from the fmell the death of any of their companions crufhed or killed about the hive, and will purfue the murderer with unrelenting vengeance.

45. They ftop up with a kind of gum-refin, called *propolis,* all the holes or crevices of their hives. Therefore the fewer there are of fuch in the hives, the more it will eafe them, and prevent a lofs of time and labour which might be employed more to our profit.

46. They foreknow impending ftorms, at fuch times crouding to their hives fo thick that the door-ways cannot admit them faft enough. They work day and night in the hive, taking repofe by turns; hanging upon each other by their claws between the combs. They alfo have figns by which they communicate their wants or defires to each other.

C 2   47. They

47. They are the moſt cleanly of all creatures (except a Dutch woman) ſuffering no dirt, filth, or any other offenſive thing in their hives. Their own neceſſary diſcharges are performed as they fly, and never in their hive, unleſs compelled thereto by an injudicious cloſing up of their hives, which generally occaſions their death.

48. They are very fierce, and prone to revenge, when provoked; as they will be by ſtrangers ſtanding too near the entrance of their hives, or when any buſtle is made near them. Their irritability proceeds from a ſuppoſition of ſome injury being deſigned againſt their ſtate; for otherwiſe they are not apt to ſting. When at a diſtance from their hive, you may beat them from flower to flower, and moleſt them while in their induſtrious purſuits; they will then bear it with exemplary patience, nor ſhew the leaſt reſentment, no not even ſhould you catch them in your hand, provided you do not preſs them.

49. They ſoon become acquainted with a perſon who frequents their hives, and ſeems attentive to pleaſe them by his calm and deliberate deportment. They readily will diſtinguiſh him from any other perſon. So far from offering him any inſult, they will often light upon him as a mark of their affection. He may even lay his hand at the mouths of their hives, and they will paſs over it without the leaſt reſentment. But ſhould this ſame perſon in any manner diſ-

turb

turb the hive, inftantly friendfhip and har-
mony are deftroyed, the pride of their little
hearts rifes, and they are filled with anger and
revenge.

50. Moft creatures grow tame to the
hand that feeds them; not fo the bees, if in
doing of it, their hive be in the leaft difturbed: for no creatures are fo fond of peace and
quietnefs.

51. Not that they will bear malice long
with the perfon they have been once familiar
with, for in two or three days they will
forget the greateft injury he can have done
them, and be as cordial with him as ever;
but not fo with cafual vifitors, by whom,
if once affronted, it is a great chance, but
that come near them whenever they will,
attempts will be made to give them the moft
exquifite pain, by ftinging their eyes or nofe.
As the ftinging of Bees is fometimes attended with fatal confequences to men and
heaft, it will by no means be improper to
make a diftinct Chapter of fo very important
a fubject.

CHAPTER

CHAPTER III.

Of the STINGING *of* BEES.

AS the Bees, though a diminutive people, are armed with weapons which,
though small, are so venomous as often to
strike men of gigantic might with terror,
it is highly proper to confider, before we
attempt any familiarity with them, how to
defend ourfelves from them; and to know
when wounded, how to apply a proper
remedy.

53. Many perfons through an unreafon-
able dread, cannot fuffer a Bee to come near
them, without being flurried; and in this
ftate of confufion and terror provoke thefe
otherwife inoffenfive infects to fting them,
by ftriking at them. This treatment always
raifes their refentment; which when thus
excited, generally continues for feveral days;
and while it lafts, the Bees will purfue the
offender from one end of a garden to the
other.

54. The beft way, where they come buzzing about you, is to wave your hand gently
before your face, and make a low retreat;
or ftooping down, to thruft your head among
herbs, fhrubs, or the like; this will be a
fufficient fecurity 'till their anger is abated,

and

and they have retired from you. This behaviour will conciliate a more peaceable demeanor towards you another time; and a repetition of it will procure you their friendſhip.

55. Not but there are ſome perſons againſt whom Bees will have an invincible antipathy, however calmly and inoffenſively they may have always behaved to them. Inſtances of this ſort have very frequently fallen under my obſervation. Neither has a change of colour in their clothes in the leaſt diminiſhed their rancour, but they would ſtill follow them in every part of the garden from day to day. Whether this diſlike proceeds from ſomething diſagreeable in the countenance, or in the effluvia of the body, is hard to determine. But it is very clear that ſuch perſons muſt never think of becoming Apiators *, or managers of Bees. Nor indeed any other perſon who cannot command his temper while employed about them.

56. The Bees are uſed to a mild parental government, to peace, and quietneſs; and like ſome of the heroes of antiquity, will never ſubmit to tyranny or violence, but will reſiſt unto death.

57. In windy or other diſagreeable weather, which diſcompoſes them, or hinders

C 4   their

---

* The adoption of this appellation I hope will be excuſed, as we have no ſingle word expreſſive of the meaning.

their labours, they become very fretful and quarrelfome; at fuch times, whoever loiters about their hives will be fure to fmart for their temerity. So likewife in very hot days, and when there is plenty of honey gathering, their eagernefs is fo great, that ftanding before their hives as it obftructs their paffage to and fro, will be deemed an affront.

58. Hair and feathers are difagreeable to Bees. But fuftian, velvet, and leather, are deftructive. For from fuch fubftances, they cannot withdraw their ftings, but, together with them, leave part of their bowels, and thus foon die. On the contrary, from linen and woollen apparel, they readily difengage their ftings; and without receiving any harm. The degree of the inflammation produced by the ftinging of a Bee, varies in a double proportion to that peculiarity found in different conftitutions, and to the quantity of venom injected. In fome people the flighteft fcratch, or fmalleft puncture, fhall prove highly painful, and be difficultly cured; while in others much deeper wounds fhall prefently heal without any inconvenience. So in fome the ftinging of a Bee will immediately occafion a very painful tumour over great part of the body; in others it will be attended with very little pain, and but a fmall fwelling, both which foon fubfide; except the wound be made in a very fenfible part, as the eyes. To me their ftinging is of trifling confequence; I had rather be ftung by ten Bees on my hands, than

once

once by a ftinging nettle. Befides, the Bees are
not at all times equally vigorous, fo that in
proportion to the heat of the weather, and
the degree of their anger, a larger or fmaller
portion of venom will be injected. Nor can
a Bee fting more than three times; as its venom will then be quite exhaufted.

59. When a Bee has ftung any one, it is
beft to have patience, and permit it to withdraw its fting, which otherwife will be left
behind, and the wound be thereby made larger.
One method of cure is, to prefs with fome force
the hollow end of a key over the wound; this
operates by forcing out the venom, and preventing its being conveyed by the abforbent
veffels into the circulation. Another method
is, with the flap of a woollen coat, or piece
of woollen cloth with the knap on, to rub
the wound brifkly backwards and forwards,
in the fame direction as the veins, now and
then wetting the wound with a little fpittle,
to prevent the fretting of the fkin, and to
continue the friction until there be a ceffation
of the fmarting. Or it will be much better
perhaps, to rub the wound with the woollen
cloth only one way, viz. downwards on the
arms, legs, and trunk of the body; but upwards on the face, neck, and breaft; by this
means the venom will be more thoroughly
preffed out and abforbed by the cloth; and
its entrance into the abforbent fyftem more
effectually prevented.

60. But if the wound be not immediately
rubbed, this method will be ufelefs, as
the

the poifon will have penetrated too far. In this cafe recourfe muft be had to fome penetrating remedy. Among a multitude of herbs, oils, chemical preparations, &c. that have been tried, the following compofitions have been found the moft efficacious, from my own perfonal experience, as well as that of many others.

Take of common linfeed oil two parts,
      vinegar of fquils one part,
      honey one part ;

thefe are to be well fhaken together. The more fpeedily this is applied, the more falutary it will prove. Rub it hard in and about the wound with your finger, as long as any fmart is felt ; and at times afterwards, if any fwelling or inflammation remains, this compofition will not wholly prevent a tumour, but it will greatly leffen it and alleviate the pain.

61. But in general, fweet fpirit of vitriol, rubbed well in, will more effectually prevent any pain or fwelling; and may be applied to the moft fenfible parts, even to the eyes, with fafety. But in proportion to the ftrength of the infect, the quantity of venom injected, the lapfe of time before the remedy is applied, and the irritability of the habit, will be the quantity of fpirit neceffary to a cure. It is not the rubbing a little on will effect it, but as long as any fwelling rifes, or any pain is felt, fo long muft the embrocation be continued ; and even

                            after

after an intermiſſion, if either ſhould return, the remedy muſt again be had recourſe to.

62. There have been too many melancholy inſtances of perſons, as well as cattle, that have been ſtung to death by Bees. Perhaps the following directions may in future, at leaſt in ſome caſes, prevent ſo fatal an accident.

When a perſon is ſuddenly beſet by theſe inſects, that have been by any means enraged, if any houſe, ſtable, or the like be near, he ſhould run and ſhut himſelf up in the darkeſt part of it, and with his handkerchief bruſh off as many of the Bees as he can. But if they be very numerous, and any other perſon within call, water ſhould be poured over him to waſh them off, as bruſhing will cauſe ſome of them to ſting. Where no aſſiſtant is nigh, after having been ſhut up a little while, and having bruſhed off all he could, he ſhould run away as ſwiftly as poſſible to get out of their ſight, and immediately afterwards apply ſome of the above remedies; or, for want of them, any kind of ſweet oil, or freſh greaſe, that can be firſt obtained, ſhould be rubbed upon the wounds, until a better remedy can be procured.

63. Where no buildings are nigh, he ſhould hide his head, and his whole body, if it can be done, in a hedge, or among buſhes, or the like. If none of theſe be nigh enough to ſave him, plunging into a pond of water will preſently free him from them. Or for want of that the throwing

up

up of water brifkly with his hands fo as to
fall over himfelf and the Bees, will induce
them to retreat, thinking it a fhower of rain.
But if no water be near at hand, the throwing
up of duft may perhaps have the fame effect.

. 64. When only a few Bees have fettled
on any perfon, let him cover his head and
neck as well and as clofe as poffible with his
clothes; and if thefe be thick enough to
prevent the ftings from penetrating, the Bees
may foon be driven away by throwing duft
or water over them. Care, however, muft
be taken to keep this covering fo clofe by
one hand, or any other faftening; that none
of the infects may be able to infinuate themfelves under it. If the head and neck be
well fecured, fuch wounds as may be elfe-
where inflicted cannot be fatal; neither can
a few ftings received in the face, before it
could be covered. And fuch Bees as may
have previoufly fettled on the head and face,
can eafily and prefently be crufhed to death
by preffing the covering againft them. If
there be nothing elfe within reach, the face
muft be covered with both hands, fecuring
the eyes, nofe, and mouth in particular.

65. Whenever any one is very much
ftung, he fhould be put to bed as foon as
poffible. And befides being bathed as before
directed, he fhould drink plentifully of baum
tea, water-gruel, or other thin cooling and
laxative drink, in which the juice of cur-
rants, apples, oranges, &c. may be fqueezed.
He fhould eat but little of any thing, and
no animal food. If there be much inflammation,

flammation, and the patient be feverish, blood should be taken away as soon as possible; and such other medicines be exhibited as a skilful medical gentleman may think necessary.

66. When a person has the misfortune to be stung in the throat, while medical assistance is fetching, with all possible speed, some mild oil should be gradually swallowed, or for want of this melted fresh butter, or even grease, if nothing else is to be had; for not a moment must be lost. As soon as the medicine composed of sweet oil, vinegar of squils, and honey, can be prepared,* the the patient must swallow some of it gradually. Where vinegar of squils cannot speedily be procured, good common vinegar may supply its place.

67. But it must carefully be observed, that the cautions and directions already given are *not* to extend to swarms of Bees, that peaceably and without any provocation leave their hives of their own accord, and settle upon any one. For then, if the eyes, nose, and mouth be secured with the hands or a handkerchief, they will alight on him without doing the least prejudice, provided he remains intirely passive and still, until they have all settled. He may then gently walk with them, until a hive can be obtained, which being rubbed on the inside, at the *top only*, with a mixture of sugar and ale, and

---

* This I have known succeed; but the sweet spirit of vitriol I have not yet had any opportunity of trying, tho' a tea spoonful or two may be taken in a little water.

and held over him as near as poffible, where the Bees are moft numerous, the greater part will foon afcend; he fhould then walk to fome diftance from the hive, and thofe Bees that yet remain upon him, miffing their companions, will foon quit their ftation to join them, unlefs the Queen fhould happen to remain behind; in this cafe, the Bees muft be taken off with a fpoon (384) and put into the hive.

68. But if inftead of obferving this peaceable behaviour, he fhould be flurried, and miftaking or flighting their intended friendfhip, fhould ftrike at, or endeavour to beat them off, they will revenge the affront fo as to endanger his life.

69. It is very probable that cattle on fuch occafions, may be excited to refentment; and although in fetling on them they do not fting, yet their crawling may give the creatures fome uneafy fenfation and caufe them to be very tefty, and by endeavouring to brufh them off, excite the Bees to fting them. In this cafe, or any other, where cattle are accidentally befet with Bees, or Wafps, &c. they fhould be driven with the greateft expedition to fome pond, where they may, if poffible, be covered with water, and the parts that are not fo, muft have plenty of water thrown on them, to wafh off as many Bees as poffible, at the fame time brifkly throwing up water among fuch Bees as continue the attack. As foon as the inraged infects are retreated, brufh off with wet twigs thofe Bees
that

that remain on the animals. When there is no water at hand drive them into a hedge, or which is-ftill better into a ftable.

70. If an animal be very much ftung, bathe the parts affected with any oil or greafe that can be fooneft got, that the poifon may have lefs time to fpread; whatever is ufed fhould be well and long rubbed in, and repeated very often until the inflammation fubfides. And if the remedies before mentioned be ufed, the cure will be more certain and fpeedy. Bleeding is proper if the inflammation be great, or the creature appears to be in great torture or convulfions.

71. A drink fhould be given him, of thin oatmeal gruel, in which two ounces of falt petre have been diffolved : this fhould be repeated at three or four hours diftance; it will contribute to diminifh the inflammation and alleviate the pain.

72. As it is impoffible but thofe that manage Bees muft fometimes be ftung, and that feverely too, unlefs they have fome proper defence; and as fuch a fafeguard may be provided at a fmall expence, no Apiator ought in good policy to be without one.

73. The fafeguard confifts of a hood made of fuch thin open cloth as milk is ufually ftrained through; any other thin light cloth will do well enough. Head armour compofed of this kind of materials will not be very burthenfome, and is fufficiently cool. It muft be big enough to go over a man's hat, and round the neck, fo as to tie before, with a

firing

ſtring running through a tape or loop holes.
That part of it which is oppoſite the face
muſt be cut out, and a piece of very open
gauze, cat-gut, or what is much better and
ſtronger a caul of which barbers make the
inſide of their wigs, muſt be ſewed therein.
Crape or muſlin will too much obſtruct the
ſight, when kept at the proper diſtance,
which muſt be ſo great that no Bee can reach
the face with its ſting The hat muſt have
narrow brims about two inches wide, and
unſtrung.

Great care muſt be taken in uſing this
hood, that it be drawn round the neck
ſo tight that no Bee can paſs underneath it,
and that the part below the neck extends as
far as the coat. If there be the leaſt opening left ſufficient for the Bees to get under,
they will find it out, and before it can be
looſened prove worſe tormentors than if there
had been no defence at all. Therefore let
the ſtring be tied with a bow knot, ſo that
if there be occaſion, it may be inſtantly un-
tied and thrown off.

74. A pair of tanned, or other thick
leather gloves will be a ſufficient defence for
the hands; but theſe muſt be long enough
to cover the ſleeves of the coat, ſo that no
Bee can get up the arms. To which let
us add, thick yarn ſtockings over another
common pair. A man thus armed is able
to encounter the greateſt army the Bees can
bring againſt him. If women intermeddle
with Bees, it will be proper to defend their

necks

necks and bofoms, by putting on a man's coat, together with the head drefs.

75. As this armour is of trifling expence, and will laft a life, no perfon who keeps Bees ought to be without it. With this defence he may turn up their hives, examine, affift, and move them, upon any occafion, or at any time, without the leaft fmart or the leaft danger. Or fhould Wafps or Bees befet any cattle, with this armour, he may fafely go among them, and deftroy them.

76. But a fmall apparatus will do, for any bufinefs about the Bees, that does not much difturb them. This may be made of a fmall hoop, wide enough to extend round the face, and three quarters of an inch deep, with a piece of woollen cloth fpread over it, and tacked to its edges, fo as to let about an inch of the cloth hang over. A piece of the front muft be cut out, and fome net-work fewed in as before directed for the hood; a narrow piece will do, placed directly oppofite the eyes. A bead, or fome fuch contrivance, fhould be fewed oppofite the mouth part to hold by, in manner of a mafk.

77. This will fufficiently defend the face, but efpecially the eyes. For fingle Bees, when they are angry, generally aim at them, and at that time, will fting no where elfe. Perfons accuftomed to the language of Bees, know what tones they ufe when they are determined to fting. The war-whoop is then founded, that every one may ftand upon the

D   defence.

defence. It is much eafier to prevent an evil than to cure it.

78. Among poor cottagers, who keep Bees, one or two of thefe fafe-guards or armour in a village or neighbourhood will be fufficient for the whole, by lending them to each other.

CHAPTER IV.

Of the APIARY, *or Place to keep Bees in.*

79. THE next object of confideration to a perfon intending to keep Bees, is a proper fituation for his Apiary. The fituation of it, whether yard or garden, fhould be as open as poffible to the fouth; that the fronts of the hives may have as much of the fun as poffible. But if the hives cannot be fet full fouth, fouth-weft is more eligible than fouth-eaft; and this laft is better than north or eaft. From repeated obfervations it has been found, that the more fun the Bees have the more vigorous they are, and that they work with the greater ardour.

80. Let them be placed fo near the dwelling houfe as to be in view of the

room

room moft occupied. · Any difturbance or
accident, will then be the more readily perceived. Neither will there be a conftant neceffity to employ a perfon on purpofe to
watch the rifing of the Swarms, but only as
occafion may require. Befides thefe advantages, the Bees will be familiarized to the
fight of the family, and thereby become
more tame and tractable.

81. The Apiary fhould be defended from
the northern and eaftern winds, either by
buildings, walls, or by clofe and high hedges;
thefe winds are prejudicial to the Bees in many
refpects. The beft hedge for this purpofe
is the quick or white thorn, permitted to
grow high, after being firft plafhed and intermixed with female lime trees, as the
flowers of thefe as well as of the quick furnifh
fubfiftence for the Bees. It muft alfo be fo
ftrongly fenced round that no cattle or poultry
can approach the Stocks. The firft, by
throwing them down, will endanger their
own lives, and occafion the lofs of the Stocks.
And the dung of the others, and their rooft-
ing upon the hives will prove fo difgufting to
the Bees, as to make them fometimes relinquifh their hives; but at beft they will
not thrive fo well.

82. Neither muft they ftand under the
dripping or fhade of trees efpecially of yews,
elders, or laurels. Nor fhould any weeds
or filthinefs be fuffered near the hives, as
harbouring numberlefs vermin, and other
enemies to thefe induftrious and cleanly in-

fects.

sects. An Apiary should not be near rivers, ponds, or large tubs of water, as many of the Bees will be blown therein and drowned.

83. The quantity of ground to be allotted for the Apiary, must be in proportion to the number of Stocks intended to be kept. Houses will be necessary if boxes are to be used. But these are too expensive for general use, or where numerous Stocks are to be kept : straw hives therefore in these cases, are preferable, being much cheaper, as they will answer the purpose as well, and require neither cot nor house.

84. From long experience, it is strongly recommended to set the Stocks at some distance apart, and upon separate stands. By this precaution much quarreling, and sometimes slaughter, will be prevented, as they will be less liable to mistake their habitations on any critical occasion, which may oblige them to return from the fields with great precipitation.

Another advantage arising from this disposition is, that by being separate they are not near so quarrelsome with each other, or with the Apiator. And not only this; but he can also go more safely and conveniently *behind* them, for which there is often an absolute necessity, without giving or receiving any offence.

85. But though the hives are to be placed separate from each other, it is by no means meant, that some should be in one spot of ground and some in another. No; they
must

muſt be altogether in one view, that in the
ſwarming ſeaſon, the Bee-herd, or perſon
who watches them, may readily diſtinguiſh
any Swarm that ſhall ariſe, otherwiſe ſome
will be inevitably loſt.

86. The country people generally place
their Bee Stocks in cots or little hovels, upon ſhelves one above another, and againſt
walls or pales, without any opening behind:
So that the getting at them is like ſtorm-
ing a lion's den. And to add to the ab-
ſurdity, the ſhelves are ſo near to each other,
that a hive cannot be raiſed, be the neceſſity ever ſo great. Theſe cots are likewiſe an
inticing ſhelter for numberleſs vermin, who
imperceptibly plunder and deſtroy the Stocks;
and the fault is laid to witchcraft, bad luck,
and other myſtical cauſes (241.). Another
great fault is the ſuffering rank weeds to grow
about the ſtands; and being ſo negligent
as not to keep the floor and ſtands clean
bruſhed.

87. The form of the ſtands for ſtraw
hives ſhould be triangular (fig. 12.). Let
three ſtrong ſtakes of ſound wood, of about
two feet in length, be drove into the ground,
conformable to that figure, ſo that from the
outſide of each ſtake there be fourteen inches
diſtance, and the ſtakes are to ſtand ſixteen
inches above the ground. The tops of the
ſtakes muſt be on a level with each other;
or rather the front ſtakes ſhould be half an
inch lower, ſo that when the hive is ſet on,
the dripping of rain may paſs freely off, and

D 3 not

not run into the entrance of the hive. Flat
pieces of wood are to be nailed acrofs the
top of the ftakes, fo that the floors of the
hives may ftand firm; but the floors are not
to be nailed on, for reafons hereafter given,
(490). Were the ftands made higher, the
hives would be more liable to be injured
by high winds, or in cafe of being thrown
down by accident, of receiving greater damage by the fall; and not only fo, but at this
heighth they are more conveniently managed.

88. The ftands ought to be five feet, but at
leaft four, every way from each other, and fet
in regular or uniform rows; where the ground
will conveniently admit of it, feven or eight feet
diftance between each hive will be ftill more
eligible; but when placed at a fmaller diftance than four feet, there is no poffibility
of going among the rows to handle the hives
without affronting the Bees of thofe behind;
and they are a people of too great confequence to be unneceffarily affronted.

89. Some gentlemen may, perhaps, difap-
prove of ftraw hives in their gardens, as being
unfightly; but, if the triangular fupporters
be made handfome, and the hives themfelves
be concealed by a wooden cafe, or only front
and fides formed of painted pannels, or by
any other fmart and pleafing contrivance, that
objection will be obviated. And if the ftands
be placed at any confiderable diftance from
the walks, there will never be any danger of
the Bees ftinging the company, provided they
do

do not incautioufly approach too near the hives. Or a hedge may foon be formed round the Apiary, of fyringoes, fo as to intercept the view. But this hedge muft be placed at fuch a diftance from the front of the hives as not to keep the fun from them. [1]

90. The bottoms of floors for the hives (fig. 6.) fhould be of well feafoned yellow deal, at leaft an inch thick, but an inch and an half will bear the weather better, and is not fo liable to warp. The fhape of the floor is to be round, or at leaft a fquare with the corners rounded off; its diameter fourteen inches. Where boards of a due width cannot be readily procured, two pieces glued, tenanted, or rabbited together, may fuffice. But to all floors two flips of wood muft be nailed underneath, to prevent the wood from cafting: this precaution muft not be neglected, it being of much confequence towards the prefervation of the Bees. And therefore, fhould any crevices, feams, or fiffures afterwards appear, they muft be timely ftopped up with putty or fome other cement.

91. The upper parts of the floors muft be planed fmooth and even, fo that when the hive is fet on there may be no vacancy between the edge and the floor. But if the floor be planed a little fhelving, or level, within half an inch of the edge, it will prevent the water from ftanding or running under the edges of the hive.

92. A fmall flip of wood, about five inches long and two broad, (fig. 8.) will be

required

required as an alighting-board for the Bees
to pitch on when they return from the fields.
It may be fufficiently faftened on by means
of two pegs of wood, or pieces of thick wire,
driven into its edge, and then fixed in the
proper correfponding holes made in the
front edge of the floor; the joining will
not be fo clofe as to prevent the rain from
dropping between, and will thereby fecure the
board from any fettled moifture that may
prejudice, the Bees. If the alighting-board
be made out of the folid wood of the floor,
many inches muft neceffarily and needlefsly
be cut to wafte; whereas any fmall piece
of refufe wood of the above dimenfions will
in fact do better, and be a confiderable
faving in a number of hives.

93. As threatening ftorms frequently precipitate the return of the Bees fo much as
to occafion their miftaking their own hives,
and thereby bring on quarrels and battles,
it will be worth while, in order to prevent
this, to paint each alighting-board of different
colours, by which the hives will be more
eafily diftinguifhed from each other by the
Bees before they pitch. And the paint will
prove both prefervative and ornamental.

CHAPTER

CHAPTER V.

Of the BEE-HOUSE.

94. THOSE who are defirous of fatisfying the laudable curiofity of minutely obferving the operations of thefe wonderful infects, muft be provided with proper boxes; as fuch indeed are indifpenfably neceffary for *this* purpofe. A *houfe* alfo will be equally ufeful to preferve both boxes and Bees from the *extremes* of the different feafons.

95. A houfe capable of containing *four* Stocks, will be fully fufficient to gratify the moft inquifitive mind in every thing relative to Bees. For real utility, ftraw hives of a proper conftruction, which anfwer the purpofe full as well, and require no houfe, are alfo much cheaper, and may be as eafily and *full* as profitably managed, as boxes of any kind whatever.

96. Directions for the conftruction of a houfe to contain four Stocks in the ftory method: The front to face the fouth. The length eight feet four inches. Height in front five feet. Behind five feet fix inches. Breadth one foot two inches. Floor, two feet from the ground. Three ftiles, each four inches wide, and long enough to extend from the roof to the bottom.

Four

Four doors, each one foot ten inches in width, and of the fame length as the ftiles, to which they are to be hung by hinges, one door to the right hand ftile, and another to the left, in manner of folding doors, fhutting in a rabbet.

Openings or paffages for the Bees, are to be cut out of the front, beginning at fix inches diftance from each ftile, and are to be in length four inches, and one inch and a half high from the fioor. Thefe are intended to correfpond with the like openings in the boxes. There are to be fimilar door-ways ten inches and a half in height from the floor. But this height fuppofes the bars of the boxes three quarters of an inch thick, and the loofe floors of the boxes the fame.

97. The boxes are defigned to ftand within fix inches of each end ; and between every two boxes, is to be a vacancy of fixteen inches ; but betwixt the boxes that ftand on each fide of the middle ftile, there will be only eight inches. The boxes are twelve inches wide; fo that there will be two boxes, and a fpace between them of fixteen inches, oppofite each pair of folding doors. If a houfe is to be made for a larger number of boxes, the fame model and proportions are to be obferved throughout.

98. The floor is to be laid one foot ten inches diftant from the ground. It fhould be upon a level, that the boxes may ftand firm, but the boards need not be planed,

if

if loose bottoms be used to the hives, as I
have recommended (90.) otherwise the house
floor must be made very smooth, and no
joinings or seams, unless strongly glewed or
cemented in those parts where the boxes are
to stand. The floors should be well sup-
ported by very strong rails; as sometimes the
weight will be very confiderable.

99. The four corner posts should be
strong and of good sound wood (oak will be
best) and well fixed in the ground.

100. The front must be boarded quite
close: but it must be particularly observed
that within side it must be quite even and
flush from end to end. Feather-edge board-
ing therefore in this part, cannot be admitted, but the boards should be rabbeted
into each other, to prevent storms of rain or
snow from driving thro' the joinings. The
reason for having the front inside perfectly
even, is because the boxes are to stand so
close against it, that a Bee cannot pass between the box and the front, and thereby
get into the house, and also because it is
necessary these boxes should sometimes be
moved to the right or left, as well as at
other times one upon another.

101. The roof may be covered with
feather-edged boards, or any other materials
that will keep out the wet. The dropping
of which is intended to be in the front, and
where it will be no inconvenience to the
Bees, if the roof be made so as to project
two inches beyond the face of the house;
but

but if the dropping be on the back, it will
be very inconvenient to the Apiator in many
of his operations behind.   The two ends
are to be intirely clofed with boards.   And
alighting-boards are to be fixed in the front
to every paffage or door-way, exactly in
the fame manner as directed for the ftraw
hives (92.).

102.   The houfe fhould be well painted;
for this will not only be ornamental, but, by
preferving the wood-work, be a confiderable
faving in the end.   Different colours fhould
alfo be painted over the feveral paffages;
which will be a very good index to the
Bees, and keep them from miftaking their
refpective habitations.   It will likewife be
very ufeful to paint the number of every Stock
over the door-way.

103.   How greatly foever, *I* may think
the ftory method preferable, there may be
perfons of a different opinion, and who may
therefore choofe the collateral method; viz.
that in which the boxes are placed fide by
fide.   To meet therefore their wifhes, we
have thought proper to give the following
defcription; and hope it will be acceptable.

104.   A collateral houfe of four Stocks,
muft be in length fix feet.   Height in the
fore front fix feet; back front fix feet fix
inches; breadth one foot two inches.   Three
ftiles, each four inches wide.

Two doors; one to each pair of boxes,
and each door two feet fix inches wide.

The houfe to have two floors.

Bottom

- Bottom floor, two feet high from the ground. . ..

Upper floor, two feet above that.

105. The door-ways or paffages are to begin feven inches from each ftile; each paf-fage to be four inches in length and one inch and an half high. But as each pair of boxes are to ftand clofe together, or fide by fide, the door-ways of each pair of boxes will be nearer together than in the ftory-houfe; and fimilar paffages are to be made for the upper floor; for two Stocks are in-tended to ftand on the bottom, and two on the upper floor.

106. No doubt there will be a defire of fetting glaffes on the tops of thefe boxes in a fimilar manner to thofe of the ftory me-thod. For this reafon it is, that a foot in height is left in each ftory above the boxes for that purpofe. But if there be no inten-tion of ufing glaffes, the houfes may be made 16 inches lower.

107. Let it be obferved, that this houfe, and that before defcribed, are formed upon a fcale adapted to the fize of my boxes. But where larger boxes are intended, the houfe muft be made in proportion to the fize. Gen-tlemen of fortune may have thefe houfes built in a very handfome manner, and orna-mented according to their own tafte; but great care muft be taken not to alter or de-part from the fcale of dimenfions. .

108. The fpaces left between each pair of boxes are for their more commodious removal,

removal, efpecially for the ftory boxes; for
when thefe are to be raifed or feparated, unlefs there be a fufficient vacancy to fet a fpare
box between, the Stock muft. be removed
out of the houfe upon a ftool, and then put
in again, which prolongs the operation needlefsly, and renders it more troublefome to the
Apiator as well as to the Bees. However,
fuch as may think fixteen inches between
every other pair of boxes, a needlefs and too
expenfive a lengthening of the houfe, may fo
contract the fcale or plan, as to leave only
fix inches between each; fo much room is
abfolutely neceffary to put the arms between
the boxes whenever they are to be lifted up
or fhifted.

CHAPTER VI.

Of BEE-BOXES, *or* BOX-HIVES.

109. WE now proceed to the conftruction of the boxes, (fig. 7.)
which, from a great variety of frequently repeated experiments, I have found in every
refpect to be the moft fimple in their contrivance, the moft eafy to manage, the moft
profitable in their produce, and the moft
moderate

moderate in price of any hitherto offered to the public attention ; at the fame time they are equal, if not fuperior, to any others, for the amufement and improvement of the inquifitive.

110. Thefe are to be made of well feafoned yellow deal, or any other thoroughly feafoned wood, that which is the leaft apt to warp or fplit, and has likewife the feweft knots, is the heft for the purpofe. Each board muft be at leaft three quarters of an inch thick after having been well planed. Thinner boards will not keep the Bees warm enough in the winter, and will therefore endanger their lives.

111. They are to be in the infide full nine inches high, and eleven fquare, from fide to fide. Therefore allowance muft be made in the height to receive three bars of wood, (fig. 7.) of the fame thicknefs as that of the box ; thefe bars are to extend from the front to the back ; the middle bar, (fig. 9.) is to be three inches and a half wide, and the right and left bars only three inches. Thefe bars are to be let into the top, fo as to have four intervals, or openings, *a, a, a, a,* of half an inch between each bar, as well as between the two fides of the box.

112. There muft be parallel grooves in the edges of every bar, and in the two fides of the box ; thefe grooves muft be one-fixteenth of an inch deep, and one-twelfth of an inch wide, in which iron fliders are propofed to run. To admit which, in the back

of

of the box, the ends of the bars are to
let in flufh with the grooves, while the up
ends are to be *rabbeted,* fo as to be even v
the upper part of the grooves; a thin fi
(*a.* fig. 9.) is then braided upon the rabb
which by this management will form f
flits or openings, (fig. *b, b, b, b,)* of
fame depth as the grooves, and in wi
three quarters of an inch, in order to rece
four fliders, (fig. 10.) nearly of thofe dim
fions.

113. But it muft be *noted* that the b
are *not* to be nailed down to the box, tl
being intended to be moveable at pleafu
The *greateft exactnefs* is required in tl
dimenfions and conftruction, or the whole
their defign will be rendered ufelefs, a
thereby bring the fcheme into difcrec
though the fault will in reality be in
bungling carpenter. Few among the coi
try carpenters (efpecially journeymen) h
tools proper for the woik.

114. For the grooves fhould be made p
fectly fmooth within fide, and of the ex
width and depth, therefore cannot be execu
by a tenant or common faw, and the uf
ploughing irons are too large. If the groo
are made rough or uneven, the fliders can
run in them with the requifite cafe. (
which is equally inconvenient, if too w
or too deep, they will caufe the fliders
run irregularly, and tempt the Bees
fill them fo full of wax or propolis,
to prevent the entrance of the flic
with

without great force, thereby greatly diſturbing the Bees, and running a great riſque of
ſpoiling the operation. After the fillets are
fitted on, they muſt be ſawed through by a
very fine ſaw between each bar, ſo that the
bars may be taken out *ſeparately*.

115. As the principal intention of the
box-hive is to view the Bees at work, and the
manner of their performing their operations,
there muſt be an opening cut in the back
to receive a pane of glaſs five, ſix, or ſeven
inches ſquare, as may be thought convenient; but in general, it will be more
eligible to have the glaſs the entire length of
the back, and but two inches and a half wide;
the upper edge of the glaſs to be within four
inches of the top of the box. But where a
more extenſive inſpection is deſired, the two
ſides and the back of the box muſt be framed,
(as for a ſaſh window) to receive as large
panes of glaſs as poſſible, conſiſtent with the
required ſtrength of the box. A greater depth
is required in the upper part of the back
frame than the reſt, the more ſecurely to let
in the ends of the bars. There muſt be alſo
three ſhutters, to ſhut cloſe over the windows, to preſerve the hive warm in winter,
and to prevent the light from withdrawing
the attention of the Bees from their
work. Boxes with only one pane of glaſs, are
alſo to have ſhutters, (fig. 7. D.) either with
hinges or to ſlide in rabbets, both ways, to
right or left; or two ſmall ſhutters to turn
upon ſcrews in their tops, and dividing to

E right

right and left ; they fhould meet in a rabbet, and be faftened by a button at bottom.

116. In the front edges of the boxes, an opening or door-way muft be cut out, four inches long, and three-eighths of an inch deep This *depth* is fully fuf-ficient for the paffage of the Bees, and if made deeper or higher, becomes capable of admitting mice and other vermin, to the great prejudice of the Bees.

117. Befides the bars to which the Bees will faften their combs, a top or cover muft be provided of the fame thicknefs as the box, to extend about half an inch over the edges, except in the front, where it muft be exactly flufh, becaufe the box muft ftand quite clofe to the front of the houfe. The cover is to be fcrewed down, not nailed ; it would be very convenient, if the fcrews had a ring or a head, projecting flat, that they might be taken out by the finger and thumb ; but as none fuch are kept in the fhops of a fize fmall enough, and to be made on purpofe may be thought too dear, therefore the com-mon round-headed fcrews, beat as flat as you can with a hammer, may be eafily taken out or in by a pair of pliers or pincers. The fcrews fhould always be greafed before they are put in, or they will ruft, and then cannot be eafily withdrawn.

The holes to receive the fcrews had better be made always in the fame places of every box, four in each cover, two in the right hand edge, and two in the left, and one inch and

and a half from the front and back ; by thefe means, the.fcrews of the boxes will indifcriminately fuit each other, without breaking the edges of the boxes with frefh holes.

118. One cover ferves for each pair of boxes, as does a moveable floor of the fame dimenfions of the cover ; one edge of which muft be planed true, that it may come quite clofe to the Bee-houfe. If boards of the above width cannot eafily be procured, narrower may be rabbeted or tenanted together, and flips of wood let in at the ends of the floors, to prevent their cafting ; but the covers may have flips nailed acrofs. Any crevices or chafms left in the bottom, will harbour earwigs and other vermin, and thus occafion, not unfrequently, the deftruction of the Stock.

119. Another important nicety in the formation of the box-hives is, that the edges, both at top and bottom, be made fo true, that any one box may be fet over or under another, and no chafm left between, to admit either an earwig or a moth, but ftand firm and level ; for they will be wanted to ftand one upon another promifcuoufly.

120. It has been obferved before, that fome perfons may prefer the collateral arrangement. Boxes for this purpofe are to be made of the fame dimenfions as the foregoing: They are unlike only in this, that inftead of the bars being on the top of the box, thefe are to be on the fide, viz. on the right hand fide of one box, and

on

on the left of the other; that when the
boxes are placed together, the barred fides
may tally and meet fo exactly, that no vermin may get between, as before obferved of
the ftory boxes. But as thefe boxes are but
nine inches high, the bars muft be made
conformable to that proportion, viz. two of
three inches and a quarter, and one at bottom
of one inch, leaving *three* openings of communication each half an inch wide.

121. The top board is to be nailed faft
down, and muft be the exact fquare of the
box, for it muft have a groove on the fame
fide as the bars, and fimilar thereto, to receive the edge of the upper flider. As thefe
bars are *not* to be taken out, they muft be
braded in faft, to ftrengthen the box. The
barred fide muft have a cover to fcrew on
when the boxes are feparated. But like the
ftory boxes, one cover will be fufficient for a
pair of boxes, as it will never be neceffary for
both to be covered at the fame time. Each
box muft have a moveable bottom, fomething
wider than the boxes, but the edges muft be
fquare and even, that they may form a
clofe joining, and alfo may fet quite clofe to
the front of the Bee-houfe.

122. As there are no openings in the tops
of thefe collateral boxes, which might admit glaffes, when fuch are defired, circular
holes may be made of half an inch in diameter, *(by a centre or fpoon bit)* in number
according to the magnitude and number of
the glaffes to be fet on. Thefe holes may
be

be covered, when not wanted, by buttons properly adapted to them.

(123.) Many contrivances have been formed to obviate the great inconvenience and danger attending the feparation of boxes in the ufual way. I fhall juft mention here fome contrivances that may greatly facilitate this operation. A more perfect method will be fhewn hereafter (605).

124. In order to prevent the Bees flying out upon the Apiator when he takes off a box, a frame (fig. 11.) may be made with bars, grooves, &c. of the fame dimenfions, and fimilar to the top of the box, (111, and feq.). But it is neceffary to obferve, that all the fides of the frame muft be of the fame thicknefs as the edge of the box.

125. Another method is, to have a groove in each fide of the box, and as near the bottom as conveniently can be made; and in the back a correfponding flit from fide to fide, to admit a fheet or plate of *double* tin, which is to be fhoved in when hives are to be feparated.

126. Thirdly, If the boxes are made with a three inch and a half bar in the middle of the bottoms, two faws, five or fix inches broad, fhoved in judicioufly at the fides of the box, will feparate them without receiving any confiderable annoyance from the Bees. The front end of the bar muft fpread out above four inches, and be levelled down to a feather edge at the ·door way, to admit the Bees.

E 3　　　127. The

127. The firft method may be objected to as being too expenfive. , The fecond will damage the Bees; as the flider cannot pafs clofe to the under hive, and muft cut through all the combs, which are generally extended and fixed to the under hive.

128. The third fcheme is the moft eligible, as there are few perfons but what either have or may readily borrow faws fit for the purpofe. And any refufe bits of wood, of the proper dimenfions, may be tacked in with little or no trouble or expence. I mean of fuch of the common people as have any œconomy or ingenuity : as to the idle and diffolute, it is a pity they fhould ever have any Bees.

129. The improved method I am emulous to introduce, is by the ufe of fliders (fig. 10.) of a peculiar conftruction, on which the whole fuccefs of the management depends.

130. They are to be four in number, and formed of milled iron; they fhould be one-twelfth of an inch thick, fourteen inches long, but not *quite* half an inch wide (*c,*) except within an inch of the end (*b,*) which muft be five-eighths wide, and terminating in a circular concave form (*a,*) the concavity of which is to be no more than one-eighth deep. The ends of the openings in the wooden tops are to be indented, conformable to that figure, to admit the fliders fo clofe at the ends that no Bee can efcape.

The

The ends of the fliders are thus conftructed, that in entering the grooves, they
may cut and throw out the wax and propolis,
with which the Bees generally clofe up the
grooves (as they do all crevices in their hives)
as they are thruft in, which otherwife would
bind the fliders and prevent their introduction, at leaft not without great difficulty.
Befides, in order the better to facilitate their
paffage, only an inch at the ends is left wide
enough to extend into the grooves; for was.
the whole length of the flider to run therein, the friction would be very confiderably
increafed.

131. Thefe confiderations are of importance,
for by this contrivance we give the Bees
fo little difturbance in their introduction,
that a child may perform the operation without danger. Whereas, in the forcible method of prior contrivances, the Bees are greatly diftreffed, as well as the Apiator; nor can
many hives be managed in a day: the uproar becoming too great, alarming, and dangerous.

132. It will be proper, and indeed neceffary, for fuch as have a great number of
Stocks, to have eight iron fliders; as fuch a
number will, in many cafes, prove very convenient, and greatly expedite the operations.

133. Should the hives be fhewn to the
fmith, before he makes the fliders, it may
perhaps give him a better idea of what he
is to do, efpecially if he has any ingenuity;
which indeed I have not always found to be

E 4 the

the cafe with thefe fwarthy gentlemen, any more than with the carpenters.

134. If in any very fortunate fituation my box hives fhould be found too fmall, they may be enlarged an inch or more in height, and an inch or more in length and width, the bars being made wider and longer in proportion. But it will not be advife-able to increafe the number of bars: as four openings will be fully fufficient, while a greater number will unneceffarily augment the trouble and expence.

135. The boxes with large panes of glafs in the back and fides, are chiefly defigned to be placed in chambers and parlours, in order to be more immediately and conftantly under the infpection of the proprietor; for this purpofe, a fhelf of the due proportion is to be faftened in the window and a proper opening cut in the edge of the fafh for the paffage of the Bees to and fro. Great care muft be taken that the door-way of the box fits clofe to the fafh, or the Bees will get into the room. If there be window fhutters, correfponding openings muft be made in them, as fervants will often lie in bed longer than the Bees. Thefe boxes fhould be co-vered with a warm cloth in winter. They may be made of mahogany where elegance is required. If the windows be at times opened, the Bees will come in and be very troublefome, which renders the introduc-tion of boxes, rather inconvenient in fuch places; fome out-buildings will therefore be more eligible. CHAP.

CHAPTER VII.

Of STRAW HIVES.

136. OF all fuch hives as are to ftand unfheltered by a houfe thofe made of ftraw are much to be preferred; as beft defending the Bees both from exceffive heat, and exceffive cold.

137. Where ftraw hives are not to be procured eafily, rufhes feem to be the beft fubftitute, but they muft be gathered when mature, and be well dried. In fome countries wicker, or bafket hives, plaiftered over with clay, cow dung, or the like are ufed. But thefe are neither fo cleanly, fo comfortable, nor fo eafily managed as the ftraw hives.

138. Trunks of hollow trees, cut into the proper dimenfions, made fmooth and clean within fide, furnifhed with bottoms and tops properly adapted to them, and painted on the outfide, will make good and very durable hives, and are much preferable to thofe of wicker or bafket.

139. However, as ftraw hives are the beft, and in general very eafily procurable, we will confine ourfelves to them. Thefe are to be made of unthrefhed rye ftraw, if it can be procured fo, for threfhed ftraw being very much broken and fhivered, occafions the hives

to

to be very rough and troublefome to the Bees at their firft entrance. Therefore the number of hives wanted fhould be befpoke before harveft, that the maker may have an opportunity of procuring pioper ftraw for the purpofe. Twice the number of hives to that of Stocks fhould be in readinefs, or there will not be a fufficiency for Swarms, and for additional hives to your old Stocks.

140. The fizes of hives vary in different counties, containing from half a bufhel, or or lefs, to a bufhel. The moft convenient fize, as I have found upon many repeated trials, is that of *half a bufhel*. Perhaps this will fuit all fituations, except the heath countries; in thofe, indeed, when only one hive is intended for a Stock, a bufhel will not be too big.

141. It is probable, that fhould the dimenfions I recommend be generally adopted, the hive makers would find it their intereft to conform to that ftandard; and confequently there would be no difficulty of procuring proper hives throughout the kingdom.

142. The ftraw hives (fig. 8, *a*) according to, my propofed dimenfions, are to be clear nine inches high, and twelve inches wide on the infide, exclufive of the ftraw. They are to be made without tops, and quite upright, fo as to refemble a broad hoop.

143. The greateft exertion of the makers fkill will confift in their being made exact to the above dimenfions, and all fo very exactly and equally alike, that every different
ent

ent hive, may be put over or under any other, and fet clofe and level; for which reafon all the edges both under and upper, fhould be made as true as poffible, rather broader than any other part, and as flat as can be. But in one of the edges the bryer binding fhould be left diftant three or four inches in length, in order for the ftraw to be cut away to form a proper door-way.

144. They are to have covers of ftraw bound together in the fame manner as the hives; thefe are to be quite flat, and broad enough to extend half an inch beyond the edge of the hive on which they are to fet clofe and even. They are to be made feparate from the hive, being intended to be put on and taken off at pleafure; one cover only is requifite to every pair of hives, viz. to twelve hives fix covers.

145. If the hive-maker fhould procure a hoop bent to the exact dimenfions, or width, it might prove a ftandard to work the whole by, to the greateft exactnefs. Should he alfo, as foon as a hive is made, place a fmooth board over it, and jump thereon him-felf, efpecially if he be a fat jolly fellow, or put a great weight thereon, it would greatly contribute to make the hive clofe, and the edges level.

146. Thefe ftraw hives, befides the ftraw covers, are to have wooden tops, which are to be formed upon the fame idea as thofe for the box hives, viz. they are to have four

openings,

openings, so as to admit four of the same constructed sliders, as those used for the boxes.

These tops (fig. 6.) are to be round, fourteen inches in diameter, and five-eighths of an inch in thickness, when planed. In each there are to be four openings, *a. a. a. a.* the two innermost are to be eleven inches long each, and the two outermost six inches long each, and all the openings exactly half an inch wide. It is to be composed of three pieces of wood each three inches wide, and which we shall call *bars, c. c. c.* and of proper length to form the circle as above described, together with two smaller circular pieces, *e. e.* to fill up the whole. These bars are to be joined together ~~and~~ the ends, *(f. f. f. f. f. f. f. f.)* by intermediate pieces of the same thickness as the bars, and wide enough to be rabbetted about a quarter of an inch into each bar, so that when glued in, the openings may be left precisely half an inch wide, and of the lengths as above specified. If the joining pieces are not rabbetted, as soon as the bars, by the heat of the sun and of the Bees, become perfectly dry, they will separate, and the whole frame become loose and unconnected. The whole being glued together, nail a piece of board across, to prevent any disunion. But, *previous to the joining,* there is a very essential operation to be performed to the greatest nicety, viz. *grooves* which are to be made

in

*until the glue
berrectly dry*

in the *edges* of every bar one-fixteenth of an
inch deep, and one-twelfth of an inch wide,
capable of receiving with eafe the iron fliders
before defcribed (130); therefore, if the
grooves are not made very accurate, the
whole will be rendered ufelefs.

147. As foon as the glue of the work is
thoroughly hardened, two flips of milled
iron, (fig. 6.) fomething thicker than double tin, and as wide as the bars are thick,
are to be *drawn nearly round the* whole edge,
as far as is dotted, and nailed firmly on.

148. This will bind the whole more firmly
together than if hooped all round; but flits
muft be cut out oppofite four of the openings, at one end, of a length, (fig. 6, *e. e. e. e.)*
juft fufficient to admit the fliders, and no
wider than neceffary; for if too wide, the
Bees will have a paffage out to annoy the
Operator. By painting the edges of thefe
wooden tops, they may be preferved for
ages, efpecially if carefully kept in a dry
place when not in ufe. It is not every common carpenter, however, that has either ingenuity or tools to make them with fufficient
nicety, but they may be very exactly and
eafily made by one that is mafter of his
profeffion.

149. It muft be carefully noted, that when
any of thefe tops are fixed on, that part
which has the flits in the edge for the fliders
to enter, muft be always fixed at the *back*
part of the hive.

150. But

150. But a cheaper method of making them, is to nail the bars together with two small side pieces, properly grooved in a hoop, made of the same depth as the bars, and slits afterwards sawed out, for the entrance of the sliders. The ends, however, of the openings in the front must be contracted about an inch by pieces of wood glued in, the inward parts being made rounding, the better to receive the ends of the sliders, so as to come close. But the ends where the sliders enter, are only to be stopped up, leaving the grooves open, otherwise the sliders cannot enter at all. If the ends are not thus managed, the Bees will escape underneath, and the cold and the vermin will have too free an admission; pieces of cork glued in will answer the purpose.

151. These tops as well as the preceding, when placed upon the hives, must have long brads, or wooden pegs, passed through each end of the middle bar, so as to penetrate about an inch into the edge of the straw, in order to keep the top steady from slipping either one way or the other.

152. Those who do not choose to have any box hives, may have a pane of glass fixed in the back of a straw hive; this is to be done by cutting four or five rounds of straw in depth, and about four or five inches in length, fixing the glass in at the ends of the straw, and stopping the joinings with putty. A cover of wood must be placed before it.

153. Those

153. Thofe alfo who cannot well afford
thefe kind of tops, need not be difcouraged.
The meaneft cottager may eafily make tops
himfelf, unlefs he had rather idly fleep-
away that time in the chimney corner, during the long winter evenings, which he
might employ in fo pleafing and beneficial a purpofe. For a *trifle* he may procure
refufe pieces of wood of three inches breadth,
and fifteen in length; or he might with only
a knife furnifh himfelf with fuch from the
branches of a tree; and with the fame knife, reduce them to the requifite flatnefs and fmooth-
nefs, though his genius be but of the moderate
degree. The ends of thefe flicks or bars muft
extend fufficiently over the edges of the hive,
fo as with nails or pegs, to faften acrofs them
bits of wood to hold the bar at half an inch
diftance, and two fmall pieces at the fides,
pegged down into the edges of the ftraw; the
ends of the openings to be filled up with
wood or cork, clay, or cow dung, even with
the infide of the hive.

154. This top will make a very good
fhift without grooves; and he will find in
the fequel feveral methods, by which he
may eafily manage with it *without* fliders,
(559, 600, 605.)

155. For want of a ftraw covering, lay
upon an even piece of ground or floor fmall
twigs (long enough to cover your hive) of
oziers, willows, rufhes, or the like; on
thefe plafter clay, cow dung, or lime and
fand; then put on another layer of twigs,
and

and another of clay, &c. when this is dry it will form a tolerable covering, and if made fhelving from the middle to the edges, will throw the water off, and keep the Bees dry.

156. For thofe who can afford it, large earthen milk or pudding pans laid over their ftraw hives is the beft covering that I know of. The largeft fort will extend fufficiently to clear the hive-floors of the water that drops from them. Cracked ones may do if the cracks be well ftopped with putty, clay, &c. thefe may be had very cheap. The ufual coverings among the country people are hackels made of ftraw, gathered to a point at the top, and fpreading down all round the hive; thefe form a tolerable covering; but unlefs well attended to, are apt, after a while, to admit the rain, and harbour mice (651.).

187. Pans are not liable to thefe inconveniences, and are more eafily removed. Befide which, as our hive floors are not fixed, the pans being heavy, keep the hives fo fteady, that no common winds will difplace them.

CHAP-

CHAPTER VIII.

STRICTURES *on* Mr. WILDMAN'S *and other prior constructed* HIVES *and* BOXES; *shewing their Defects and Inconveniences, with a Comparison between them and those of my* PLAN.

158. IT is now much more than a century since the first attempt was made by the means of box hives, to manage Bees without destroying them. Several ingenious gentlemen, in succession, have very laudably endeavoured to improve upon each other. Among these were, Messrs. Mew, ~~Goddy.~~ Wolridge, Rusden, Warder, Thorley, White, and last of all, Mr. Thomas Wildman.

159. However praise-worthy their design the public at large has been but little benefited. The expence of box hives and houses has hitherto, and is always likely, to confine this improvement to the wealthy, as they are by no means adapted to common use. Warder, indeed, foretold this when he wrote, and facts have verified it to this day; unless therefore we can introduce a scheme which may come within the compass of the farmer's and cottager's abilities and attention, we labour in vain.

F   160. The

160. The perfection of this art does not confist merely in taking the honey and wax, without deftroying thofe that procured them; it extends alfo to the doing it with the leaft poffible difturbance and damage to the Bees, with the greateft cafe and fafety to the Operator, and with the fimpleft and cheapeft apparatus.

161. It will be proper to make a few remarks upon the moft noted of thofe apparatus' which have already been introduced to the public.

We will begin with octagon box hives. Warder and fome others have recommended thefe in preference to every other kind, on a fuppofition that as they will be warmer, fo the Bees in the winter, and the brood in the fpring, would thereby receive the greater benefit. But if we turn fiom theory to practice, it will be found (at leaft with me it has) that the Bees and brood thrive as well in fquare boxes as in round ftraw-hives, which are much warmer than any box hives whatever.

162. The *fize* of a hive indeed is of confequence, but not fo the fhape. Large hives are very troublefome to handle. In winter, alfo there will be too much vacant fpace in them, whereby the Bees will be too much chilled. In fummer, the Swarms will be too late; nor will they be able to fill two fuch hives in a feafon, except both that and the fituationbe uncommonly advantageous.

163. On the contrary, fmall hives not having fufficient room for a great number,

the

the Bees are obliged to ſwarm too ſoon and in too ſmall a quantity, room being wanted for the continual encreaſe of the young. Nor are they capacious enough to hold a Stock of Bees ſufficiently large to perform the various operations requiſite in the ſpring, nor will they be ſo well preſerved from the winter's cold. For the greater the number the greater the warmth will be, provided the hives be well filled; for on this alone the great benefit depends, and not on the *ſhape* of the box. Much leſs does it depend upon the nature of the wood of which the box is made; for it is of no real conſequence whether it be of deal, mahogany, or cedar. The Bees are not fanciful enough to ſtand upon ſuch niceties. Let any gentleman keep two good Stocks of Bees, one in a deal box, and the other in a hive made of any other materials, and he will be convinced that this theory is without any foundation.

164. Prior to Mr. T. Wildman there has been no conſiderable variation in the conſtruction of boxes, except in Mr. White's; for Ruſden, Warder, Thorley, and ſome others, are of the ſame ſentiment reſpecting the openings of communication; viz. to have theſe in the middle of the tops of the hives, about ſix inches long and four inches broad.

165. This conſtruction has appeared to me very injudicious; nor has Mr. T. Wildman's

narrow

narrow bars * appeared lefs fo; as it clafhes with the generally received doctrine, *that the Queen Bee chiefly refides in the center of the hive : There fhe fixes her palace and throne, as being moft fecure,* moft warm, and moft fecret, and which fhe feldom quits but to depofite her eggs, returning again immediately afterwards to her wonted privacy. If fo her life muft be in imminent danger at the time of driving the wooden flider in; for upon any difturbance fhe generally afcends towards the top, and therefore may be crufhed by the flider, which cannot be introduced *gently,* becaufe it will be obftructed by the extenfion of the combs thro' the openings from the upper to the under part. Nay, even the feparation made by a tin flider, will not prevent the honey from running down among the Bees, in the very center of the box; this will likewife befmear the openings, and deftroy many of the Bees, nay, not unfrequently, the Queen herfelf; and thus occafion the ruin of the Stock.

166. Thefe dangers, I have the vanity to think, are obviated by the nature and difpofition of my fliders and tops : For the middle bar is three inches and a half wide; to this two combs will be always made, and a fpace left between for the Queen's refidence, over which there being no opening fhe will be in perfect fecurity from the fliders, which are to run on the fides

of

---

* Management of Bees, 1770.

of the combs.   To, which may be added,
that theſe ſliders can always be introduced by
the *hand*; whereas the wooden ones muſt
generally be forced in by a hammer or
mallet, greatly diſturbing and hurting both
the combs and the Bees; nor is it likely
that the Apiator himſelf will eſcape quite
free.

167. Another great inconvenience attending theſe middle openings is, the giving the
Bees much unneceſſary labour, by making
them crawl up the ſides, &c. before they can
get to them, and many of them are a long
while before they can find them out.   In Mr.
Daniel Wildman's, (nephew to Mr. Thomas
Wildman) box hives the communications
are near the back.   The Queen indeed by this
alteration is not in quite ſo much peril, but
it increaſes the taſk of the Bees.   For theſe
inſects uſually and through choice aſcend by
the front of a hive, and the neareſt combs;
conſequently the way is conſiderably lengthened by their being obliged to go to the
back before they can aſcend.   Theſe are perhaps the principal reaſons why Bees in
theſe boxes ſhew ſo great a reluctance to
begin to work in an upper hive.

168. Let it alſo be conſidered, that when
an empty hive is ſet under another, the Bees,
heavily laden, muſt firſt crawl up its ſides to
the top, and when there, muſt ſearch about
ſome time before they can find the opening,
and when found, it leads not to the diſtant
combs, where their ſervice is now moſt

F 3   wanted,

wanted, but to the place already filled and thronged with the Queen and her numerous retinue. And not only fo, but this dif-agreeable tafk muft, perhaps be continued fome weeks, before they will be ready to work in a lower hive, or have made combs in its center to afcend by. So that here is a great wafte, both of toil and time.

169. Actuated by the defire of difcovering a method to remedy thefe great inconve-niences, and to preferve with more cafe and certainty the young brood, the Rev. Mr. White paid great attention to this fubject. The refult of his care and trouble was the ingenious and fimple invention of collateral boxes.

Madam Vicat, a no lefs ingenious lady, of Switzerland, has endeavoured to improve upon him. And a gentleman under the fig-nature of *A Lover of Bees,* in the appendix to Mr. T. Wildman's treatife, has propofed an improvement upon both.

170. Undoubtedly, by having the commu-nications in the fides, the Queen can be in no danger, and was there no other method of obtaining this advantage but the collateral, we fhould not hefitate to give it the pre-ference.

But by keeping Bees both in ftory and collateral boxes at the fame time, I have conftantly found that they will not fo rea-dily extend their works lengthways as per-pendicularly. Befides, in Mr. White's boxes the openings are not fufficiently numerous

to

to tempt the Bees that way. And, not only so, his method of sliding a sheet of tin, to separate the boxes, irritates the Bees more, and the Apiator is in greater danger than if he had precipitately forced the boxes asunder without it; as any one upon trial may be feelingly convinced of. Upon the whole, the operation is much more awkward and inconvenient to be performed this way than story method.

171. But the grand point, which these several improvements seem to have more immediately in view, is the better nurture of the brood, which they suppose, with some other authors, are placed in the middle of the hive, and unless so placed will not arrive at maturity.

172. This perhaps is carrying our refinements too far. That the Queen, in general, lays most of her eggs, especially the Drone eggs, in the center of the combs, is true. But if room be wanted, she will lay them in any other parts, even close to the windows, not excepting the royal cells; nor has it been observed that any failed the more on that account. Of the truth of this I have had yearly demonstrations ever since I have kept Bees. Nay, the contrivance itself defeats its principal design, viz. the procuring a greater degree of warmth for the brood. For by adding these side boxes, the Queen is induced to lay her eggs nearest the entrance, consequently the brood must be much more subject to the influence of the

air

air than if the brood were in a box
behind, or in an upper one. The truth is,
we much oftener want early honey than
early broods; and frequently both the old
and young perifh in the fpring for want
of food, and not for want of a warm fituation.

173. The *Lover of Bees* propofes that
a fuit of three boxes be placed *before* each
other, inftead of fide by fide. This does
not feem to me to promife more fuccefs
than the others. For, in the firft place, we
cannot fo conveniently fee how they thrive in
the middle box. Secondly, when an empty
box is placed before another, the Bees muft
pafs with their loads through it, fome weeks
perhaps before they will have occafion to
build therein, or otherwife frequent infpection is required, to fee when they want an
additional box, or they may want room before it be known that they have need of it;
whereas in the collateral and ftory plan,
they may have admittance to either without that inconvenience. Sliders are alfo to
be ufed in the feparation; but as we have
neither been favoured with the particulars
of this arrangement, nor with any account
of his fuccefs, we can fay nothing very decifive concerning it. This we lament, as
the writer feems to be a judicious obferver of
Bees, and has made fome very pertinent remarks upon Wildman.

174. But I find that all thefe, and feveral
other methods, have been tried by a very
ingenious

ingenious gentleman, who publiſhed in 1675, under the ſignature of J. W. Gent. *, and had been then found as inadmiſſible for general practice as they have ſince.

To remedy the inconveniences of theſe methods I contrived mine, which is much leſs complicated, and much leſs expenſive; requires but little attention and trouble in the management: far leſs indeed than Madam Vicat's, whoſe Boxes cannot be ſeparated without the introduction of ſmoke; (not to ſay any thing of the expence) which renders the operation ſtill more troubleſome and offenſive to the Apiator and Bees than any of the other modes before-mentioned.

175. Mr. Thomas Wildman's boxes † are the next that merit our attention. And although he has diſtinguiſhed himſelf very eminently in the *Bee-walk*, and enlightened us in ſome things, yet we muſt not depend upon him as infallible.

176. His plan conſiſts of a double ſquare box, the lower one to have ſix bars acroſs, for the Bees to fix their combs on; the upper box inſtead of bars is to have two frames, and each frame to have four upright ſliders. There is a wooden ſlider to be put in between the upper and lower box, and a ſimilar ſlider at bottom. There are three windows with ſhutters to each box.

177. A

---

*. Which I ſuppoſe to be Worlidge.
† See his Treatiſe on the Management of Bees, p. 112.

177. A drawing is given of thefe boxes and frames, but it is too inaccurate, and his defcription too defective, to be underftood by common underftandings. At leaft, neither myfelf, nor feveral of his friends, to whom I have fhewn it, were able to comprehend it. However, the purport feems to be, that each of thefe frames are intended to hold three combs, and when filled are to be drawn up at the top.

178. Something analogous to thefe are thofe of his nephew Mr. Daniel Wildman. *. But thefe have three frames in a box, and are to be drawn out at the back. Others I have feen formed with three drawers, to be pulled out like thofe of a cheft.

179. All thefe are very pretty contrivances in *fpeculation*. But let me here obferve, that when any of the frames, or divifions, are *drawn* out, a whole regiment of Bees will *draw* upon the innovator in defence of their property (48.). The difturbance is great, and their fury ftill greater. But fuppofe the Bees can be confined in the frame until that is taken out, the expence of fo many frames is needlefs, becaufe the box itfelf may be feparated, and any combs taken that are proper to be fo, and the box afterwards returned.

Befides, the Bees will extend their combs over the joinings of the frames, and if they do

---

* Complete Guide, &c.

do not fit very cloſe will cement them ſo
firmly with propolis as to render it im-
praƈticable to draw them out at all.

180. Neither can I agree with Mr. T.
Wildman, ·' .'t repeated tappings upon the
glaſs will áuſe the Bees to quit a box; ſo
far from .'t, they will flock to that place
in greater numbers. But ſuppoſe the greater
part do aſcend into the upper box, ſome
will remain, and conſequently when the
pane of glaſs is taken out, (as he direƈts) in
order to come at the combs in the lower box,
the remaining Bees will certainly revenge
the theft: for no tappings upon glaſs can
be ſtrong enough to intimidate the Bees like
driving. Then to take the pane of glaſs
out firſt, and afterwards the combs at the
back, muſt be a very awkward, inconvenient, and alſo a ſlovenly method, for
much of the honey will be ſmeared about
the box.

181. The ſame objeƈtion that has been
made againſt the frames, holds equally good
againſt the ſliders in the middle and bottom
of the boxes. For being of wood, and the
whole breadth of the box, they will be far
more difficult to introduce than any we have
yet mentioned.

182. Mr. T. Wildman aſſerts, (page 156.)
" that as there are but three combs in each
ſeparate frame, the Queen at any time may
be diſcovered." It does not appear ſo to me;
and moſt connoiſſeurs in Bees know, that except at the moment of depoſiting her eggs,

if

if there be but two combs, the Queen will
be in the middle, and fo furrounded by her
attendant Bees as not to be feen, unlefs
through mere chance, by the beft pair of
philofophic eyes in the kingdom. If a hive
conftructed entirely of glafs (as a globe) will
not prefent us with an opportunity of beholding her Majefty, much lefs can we expect it from fo partial an opening as that of
a fide or back window.

183. But the grand object principally intended by his plan, and that of feveral others,
is the taking the honey frequently; as he-
ing then, fay they, much fuperior in goodnefs than it would be if left 'till the end of the
feafon. Conformable to this defign is the
conftruction of Mr. T. Wildman's ftraw
hives as well as of his boxes, confequently
the fame ftrictures will fo far apply to both.

184. That honey taken in the fummer
is better than what is taken in autumn is
by no means fo clear a point. Becaufe, as
foon as cells are filled with honey, they
are fealed up with wax; which is full as
effectual to preferve the fpirit and fragrance
of the honey, as the beft glafs phials, even
though they have ground glafs ftoppers. If
honey be depofited in virgin cells it will
fuffer no diminution of its goodnefs, nor
alteration in its colour, however long it may
be kept there; but if laid up in old cells,
it will in a very few days become darker coloured.

185. I

185. I acknowledge, that honey taken at the time when the moſt aromatic flowers are in bloom, is preferable to any other; but then this may be done, and beſt done too, by glaſſes, or other ſmall veſſels placed upon the tops of the boxes or hives (431, 452, 462.) without any additional expence, and with very little trouble. In other reſpects, one of my hives or boxes, taken when full, will have honey and wax equal in quality to any from his ſhallow hives.

186. Beſides, there will often be brood in the ſhallow hives when taken off, nor will they yield ſo much virgin honey as might be ſuppoſed I tried Mr. T. Wildman's ſhallow hives three ſucceſſive years, but they afforded me not near the profit I gained from thoſe Stocks of the ſame years which were managed in my own way.

187. Mr. T. Wildman has introduced into his practice tops for his ſtraw hives with circular holes; theſe I am apt to think are rather diſagreeable to the Bees, as they oblige them to build their combs out of the uſual ſtile of parallel lines, and to vary them, in many curved directions, according as the holes interfere. If holes are thought moſt proper, they ſhould be made in double rows as near as poſſible to each other, and in ſtraight lines, leaving proper vacancies between every double row, for the combs to be fixed to.

188. It will not, I hope, be thought impertinent if I here make a ſlight digreſſion,

for

for the fake of obferving, that when fuch Swarms as came from the Stocks of thefe hives that had tops with holes in them, were put into hives with bars, they neverthelefs made their combs fome curved and fome oblique, and this for two years in fucceffion; which evidently proves, that the old Bees go out with the Swarms, and that thofe young Bees of the fecond year, which faw the manner of building in the hive they left, purfued the fame plan when they formed a part of the next fpring Swarm *. It alfo proves, that the elder Bees are the principal architects.

188. Perhaps it may not be improper to make fome further brief remarks upon Mr. T. Wildman's ftraw hives, and by comparing them with thofe I propofe, fome judgment may be formed which is the fimpleft, eafieft, and moft beneficial; and from thence inferences may be readily and juftly drawn refpecting all other kinds of hives and boxes.

189. His ftraw hives are feven inches high and ten wide; in the upper row of ftraw a hoop is faftened, and to this are nailed five bars, each one inch and a quarter wide. In one of thefe hives a Swarm is firft to be put, and another placed under it the

next

---

* From this circumftance a queftion may arife relating to Inftinct, which is fuppofed to act invariably. For how is it poffible that faculty could impel thefe infects to deviate from a ftraight line, and to carry on their work in directions fuited to their new habitation? Was there no ratiocination employed?

next morning. This next morning's work·
my hives do not require. But why the
morning, when in the next evening it may be
done with more eaſe and ſafety ? Soon after
a third hive is to be placed under the two
former ; but whether at night or in the
morning we are left in the dark. At the
end of about three weeks, the top hive is to be
taken off, at the noon of a fair day (611),
and a *fourth* hive is then to be placed under
thoſe that are left. After a while another
hive is to be taken off and a fifth added,
obſerving that the firſt hive taken off, is to
be reſerved, leſt it be wanted to be replaced
again in the winter.

196. To perſons who have nothing elſe
to do but tend Bees, like Mr. Wildman,
theſe repetitions of *taking off* and *putting
on,* may be a very pretty amuſement. *Provided,* however, that the Bees be like
the common flies, that is, without ſtings.
For moſt aſſuredly, the combs of theſe
ſhallow hives will be ſo extended and
fixed down to the bars of thoſe underneath,
that in taking one off (the manner of doing
which however we are not made acquainted with) force muſt neceſſarily be uſed to diſ-
engage the combs, part of which breaking,
clumps of them will be left upon the bars
of the under one, and prevent a cover being
placed on, until they be removed; during
which time, the Bees of the hive taken,
and of thoſe left, having free egreſs and re-
greſs, will ſoon make the Apiator heartily
ſick

fick of his operation, and Mr. Wildman's in= vention.

191. But ferioufly, can it be thought, that farmers and cottagers will or can fpare the time and attention that this method requires, or indeed that the profit, efpecially in counties confiderably diftant from the metropolis, will anfwer the expence and trouble. Moreover, the difturbing the Bees fo much, together with the fhaking of the combs, and perhaps caufing fome to fall out (being done in the heat of fummer) fo intimidates and difheartens the Bees, that they feldom work with their wonted vigour and alacrity the whole feafon after.

192. My propofal is to have only two hives to a Stock. Fewer can by no means be difpenfed with upon any plan to perferve the Bees. Thefe require but one removal. By means of the fliders, the Bees of the hive left are always confined during the operation; and where an additional frame is ufed, thofe of that taken off will be kept in alfo. But if this be thought too expenfive; feveral methods are pointed out in the following fections (592, 599, 600, 602, 605.) of doing it with fecurity, and with little or no apparatus. And the time of adding or taking a hive will require no other infpection than the cafual one of the Apiator, or fervants of the family as they pafs the Apiary *.

193. Mr.

---

* I would juft obferve here, that the combs of that hive which Mr. Wildman directs to be taken off in

order

193. Mr. Wildman further obſerves, " that
" the Queen will lay ſome eggs in the up-
" per hive, but ſo ſoon as the lower hive is
" filled with combs, ſhe will lay moſt of
" them in it. In little more than three
" weeks, all the eggs laid in the upper hive
" will be turned into Bees." Very often it
will be ſo, but as often the cuntrary. I
have taken not only his ſhallow hives, but
alſo common round top hives, that had been
raiſed three *months*, and yet when taken
were as full of brood as though no under
hives had been placed (106, 193, 472).
Which proves this theory fallacious. There
is no certainty in any of theſe methods of
not having brood in additional hives, placed
either by the ſide or underneath. The only
ſure way may be ſeen (473).

194. The inconveniences of narrow bars
I have already taken notice of (190) as being much worſe than where the openings
are only in the middle. Straw hives have
been formed upon that principle both here
and in France, and ſmoke uſed to cauſe
the Bees to aſcend into an upper hive. But
as we can perform it with more facility and
and leſs offence, (592, 605) it will be unneceſſary

___

order to be replaced in winter or ſpring, left the Stock
ſhould have ſhort commons, will be liable (however
well ſecured) to become mouldy, and the honey can-
died; or the moth may get in and deſtroy the whole.

G

ceffary here to enlarge further upon the impropriety of it.

195. My hives have four openings, in the whole of thirty four inches, which though not equal to Mr. Wildman's barred hives, are yet fully fufficient for the Bees paffage, as every comb will have a free paffage of communication from it, either upwards or downwards. The communications of my boxes are alfo forty-four inches in length; whereas thofe boxes that have no bars, feldom have more than eighteen inches. So that they have here a fuperiority of twenty-fix inches. But what is ftill of more advantage, the Bees can crawl up and down the fides and ends of my hives and boxes, without obftruction. And when the combs are built, can defcend by them in direct lines to an under hive, as though it were but one hive, and adapted to their own peculiar mode of architecture. Nor is this chimerical: the Bees have often furnifhed me with demonftrative proofs of the truth of it, either working upwards or downwards as I chofe to have them. (473, 492.)

196. My fliders have alfo the advantage, for, being four in number, and furnifhed with fharp edges, they are introduced, not like the large wooden fliders, all at once, and with great violence, but gradually and alternately fliding in eafily, and with little or no difturbance; efpecially in boxes fet in a houfe. The Bees will neither know
the

the cauſe nor the invader. This operation therefore does not require even ſo much as a pair of gloves to perform it in. Neither ought we to forget the advantages ariſing from the ſecurity of the Queen; of which we before obſerved (165, 166,) the very great importance.

197. By means of theſe ſliders, glaſſes may be ſet equally as well on the ſtraw hives as on the boxes (452) without any ſort of danger or difficulty. My ſtraw hive tops have alſo a great ſuperiority over all others, of allowing an inſpection into the ſtate of the Bees works at the top; for by putting the ſliders in at any time, than taking off the cover, and, after placing a ſlip of glaſs over either of the communications, with-drawing the ſlider, not a Bee can come out, and curioſity may be ſatisfied without any danger; which will not only be entertaining but, on many occaſions, uſeful.

198. The laſt point of compariſon we pro-poſe to examine, is the expence or differ-ence of value of Mr. Wildman's ſtraw hives. Five are required to one Stock; and each hive will coſt one ſhilling, which is five ſhillings the ſet. Of mine two only are neceſſary for one Stock; the expence of which is two ſhil-lings. His hives have ſtraw tops; ſo have mine. But each of his hives has a hoop faſtened in it with ſeven bars, which I will eſtimate ſo low as only ſixpence each: this is two ſhillings and ſixpence more.

Each

Each grooved top of mine will coft two fhillings; which with the hives amount to fix
fhillings for my fet; while his fet comes to
feven fhillings and fixpence.

199. But there is ftill a greater difference
in this refpect. For his hoop and bars, being
fixed, are not applicable to other hives; and
as ftraw hives in two or three years are not
fit for fervice, the whole muft be new. My
tops, on the contrary, being moveable at
pleafure, and fuiting each hive indifcriminately, will with care be durable, perhaps
for centuries, and therefore ought not to be
eftimated with the prime coft of the hives;
the fame may be faid of my fliders. The
extraordinary expence for each Stock, the
firft year, will be four fhillings for tops, and
two fhillings and fixpence for fliders.

200. But for every fucceeding year, the
expence will be but two fhillings at moft,
reckoning a hive for a Swarm, and another to
raife the Stock with; and this will frequently
be unneceffary, becaufe an additional hive
will not often be above three or four months
in ufe before it be taken away, and therefore
will be hardly the worfe for ufe; fo that
upon the whole, it is but a trifling advance
more in keeping Bees this way than in the
old one of *fingle hives.* Nay, the expence
may be ftill very confiderably leffened to perfons that make their own bars without
grooves, as directed, (153).

201. But

201. But let us now fuppofe that only twenty pounds extraordinary of honey and wax be obtained the firft year from fix Stocks; will it not be a fufficient compenfation for the extra expence? Moft certainly it will; and therefore the whole apparatus may, the next year, be fairly confidered as cofting nothing. Nor is this all, for the pleafure of managing the Bees more profitably and with greater eafe, may furely be added. All thefe confiderations ought, I think, to have fome weight with every prudent and fenfible perfon.

202. As to the price of Mr. Thomas Wildman's boxes, I am not acquainted with it. But as they are more complicated than mine, it is reafonable to fuppofe, that the expence muft be greater in proportion. We may, however, give a fhrewd guefs at this, from obferving the price of his nephew's boxes. In his Treatife, Mr. D. Wildman, though he calls it *complete*, has forgot to give the dimenfions either of his hives or boxes; but the laft I take to be rather more than a foot fquare. One of thefe with four glaffes, each containing about half a pint, and one about three times as large in the middle, together with a cover to put over them, comes to two guineas. The wood-work is of mahogany.

203. His ftraw hives, about fixteen inches diameter, and eight deep, with feven glaffes and ftraw cover, half a guinea. The expence

of

of one of my ſtraw hives, with barred top, and fix half pint tumblers, ſingle flint, and one quart tumbler for the middle, will be eight ſhillings, viz.

Glaſſes	5s.
Hive -	1s.
Barred Top - -	2s.
	—
	8s.
	—

204. A pair of my boxes, made of painted deal, with moveable top and bottom, will be twelve ſhillings.

205. A pair with three large panes of glaſs in the three ſides, braſs hinges, moveable top and bottom, all of painted deal, one pound four ſhillings.

206. Theſe are the extreme prices for which any ingenious carpenter will make them. No further comment is here wanted, every one's reflection muſt readily make it.

CHAPTER

CHAPTER IX.

RULES *and* CAUTIONS *to be obferved in the Purchafing and Removal of* BEES.

207. THE two feafons moft proper for purchafing of Bees are, the fpring for Swarms, and the autumn for Stocks. The beft fwarms ufually rife from the middle of May to the middle of June.

208. If a perfon commences Bee-mafter, or Apiator, in the fpring, he fhould fend his own hives or boxes to the neighbours he intends to purchafe of any time before April, that they may be in readinefs againft the Swarms rife. But there will be danger of impofition unlefs the bargain be made for a Swarm that will at leaft meafure a peck; and therefore a fmaller Swarm ought by no means to be put into the hive.

209. When the hive is furnifhed, and before it is brought away in the evening, 't fhould be held up and examined whether the clufter of Bees be as bulky as it ought to be, if not, it fhould be ftruck out upon a cloth, and another hive fet over it (260). In this cafe, a better Swarm muft be patiently waited for; otherwife, the firft large Swarm that fhall rife, may be bargained for among the neighbours; this fhould be brought home the fame evening, when being difplaced from

G 4

the

the hive they are in, the intended hive ſhould be placed over them, and they will ſoon aſcend therein.

210. A ſmall Swarm will not only yield no profit the firſt ſeaſon, but if the weather be unfavourable, and the ſituation bad, it will be very likely to periſh before the next ſummer. A Swarm that will nearly fill one of my ſtraw hives, may be called a very good one, and will turn out ſweetly profitable before the autumn comes on. If a large Swarm cannot be procured, two ſmall ones, united in one, (260, 366.) will anſwer the purpoſe as well.

211. If the Bees be not brought home the ſame evening that they ſwarmed, many of them will return to the place were they ſtood; and not knowing where to go, will be loſt.

And not only ſo, but if kept two or three days before they are brought home, ſeveral combs will be formed, which being new, and conſequently very tender and warm, a ſlight motion will cauſe them to fall, ſmothering many of the Bees, perhaps the Queen herſelf, and thereby occaſion the loſs of the whole. But if through neceſſity of any kind, the Swarm be kept ſo long, two or three o'clock in the morning will be the ſafeſt time to bring it away, as then the combs will be the cooleſt.

212. September or October are the two beſt months to buy Stocks in. But it will be proper, if you are not converſant in Bees, to

take

take the judgment of fome fkilful and difin-
terefted neighbour. For it is abfolutely
neceffary that the Stocks fhould be examined before they are purchafed. Perhaps
by attending to the following directions
you may become a competent judge yourfelf.

213. For performing this bufinefs, a cool
day, or a fine calm evening, or rather than
either, the break of day, as at this time the
power of ftinging is weakeft, is to be preferred. Windy or rainy weather is improper
for this purpofe, as it makes the Bees very
fretful and quarrelfome. The armour (73)
will here be proper, or at leaft the face
fhould be well fecured. Gently turn the
hive up upon its edge, high enough to have
a full view of the Bees and combs; if there
be many Stocks you want to examine, as
foon as the Bees become too troublefome,
leave them for about half an hour, or until
they feem tolerably quiet; and then in like
manner proceed with the reft. But the beft
way will be to ufe the mefh or grated board,
hereafter mentioned (600, 602.)

214. Obferve that if the combs, as far as
you can fee, be of a white colour, or of a
flight tinge of yellow, they are the produce
of a Swarm of this year; but if of a very
very deep yellow or brownifh colour, the
Stock is of the preceding year. When the
combs are of a very deep brown, or black,
the Stock is certainly an old one, perhaps
three or four years old, and totally unfit for
your

your purpofe. Thefe require a more clofer infpection, as a fudden glance will not difcover the truth; for the bottoms and fides of the combs, though apparently new, are often made by old Stocks, while the reft of the combs may be of three or four years ftanding.

215. The fpaces, or ftreets, (if I may be allowed to call them fo) between the combs, fhould be well crowded with Bees, and the combs themfelves well ftored with honey, down to the floor, or nearly fo. If this is not the cafe it is a fign it was a Caft, or a Stock too poor to form a thriving Apiary with. A good Stock will weigh from twenty-five to forty pounds; but in old Stocks, the weight cannot be depended upon, (628.) which is another reafon againft buying fuch.]

216. It will be more advantageous to purchafe a good Stock in autumn, than a Swarm in fpring. For there will be little rifk of fuch a Stock's profperity until the next feafon, when moft probably it will afford a Swarm; fo that for the fame price, you may be faid to have both Swarm and Stock. Whereas, if a Swarm be bought in the fpring, there will probably be no advantage until the next year.

217. In the vicinity of London, the price of a Stock or Swarm is ufually half a guinea; but in diftant counties feldom more than half the money; though fome country people are fo ridiculoufly fuperftitious as to fuppofe, that Bees will not thrive unlefs *gold*

be

be paid for them. What abfurdities are there, however grofs, which the human mind has not adopted at one time or another?

REMOVING.

218. It muft be in the dufk of the evening, when all the Bees are at home. But fome hours previous, the hive fhould be raifed a little from the floor, by bits of fticks, or tiles, &c. otherwife, when the hive is fuddenly taken off, a great number of the Bees will remain on the floor. A cloth that is not of a very clofe texture, fhould be laid ready upon the ground before the Stock, then gently lifting up the Stock, fet it upon the cloth, and immediately gathering the corners up very tight, tie them together at the top; and laftly, tie a cord round the body of the hive; this will effectually prevent any of the Bees efcaping, or crawling up to the top. When brought home, fet each hive upon the ground, near the ftand it is defigned for, untie the cloth, and lifting the hive off, fet it upon the ftand, and lay the cloth with the Bees on it over the hive; before morning they will go down into the hive, and none be loft. If the hives are to be placed in a Bee-houfe, they muft not be fet clofe to the front, for then the Bees on the cloth cannot have entrance at the door-

way;

way; but the next evening they fhould be fhoved clofe.

219. As the ftraw hives in common ufe projeдt more in the middle than at bottom, confequently when placed in a Bee-houfe, a vacancy will be left between the hive and the front. This chafm fhould be filled up by cutting or hollowing out a piece of wood in the middle, fo as to be very thin there, and about three inches long, leaving the ends fufficiently thick to fill up the vacancy; if it does not exaдtly fit, a little clay, or cow dung, will fupply the defeдt, as it is only to be uifed at firft, until the Bees have worked themfelves into a box.

CONVEYANCE.

220. The beft way of conveying Swarms or Stocks from one place to another, is in a hand-barrow between two men; the next to that is by a milk yoke, with a hive on each fide, or one or more hives may be hung upon a ftout ftick, refting upon two men's fhoulders. But where many are to be removed, or when they are to be carried fe-veral miles, a poft chaife, coach, or any other vehicle that has an eafy play upon fprings, is to be preferred: the hives muft be carefully placed upon a thick bed of ftraw, and the motion of the carriage flow and gentle.

For want of thefe, a cart may do; adding the more ftraw, and taking care that the

horfes

horſes proceed only in their ſloweſt pace; otherwiſe the combs will probably be moſtly ſhaken down, and the Stocks ſpoiled.

CHAPTER X.

Obſervations on the Increaſe of BEES, *and Nature of* SWARMS.

221. THE increaſe of Bees is of very great importance to the owners, for in proportion to *that* will be the profit, and therefore every thing relating to this deſerves a minute detail.

222. The breeding of young Bees is begun ſooner or later, in proportion to the prolific nature of the Queen, the ſtrength of the Stock, and the ſtate of the weather. The more numerous the Bees are in a hive, the greater the heat, which enables the Queen of ſuch Stocks to begin breeding much ſooner than the Queen of thoſe that are poor and weak; the brood of which increaſe but ſlowly, and are therefore later. If the weather be mild the Queen will ſometimes begin to breed in January, but often in February, except the ſeaſon has been very cold, and is

very

very backward, and then it will be March firſt.

223. For a long continuance of cold wea‑ ther, or of both cold and wet, greatly retards the hatching of the brood, and cauſes many abortions, which may be ſeen thrown out of the hives in ſuch unkindly ſeaſons. But when the ſpring is neither very early nor very late, there will be the greateſt brood, and conſe‑ quently the moſt numerous Swarms.

224. For as the influence of a mild ſpring haſtens the brood, it no leſs haſtens the bloſſoms. The fallows, the ſnow drops, and crocuſſes, thoſe welcome harbingers of joy and abundance to the Bees, (512.) afford them at this time plenty of farina, without which their young cannot be ſuſtained or fed. But ſhould wet weather ſet in, while theſe are in bloom, ſo as to prevent their going out to collect it, thoſe already bred, will pine for want, and very few will be added to the number until a more propitious change. So that we ſee there muſt be a co‑ incidence of weather and flowers to produce timely and large Swarms.

225. It often happens that there is a long ſeaſon of proper weather for gathering farina, (515.) even to the latter end of May ; but too cold for any flowers to afford honey. During this tedious interval, the Bees having nothing elſe to do, their whole attention will be fixed ſolely to the increaſe of their family, not conſidering that famine will ſoon begin to ſtare them in the face.

226. Like

226. Like too many of our own unthink-ing ſpecies, who eagerly ſeize the bliſs of propagation, ſupport the offspring who may! Thus the Bees, having already a large fami-ly, and that encreaſing daily by hundreds, at the ſame time that the honey is wholly or nearly exhauſted. In this perilous di-lemma, they muſt either ſtarve or leſſen their numbers. Irreſiſtible neceſſity compel-ling, they divide, and a Swarm riſes; which ſurely dies, if a warm ſeaſon does not im-mediately ſucceed.

227. But if no young Princeſs be ready to lead a Swarm; the ſuperabundance of Bees will in a ſhort time conſume the ſmall remains of honey, and the whole will periſh by famine, at a time, and from a cauſe the leaſt ſuſpeĉted, and often ſo late as the end of May.

228. May and June are accounted the two beſt months for Swarms; for thoſe that riſe much ſooner or later are either too few to form good Swarms, and are in danger of being ſtarved, or by coming too late, im-poveriſh the old Stock by too large a de-creaſe; and themſelves not being able to lay in a ſufficiency of ſuſtenance for the winter, will run the utmoſt hazard of dying alſo. To the middle of July I have had Swarms, and known many others, that have ſucceeded; but later than this none ſhould be ſuffered to ſwarm. The beſt method of accompliſh-ing this is to raiſe the Stocks (231).

229. If the ſpring has been good for
breeding

breeding, but no honey gathered until late, as perhaps until the middle of June, however *capacious* their *hive* may be, the Bees will certainly fwarm.   This is repugnant to what fome writers have taught; trufting to whom I have loft many Swarms, by neglecting to have them watched; and there is no doubt, but many others have done fo too, and fuffered the fame lofs.   Long and great experience has fince fully convinced me of the fallacioufnefs of this principle.

I have had Bees both in boxes and hives that increafed fo faft, and feemed fo crouded, that to prevent their fwarming (as I then thought) they were raifed gradually three ftories high.   But notwithftanding all thefe precautions, every one of them fwarmed, nay fome of them caft befide; and in fuch indifferent weather, that no one could have fufpected any Swarms would have rifen.   One year in particular, though my Bees were fo prone to fwarm, feveral of the neighbouring Stocks, being over charged with young, were obliged to lie out for want of room, and did not fwarm at all.   In this inftance we obferve, *plenty* of room induced mine to fwarm; while others for *want* of room, laid out, and never attempted to fwarm.

We may further notice, that in hollow trees, and under the roofs of houfes, which afford the Bees unlimited room, yet it is well known that even in thefe fituations they always fend out Swarms.

230. On the contrary, when *honey* is to be met with *early,* and in *plenty,* and the Bees have abundant fpare room, it is a great chance if they fwarm at all; not being willing to leave a houfe well furnifhed to go in queft of a new habitation, as here every thing will be wanted. What more confirms me in this opinion is, that in the fummer of 1779, a very remarkable one for the production of honey, only two of my Stocks, which I purpofely had not raifed, fwarmed. The reft filled their hives fo faft, that I was obliged to raife them twice. While the Stocks of the country people in the neighbourhood, fwarmed, and caft feveral times; nay Swarms produced Swarms; (or as the country people phrafe it) had maiden Swarms.

231. This was owing to there being plenty of Drones, and of young Princeffes ready to lay; fo that their hives being too fmall to hold them, the honey, and young brood, and their owners not. poffeffing ingenuity enough to affift them, they could do no otherwife than divide. To this caufe alfo it is owing, that Stocks are obliged to fwarm and caft fo often as to impoverifh themfelves intirely. Similar obfervations were made by Butler in the year 1616. Herein the Bees act like parents affectionate to exccfs, who ftrip themfelves to enrich their offspring, and by that means become expofed in the winter of old age to all the rigours of poverty.

H

232. The

232. The more pregnant Princeſſes there are, the more eager the Bees are to fwarm (other favourable circumftances coinciding). On the contrary, if none of *thefe* are ready, be the quantity of the Bees- ever fo many, no Swarm will rife, but will rather die than quit the hive. This fact has been fully af-certained by the examination of Stocks, which could by no means whatever be induced to fwarm, and were always found with only the old Queen ; the royal eggs, or embryos, hav-ing failed, or been deftroyed by accident.

233. Early Swarms are not always beft, viz. from the entrance of April until the middle of May, the weather often changing from one extreme to another; which either ftarves or otherwife fo reduces them, that they become of little worth. But there is no rule without exceptions. For I have known early Swarms which multiplied fo much as to produce a maiden Swarm fo late as the 30th of July, and profpered. I alfo knew two old Stocks that produced fix Swarms the fame feafon, moftly good. But it was in an excellent feafon and fituation, and no other Stocks near them. Such Stocks with me, inftead of thus increafing, would not have furvived the winter. Moreover, in fuch favourable fituations, many Swarms have rifen about the ninth of May, though very cool weather, with northerly winds, and which continued fome weeks. From thefe circumftances I inferred that they would

not

hot be able to procure fuſtenance. They deceived me however, for they not only lived but proved vigorous and proſperous. Such difference is there in ſituations!

234. A large early Swarm, with favourable weather ſucceeding, will be far ſuperior to one that is later; for having ſo much time before them, they will be well repleniſhed with ſtout young labourers, ready to reap the honey harveſt, the ſweet reward of all their toil. The Mother Stock, at the ſame time, will be in the ſame thriving condition : the old proverb applying here moſt admirably, viz. " Many hands make light work." If bad weather, indeed, ſhould ſupervene they will require a little attendance and expence in feeding; for which their future toils will more than doubly compenſate.

235. Butler has given us a judicious ſtandard to judge of the propriety of the time of Swarms riſing, viz. " that Swarms be- " fore the blowing of *knapweed*, are in good " time. Thoſe before the blowing of black- " berries may proſper. But blackberry " Swarms, eſpecially Caſts, will be ſeldom " worth keeping, as being too late to lay " in a proper ſtore for the winter. Such " ſhould be returned back to the ſtock."

236. In another place he obſerves, " that " in ſome backward years, as was 1621 " and 1622, there have been Swarms the " latter end of July that proſpered. For it " is remarkable, the bramble did not blow

H 2　　　　" until

" until that time, which uſed to blow a
" fortnight ſooner.

" So in warm countries, and a kind ſpring,
" Swarms have come early in May; whereas
" in the heath countries Swarms are as late
" as near the end of July, which often prove
" better than the early." Near woods the
Bees obtaining from the trees plenty of farina
to feed the brood with, is the reaſon why
Stocks, in ſuch ſituations, have large Swarms,
and early.

237. The common working Bees are firſt
bred, then the Drones and Princeſſes. In general, the Drones do not appear until the middle
of May, but large Stocks will ſometimes have
them as early as March, in April very common. Hives will often be ſo full of Bees as
to cluſter out before any Drones ſhew themſelves; and, for want of which, they will not
ſwarm; not but there may be a few Drones
in the hive, though not ſufficient in numbers
to make their appearance: or the air may be
too cold for them, though not for the Commoners; for the Drones are much tenderer
than theſe. When they are moſt numerous,
the Swarms are moſt likely to riſe. If this
happens early, in general ſo will the Swarm
be; if late, the contrary.

238. Butler obſerves, that ſometimes the
firſt brood of Drones in the ſpring will be
killed, and caſt out. I obſerved a ſimilar inſtance in a Stock, which in the beginning of
May was full of Bees and Drones, but the
middle of the month affording plenty of honey,

ney, to make room for it, they not only killed the Drones, but the brood alfo; hundreds of which lay before the hive.

239. The generality of country people are fo ignorant of the nature of the Drones as to imagine they are doing great fervice in deftroying them as foon as they appear; which is full as wife, as if they were to kill *all* the males of their flocks or of their poultry, in order to have the more chickens or lambs. Good dames! if you love your hufbands, cherifh the Drones, for they cherifh the Queen, even as your hufbands cherifh you!

240. I have experienced, that in a fummer, extremely dry, few Princeffes were born, and many of the Queens dying of old age (as I fuppofe) there were but few Swarms, and many Stocks deferted their hives for want of Queens. Though this was the caufe, few perhaps knew it, and therefore other caufes were affigned.

241. As witchcraft in feveral counties is fuppofed to do a great deal of mifchief; in thefe, and fimilar cafes, fuch loffes will be attributed to it; and he who fhall dare to difbelieve it, will be confidered as an atheift. But what is this witchcraft? a power fuppofed to be communicated by the devil, or by many devils (for the chief cannot be omniprefent) to fome ugly crofs old woman, to do what mifchief fhe pleafes to her neighbours, who do not pleafe her; an opinion founded in paganifm, nurfed in fuperftition, propagated by oral tradition, and believed with as

H 3   fteady

steady a faith, by these credulous simple ones, as the most sacred tenets of the Gospel. Such people should consider, that if Providence " suffers not a sparrow to fall without his " permission," it must be the height of absurdity to suppose, that infinite wisdom and goodness will permit, much less give a power to dæmons, or women, because they are *old* and *ugly*, to injure their neighbours, in a supernatural manner, according to their own capricious, foolish, and unjust resentments.

242. Doubtless the lovely females, blooming in virtue, youth, and beauty (such is the will of Heaven) have always had an inherent power of fascinating the mind and body of man : and this has been exerted not only among the gentle rustics of the peaceful village but emperors and heroes, philosophers and divines, recluse monks, and men of business, have all *felt* and yielded to its irresistible sway.

But from such a wonderful influence the Bees are entirely exempt. What disasters befal them generally arise from the ignorance or indolence of those who superintend them.

243. A Swarm consists not of all young, as many falsely imagine, but of a Queen, of Drones, and of working Bees, both old and young ; and such as happen to be at the doorway, when a Swarm rises, go off with it.

244. The lying-out, or clustering of Bees, on the outside of the hive, is often a great diminution of the expected profit ; and also accustoms them to habits of idleness. It is occasioned by the continual and large increase of
young,

young, whereby the hive becomes fo crowded, and in the day time fo hot, as to oblige great numbers of Bees, to lodge or clufter on the outfide, and about the door-way and front of the hive. Frequently at firft they only lie out in the day-time; at night the hive being cooler, they are collected clofer together, whereby the whole are admitted: but unfavourable weather, the want of a Princefs, or of Drones, preventing their fwarming for fome time, they become too numerous for the habitation to hold them, either night or day.

245. Pure neceffity obliges them at firft, but afterwards they contract a liking to their new fituation; others alfo daily join them in their idlenefs, and in fuch numbers, that often there are as many Bees on the outfide of the hive as within. In confequence of this, the young Princeffes, who always refide within, not having a fufficient number there, or inclination to form a Swarm, none will rife; until growing too late in the feafon for fwarming, they at laft betake themfelves to build fome combs by the fides of the hives, or under the floors, and there remain until autumn: not but there may be fome exceptions. I have known Stocks increafe fo faft, that notwithftanding thefe exterior clufters, they have fwarmed, and left the idlers behind; who afterwards perceiving room enough within, quitted their ftations, and entered the hive again.

246. It not unfrequently happens that their lying out, and that for feveral weeks, and

H 4 with

with favourable weather, is owing to there being no Princefs yet born, or in a condition to lead them. This I conjecture from having many times obferved my box-hives crowded, well ftored with Drones, and the Bees feemingly defirous of fwarming, but yet did not, for a confiderable time. Now as feveral royal cells were clofe to the windows during this time, but not finifhed or fealed up, no Swarm rofe until fome time after they were fo: on the contrary, when there is a very forward Princefs, or perhaps feveral competitors, a Swarm will rife without any previous indications, and when the hive is far from being crowded; confequently fuch Swarms will be always fmall.

247. It is obvious, that a large quantity of Bees lying out inactive, at the moft critical time, when their labour might be of the greateft fervice, muft be a very confiderable lofs to the owner. For inftead of this, if they had fwarmed in that time they might have filled a hive with honey; or produced as much in an additional hive, had one been furnifhed them. A ftrong indication this in favour of our double method. Another inconvenience is their hindering and obftructing the paffage of the other Bees, and by their example inciting many others to be as idle as themfelves; No uncommon cafe among idlers of the human race! Nor is this all, for having obtained this indolent habit, it will be communicated to the next generation; for it is obferved,

that

that Bees from thefe Stocks are much more apt to lie out than any others. For the prevention, fee (249).

248. Many perfons on feeing fuch clufters of Bees upon their hives, have imagined, that by getting them into an empty hive, they fhould have a complete Swarm; but thofe attempts have always been unfuccefsful, all the Bees uniformly returning home again, and cluftering as before. The reafon is, they have no Queen with them: without whom no feparate Swarm can poffibly be eftablifhed. For the treatment of Bees that lie out for want of previous care, fee (282).

249. An objection perhaps may be made againft the raifing of hives, in order to cure them of lying out, viz. that it will prevent their fwarming. It has been fhewn, that it has not always that effect (229). But if it had, they had better not fwarm at all than lie out. The Bees themfelves will be the beft judges; but, fuppofing they do not fwarm, they are not idle, but fully and continually employed in compleating their own hives, and filling the new apartment you have enlarged their habitation with. We will likewife fuppofe fo bad a feafon, that they cannot fpare you a hive of honey the prefent fummer: Notwithftanding this, as their increafe of brood has been continual, the next year they will make you amends for your forbearance: by being not only a powerful Stock, but alfo by complimenting you with a large and

early

early Swarm; and probably, with a hive of honey, as an additional recompence.

250. Several ſigns or tokens are deſcribed by different authors, portending the *riſing of Swarms.* Thoſe of moſt note, I ſhall preſent to my readers. The firſt ſymptom of a Stock's being nearly in a condition of ſwarming, is their populouſneſs, and the appearance of Drones. The firſt is known by the more than ordinary concourſe of Bees going in and out. Alſo, by rapping againſt the body of the hive in the evening, judgment may be formed of their ſtrength by the buz; and when many of the Drones are ſeen, it denotes that there has been plenty of Bees for ſome time.

251. Hives that are very full of Bees will make a noiſe almoſt approaching to roaring; ſo much ſo as to induce one to imagine they are juſt going to ſwarm, it ſhews indeed their impatience to ſwarm, but alſo that they have no Princeſs as yet equal to the taſk; and therefore this noiſe may be continued ſeveral days before their flight.

252. Should a Stock in the morning, inſtead of working, remain playing about the hive, it is a ſure ſign they intend ſwarming that day, the weather permitting; but they as frequently riſe at the very inſtant that multitudes are going in loaded, many of whom go off with the emigrants. Uſually before their flight, there is an uncommon buz, that may be heard at a conſiderable diſtance. Hives that ſtand fronting the morning Sun will riſe earlier in the day than thoſe that ſtand to the ſouth or weſt.

253. Lyi

253. Lying out is a fign of their defire of fwarming. Firft Swarms frequently rife without fhewing any *other* fign than an increafe of numbers. Firft Swarms are often divided or broken, by fome cafualty, as a fudden ftorm, dark clouds, fhowers, thunder, or by tinkling before they have all done coming out. By thefe noifes the remainder are intimidated, and ftay behind; or if the whole be out, either fearing a ftorm, difliking their pitching-place, being too much difturbed in the hiving, or lofing the Princefs, they return back again. The Princefs going out with them, being fometimes too weak for flight, drops down by the way ; in this cafe, fhe may be often found, when if placed in fight of the Swarm, the Bees will prefently fettle round her.

254. A firft Swarm, except it happens to be broken, is worth two or three after ones ; or, as they are generally called, Cafts and Colts : but when this accident befalls it, if the next comes forth one entire Swarm it will be better than the firft, though perhaps it may leave the mother Stock too poor. (231)

255. Butler obferves (as do alfo feveral other writers both before and after him) that three or four nights before a fecond Swarm rifes, there is a peculiar noife in the hive, very different from the ufual buzzing of Bees, and which is heard upon no other occafion. Mills, * (who feems to be no Bee-Mafter) treats this as an illufion of the imagination, ; I was of the fame opinion, until accidentally ftanding

by

---

* Effay on Bees.

my bee-houſe about ten o'clock at night, I was attracted by theſe very unuſual aud muſical ſounds. Perſons verſed in muſic can tolerably judge of an octave; ſuch theſe reſpective notes appeared to me, and ſuch alſo as could not be made by the wings, but ſeemed as if proceeding from a tube. What the intention of theſe notes might be I pretend not to determine; whether they be made at ſtated periods before ſecond Swarms riſe, is not much to our purpoſe; becauſe it is not likely that many Apiators will have either time or inclination to watch theſe notices, therefore it is a matter rather of curioſity than of utility.

256. Butler indeed, writes, that, " Firſt " Swarms riſe without theſe notices; but " after Swarms or Caſts hardly ever without. " From the 8th to the 11th day after the " firſt Swarm is departed, the other young " Princeſſes that are pregnant, will make " the like petitions. Conſent being had, " the young Queen the next morning comes " down near the floor, and there calls much " louder, and at the moment of ſwarming, " the notes are more frequent and ſhriller; " and then iſſues the buzzing multitude."

257. " If rainy or tempeſtuous weather, " prevents their ſecond or third Caſts, until " beyond the 14th day, one of the young " Queen's is ſlain on the morning of the 15th " day, leſt a ſedition ſhould be raiſed, and a " civil war overturn the empire.

258. " So ſenſible are the Princeſſes of " their tragical fate, if left behind, that ſome-
" times

" times two or three will accompany a fingle
" Swarm; or if the weather continues indif-
" ferent a confiderable time, often one more
" bold than the reft, will coax as many com-
" panions as fhe can, and though only a few,
" will lead them forth, trufting to fortune
" for fuccefs.

" If the firft Swarm be divided or broken,
" the fecond will call, and fwarm the fooner,
" probably the very next day, and there-
" by occafion a third, or fometimes a fourth,
" but all within a fortnight after the firft;
" unlefs prevented by bad weather, or ex-
" cept in fome extraordinary plentiful years
" and fituations both for brood and honey
" gathering."

259. When two or more Princeffes accompany one Swarm they ufually fettle in different clufters; but thofe of the fmalleft feldom tarry, joining themfelves to the larger
body, the young Queen following.

260. As to fecond Swarms, much lefs
Cafts, very few are ever worth keeping, without the fituation and feafon have been uncommonly favourable. The reafon is, the Bees of
every Stock have to provide for, and take
care of, a numerous brood, as well as to collect honey; but as after-fwarms are but few
in number, compared with the firft, they
muft fall fhort, in performing both thefe
tafks in any degree adequate to what the firft
can do; but as they are more intent upon the
increafe of the brood than procuring honey
in autumn they will not have a fufficiency

of

of honey to fupport them until the next feafon, and therefore will die of famine. Or if takeñ, the honey will be but trifling ; whereas, had they been united to a Stock, or feveral of thefe Cafts incorporated together fo as to form a good Swarm, it would not only preferve them for next year, but alfo yield a good profit.

261. It is ufual with the Bees before they fwarm, to fend out meffengers or quarter-mafters to feek out and prepare proper habi-tations : empty hives left in a garden, will fometimes be chofen. In fuch a cafe, two or three hundred Bees may be feen going in and out, to clean the hive : on feeing this, you may depend upon a Swarm entering into it within a few days. I have often experien-ced this myfelf, as well as fome of my neigh-bours. The fame may be obferved of hollow trees, vacancies under the roofs of houfes, and other fimilar places.

262. It may be readily known that a Swarm has efcaped, if the Bees in going in or out od not feem near fo numerous as before.

263. Notwithftanding all that has been writ-ten refpecting the figns and tokens of the rifing of Swarms, I am fully fatisfied from my own experience, that they are very fallacious, and not to be trufted to, without running the ut-moft hazard of lofing fome of the Swarms ; and I am well perfuaded that the only fecurity is keeping a conftant and clofe watch over them, (278) from the time they begin to be confiderably

fiderably increafed until the fwarming feafon
be over. For they will frequently rife in fuch
very indifferent weather, and fometimes fo
very early in the feafon, that no one could have
fufpected any fuch thing. In thefe circum-
, ftances they frequently fly quite away without
fettling at all; and without giving any previous figns, or intimations of fuch a difpofition.

264. As no Swarm ought to be kept unlefs a good one, whether it be a firft, a fecond, or any other; but muft be returned again (370) or united (366) it may be
both ufeful and amufing to eftimate the
weight, meafure, and number of Bees, fufficient to make what may be truly called a
good Swarm.

265. " It has been found, (fays Butler)
" that a larger number than 40 or 50,000
" will not thrive together in one hive.
" Swarms often amount to 30,000. A large
" Swarm may weigh eight pounds, and gra-
" dually lefs to one pound; confequently, a
" very good one weighs five or fix pounds, a
" moderate one four pounds. No Swarm
" lefs than this fhould be kept, but united
" with others."

266. I difagree with Butler in this. For
— I think a fix pound Stock is full little enough
to turn to a good account; efpecially in the
double mode; where they ought never to
want room, confequently fuch a Swarm in a
tolerable feafon will furnifh a hive of virgin
honey. Therefore, all Swarms, lefs than *fix*

pounds,

pounds, eſpecially in moderate ſituations, I would recommend to be united with ſmall Swarms or Caſts. If there be enough to make half a buſhel, it will be ſtill more eligible.

267. The following eſtimate is given us by different writers of the weight and number of Bees:

BUTLER.
280 to an Ounce
4,480 - - a Pound
40 or 50,000 to ten or eleven Pounds.

Natural Hiſtory of BEES.
336 to an Ounce
5,366 - - a Pound
43,800 - - 8 Pounds.

WILDMAN.
308 an Ounce
4,928 a Pound.

According to my own Eſtimate.
290 an Ounce
4,640 a Pound.

		oz.	dr.
915	Half a Pint	3	$2\frac{11}{16}$
1,830	a Pint	6	$5\frac{3}{8}$
3,660	a Quart	12	$10\frac{3}{4}$
		lb. oz.	dr.
29,280	a Peck	6 5	6

Wincheſter Meaſure.

268. The diſagreement of weight and meaſure in theſe ſeveral experiments ſeems to ariſe from the different ſtate of the Bees at the time of examination; for certainly they muſt weigh and meaſure more when their bellies are full than when empty, the caſe of Stocks that die; alſo thoſe loaded with farina, weigh and meaſure more than thoſe only with honey. This was fully confirmed to me by experiments made at different times, which always varied; but from the average

average of the whole, the calculation given feems nigheft the truth, at leaft it is fufficient for any purpofe the practitioner may require.

CHAP. IX.

PRECAUTIONS *and* RULES *to be obferved in the Managing and Hiving of* SWARMS.

269. IT will be highly prudent to have your hives in readinefs before the Swarms are likely to rife. For want of this neceffary forethought many Swarms have taken French leave, and been heard of no more.

270. The infide of ftraw hives fhould be rubbed with a ftiff hair brufh, or coarfe cloth, to get off the little bits or fnags of ftraw; which otherwife will occafion the Bees a great deal of trouble and lofs of time to gnaw off, when they might be more ufefully employed in building their combs.

271. Boxes alfo fhould be cleaned from all little fplinters, or other roughnefs, and made as fmooth as poffible; every hole or crevice muft be ftopped up with putty, or the Bees, to keep out the air and vermin, will be

I   obliged

obliged to do it with propolis; for what you may do with one ftroke in a moment will coft them many minutes, and perhaps the labour of hundreds.

272. I ufe no other preparation to my hives; but perchance fome good dames may not be fatisfied with this fimplicity, and therefore I would recommend to them if they muft do any thing more, to rub the top of the hives with a mixture of ale and fugar, or of ale and honey : but in boxes, the rubbing the upper part and fides with wax will be beft, as being not only agreeable to the Bees, but alfo enabling them to crawl up the hive with greater cafe. Rubbing hives with fweet herbs is of no ufe, for it is the honey at the bottom of the flowers that the Bees are fond of and not the leaves. How ridiculous to ufe *fennel,* a plant they hardly ever approach, as if *that* would intice them. In fhort, they feldom diflike their hives if they have got a goodly company, and a good *miftrefs.*

273. Thofe that continue to ufe common hives, fhould have feveral of them, from two to three pecks each, in readinefs; becaufe Swarms differ fo much in magnitude, that a two-peck hive may often prove too fmall; but no Swarm fhould be put into a hive lefs than half a bufhel. However, after the Bees are hived, if they be not contented and quiet, or lie out, it will be proper to raife the hive by placing two or three rounds or more of an old hive underneath fo as to make it high enough to receive the whole.

274. Straw

274. Straw hives or boxes, with openings at top, have this advantage, that if not sufficiently large, another can be immediately added without any difficulty. After having once put a large Swarm in one of my boxes, I perceived the Bees to be very much difpleafed, and in great confufion; I immediately placed another box over them, but ftill the uproar not only continued, but increafed, and the Bees began to pour out of the box: conjecturing then, that they had loft their young Princefs, I examined the ground near the box, and found a fmall clufter of Bees, in the midft of which was the Royal Lady. I immediately took her up, and placed her at the door-way of the box, from which the Bees were running; a ftop immediately enfued, a retreat was founded, the emigrants returned, and nothing was to be heard but acclamations of joy.

275. If for feveral years together Swarms come late, and perhaps fome Stocks do not fwarm at all; though the feafons be tolerably good, it may be taken for granted that the hives are too large, or the Stocks too many: on the contrary, if the Swarms be too early, and but fcanty in number, it indicates the hives to be too fmall: a fingle year cannot determine this, feafons being fo very different from each other; fomething therefore muft be left to experience, and each perfons fagacity.

276. Hives are generally fpleeted, that is, fmall fticks are placed within the hives to

support the combs, and keep them steady. Country people fix too many, and these also so improperly as to render it impossible to take the combs out without smashing and mangling them, by this means fouling and wasting the honey. The Bees are endowed with ability sufficient to fasten their combs, provided the hives are not to be moved; but as this is requisite, one stick fixed across the hive, within about two inches of the bottom, and from right to left, will fully secure the combs, upon any necessary removal or inversion.

277. For as the Bees generally build their combs in parallel lines to the door-way, the spleet or stick being placed at right angles, or the reverse of the combs, each of these will necessarily rest, and be fastened by the Bees to the spleet, thereby rendering any more superfluous. When the combs are to be taken out, a notch is to be cut in each comb as far as the spleet, which may be then pulled up, and the combs taken out entire.

278. During the whole season of swarming the Bees should be carefully watched. This season is sometimes very long. In the year 1779 my Bees were obliged to be watched from the beginning of April until the end of July; but this is seldom the case: however so long as any Stocks have not swarmed, they certainly require to be attended to. In some years a month will be long enough. Those who keep half a dozen Stocks or more may get poor children to watch them for a
trifling

trifling reward; and thus at a fmall expence ferve th mfelves and a poor family at the fame time. In the *longeft* feafon it cannot *exceed* half a guinea. Suppofing only one Swarm to be faved by this means, it will pay the whole; but in general the expence will not be near fo much. A conftant watch however ought moft certainly to be kept: For Swarms very frequently rife, as has been obferved, without fhewing the leaft fymptom of their intention. Many Swarms I have loft formerly by not attending to the profitable doctrine of conftant watchfulnefs: for as Swarms often rife fuddenly, if a perfon be abfent but five minutes the Swarm may be gone.

279. The fwarming hours are generally reckoned to be from nine o'clock to two. This is very wrong, for Swarms frequently rife as early as eight, and as late as four. Whoever therefore trufts to fewer hours will often fuftain a confiderable lofs; as will alfo thofe who truft to their not fwarming in indifferent weather: I myfelf have had, and know many others who have alfo had Swarms rife in what we may call cold weather in May, and in mifling clouded days. The Bees are a people fo uncertain in their motions, that a conftant eye muft be kept upon them in all weathers, except indeed a hard fhower of rain, hail, or fnow. Let us not therefore to fave a few fhillings, run the hazard of lofing pounds. No one ought to expect to be fuc-

I 3   cefsful

cefsful with Bees, any more than with pigs or poultry, which profit but little without care and attendance.

280. The difadvantages of the Bees *lying-out*, have been already treated of, (244) we now proceed to point out the only remedy againft this vicious habit that can turn to any profit.

281. When a Stock is not wanted to fwarm, it fhould be *raifed* as foon as the Bees begin to work brifkly, ftopping the bottom door-way until full fwarm-ing-time; for if they are not raifed until they feem to want it, the doing thereof will often occafion them to Swarm; on the con-trary, when a well replenifhed Stock is in-tended to fwarm, but the Bees begin to af-femble in idlenefs, they may be permitted to do fo four or five days, but no longer.

282. This idle habit fhould be broken by raifing the Stock, rather than fuffered to increafe, though fwarming during the whole feafon, fhould be prevented by this proceed-ing: for frequently the difturbance of raif-ing provokes them to fwarm in a day or two afterwards; and therefore a ftrict look-out muft be kept.

I once had a box Swarm, which after-wards layed out, notwithftanding as many glafs veffels were fet over them as amounted to a peck; much work being done in the glaffes, I did not choofe to take them off, and therefore a little box was fcrewed on over the clufter and door-way; and a frefh door-way made

made therein. They built in that box, and succeeded well, when taken away as soon as honey-gathering ceased. Where Bees are kept in common hives that cannot be conveniently raised, any convenient vessel placed over the largest cluster, and fixed as near the door-way as possible, will answer the same purpose; the heft time to do it, is after the close of the day, either by moon light, or by a candle and lantern; but at no nearer a distance than just to see how to perform the business.

283. But should this not succeed, having put on a pair of gloves, and secured your face with a mask, at the close of evening, or rather at day-break, hold a hive, or other vessel under the largest cluster that lie out, gently pushing the empty hive upward, that as much of the cluster may hang in it as possible; then with a stiff wire, slip of tin, or thin stick, drawn closely and very gently against the bottom of the floor or stool, separate the Bees therefrom, so as to fall into the hive underneath; or, the vessel or hive itself drawn by a skilful hand against the bottom, will have the same effect.

284. But if they cluster *round* the hive, and not underneath, hold the bottom edge of an empty hive, so as to be even, or upon a level with the stand; then with a brush or rather a wing, gently move the cluster forward, until they fall into the hive; but if they hang about so inconveniently that this cannot be effected, they may be taken up by

I 4

a spoon

a fpoon and put into the hive (384). Should there be danger of fome of the Bees falling on the ground during the operation, a cloth fpread thereon, will receive them, and being afterwards laid over, or about the fkirts of the hive, the ftragglers before morning will be returned home.

285. The Bees you have taken may be returned to the Stock, which in the interim fhould be raifed by an ekeing, or lift, that is, two or three rounds of another hive placed under them; or, for want of thefe, by ftones or portions of bricks laid at proper diftances underneath. Then take the hive or veffel that has the outliers in it to the old Stock, turn it upfide down, and ftrike the edge forcibly upon a floor or ftool, clofe to the Stock; the Bees will fall out and join the family before morning; then clofe all the openings with clay or cow dung, leaving only the ufual entrance. Thus having fufficient room, they will either immediately begin to extend their works, or fwarm in a day or two after. A cover fhould be fufpended over them during the night; and alfo over fuch Bees that lie out, left hafty fhowers wafh them down, and deftroy them.

286. Another method is to take the old Stock off the ftand, raife it as before directed, and fet it upon a ftool about a foot diftant from the ftand. Then lay a fmall piece of board from the Stock to the ftand, to ferve as a bridge. Let them remain in this fituation all night. The nolfe of the Stock, occafioned

cafioned by the removal will alarm the clufter of idlers, who miffing the heat and connection they before had, will prefently be in motion and anxious to find their compa-nions; this they will foon do by paffing the bridge; and now finding ample room, will be received with joy. The Stock the next evening may be fet in its ufual place.

287. But if vou want Bees to ftrengthen a weak or backward Stock; ftrike them out (260) at night before the Stock, and by the morning they will be incorporated; or, (and which is the beft mode) take a bucket, pail, &c. or four or five rounds of ftraw cut out of an old hive. On either of thefe, turn the hive of idlers upfide down, and imme-diately fet the Stock over them.

To Hive Bees *properly.*

288. I would recommend no other defence than what I ufe myfelf, and which few perfons will probably object to or think extravagant. My meaning is, to drink a cup of good ale, and to rub fome of it over your face and hands, for as the Bees love the fmell of this liquor, when good, it will be no fmall recom-mendation to their favour. While this agree-able exhalation therefore is rifing from you, caft away fear, for you may hive them with fafety, provided it be done with care and proper precautions. Boldnefs and gentlenefs are now equally neceffary, every motion muft be deliberate, and without any hurry. Be particularly careful not to crufh any of the

Bees,

Bees, for the fmell of their bruifed bodies will excite the reft to fury and vengeance. Great care is at this time peculiarly neceffary, as without circumfpection, you may even kill the Queen herfelf, as is too often done, and which will infallibly occafion the Swarm, though well hived, to return home.

289. There is little danger to be apprehended from the Bees when they fwarm, becaufe at that time they have many fears and apprehenfions, and are therefore uncommonly gentle and pacific. At fuch times I have thruft my naked hand up into the middle of a Swarm as they hung upon a bough, without the Bees fhewing the leaft refentment : which, had they been in their hives, they would not have fuffered without the utmoft indignation. But in bad weather, efpecially if it be windy, they become more irafcible, and will not fuffer any one to be quite fo familiar with them ; a pair of gloves will then be neceffary.

290. Some are fo very fimple, as either to fumigate the Bees with fmoke, or throw water on them, from a notion of making them fettle and become more quiet. But fo far from anfwering this purpofe, it deftroys many of them, and makes the reft fo defperate as not to be hived without great danger. And even when this is accomplifhed, they are fo irritated at fuch uncivil ufage, that they frequently rife out of the hive, and fly quite away. Whereas, let the bufinefs be done with patience and circumfpection,

they

they may be hived, however badly fituated, without any of thefe inconveniences.

291. Swarms are often divided by fuch injudicious management; part of them returning home, while thofe that remain, being fo much diminifhed, form but a feeble Swarm, and of little value.

292. It fometimes happens that a Swarm divides while hovering in the Air, and fome fall to the ground. You muft examine in this cafe with great care, for if you find any, it is very likely the young Queen is among them; if fhe is, place her *upon* the empty hive, and take it as near as you can to the Bees fwarming: if only a few fee her, they will give notice to all the reft, and prefently fettle upon the hive, over this another may be placed, into which they will afcend, without further trouble. But if the Queen be not found, the Bees, though well hived, will not remain but either fly quite away or go back to the Mother Stock, or endeavour to gain admiffion into fome of the other Stocks, thereby occafioning tumult and flaughter.

293. It has been an ancient cuftom to make a tinking noife upon a pan, kettle, or the like, when a Swarm rifes, as being thought conducive to make them fettle the fooner, and prevent their flying away. This has been objected to as of no ufe. I once thought fo, and thereby loft feveral Swarms. Many times I have forebore tinkling until they were almoft out of my premifes; but on ftriking up a ferenade upon a large watering

pt,

pot, they have always fettled; and I have never loft a Swarm, fince I have ufed this method, · or had them fettle at any great diftance.

294. I have known of feveral Swarms flying over large commons, that merely by the tinkling of a key upon a fork, have been immediately ftruck with attention, and their flight being ftopped, have fettled on the ground very near the ruftic mufician.

295. The reafon may be the fame, as that which induces Bees to return precipitately to their hives at the approach of a thunder ftorm. Tinkling has the fame effect, as far at leaft as the found extends; the explofion of fire-arms produces the fame, but in a much fhorter fpace of time; as it will caufe them to fettle almoft inftantly; and confequently within due bounds, provided the explofion be made on that fide to which they are ftraying too far.

Not that the Bees are fond of mufic as fome fondly imagine, for my Bees have often had variety of *that* near their hives, without taking the leaft notice of it. ·

296. As the practice of tinkling has been of a very long ftanding, and is no ways hurtful, I fee no good reafon for its difufe; befides, it is abfolutely neceffary in another point of view, viz. to afcertain your property, which otherwife might be difputed, if the Swarm fhould fettle in another perfon's premifes. For the tinkling fecures a *legal right* to follow your Swarm upon another perfon's
grounds

grounds in order to hive them ; making good any damage you do thereby.

297. Particular care muft be taken, not to *begin* tinkling until the Swarm is all out, left you intimidate the others, and prevent their rifing.

298. If notwithftanding your noife, they feem not difpofed to fettle, or they fly too high, throwing up fand or duft among them, will caufe them to keep within bounds, and the fooner defcend. As foon as ever they begin to fettle, immediately ccafe all noife, that thofe on the wing may hear the founds of thofe that are fixing, and be allured to join them.

Whiftling or any other noife is then highly improper ; for the more filence, the fooner they clufter. For when once a part is fixed, there is no danger of the reft not following.

299. Before Swarms are put into one of my hives the barred top fhould have a hole made at each end of the middle bar, to admit a four-penny brad, long flender nail, or peg, to pafs through into the edge of the hive, in order to keep it firm in its place ; the ftraw top muft be faftened on ; this is beft done by making four loops with a ftrong pack-thread, drawn through the hive, near the top edge, at equal diftances, and long enough to meet at top within three or four inches, and drawn together by a other piece of pack-thread, and faftened by a knot upon the
top.

top. If a box be ufed, the top muft be fcrewed on.

300. If a Swarm or Caft is rifing from a Stock, contrary to your wifh, immediately with a handkerchief; or the like, ftop the door-way for fome time; this will baulk and perhaps deter them from fwarming afterwards. But if the young Queen rofe with the few that firft iffued, thefe will not return again.

301. When a Swarm is upon the wing, have an eye to your other Stocks, and if any are preparing to rife, ftop them, until the Swarm is fettled. Then, if another rifes, and attempts to unite with the firft; cover thefe immediately with a cloth, until the other is alfo fixed; and fo for any others. For if double Swarms be hived together, there will be a terrible flaughter, until one of the Queens be killed; or fometimes the whole Swarm will quit the hive, and fly quite away.

302. Although Swarms will often rife at the very inftant when the greateft bufinefs is çarrying on; yet, when it is a favourable day, and they are obferved not to work, and but little noife in the hive, a Swarm will furely take wing in an hour or two afterwards. Sometimes, alfo, there is a fudden throng of Bees at the entrance, making loud alarms, as though going to fwarm, when it is only the expreffion of joy for the appearance of a large delivery of young at once.

303. If

303. If a Swarm rifes and returns back again to the Stock, and you perceive them before many are got into the hive, immediately take, the old Stock away, and fet an empty hive in its place; by this manœuvre, the Swarm will be deceived, and fettle quietly therein. It fhould then be placed at the moft diftant part of the Apiary, and the Mother Stock fet in its own place again. But if the Swarm fhould be tumultuous and uneafy after it is in, fet the old Stock clofe to them, and they will foon be re-united to them again. For in this cafe, it is plain, they either had no Queen with them, or had loft her in their flight. Though there are other caufes of a Swarm's returning, as too much wind, clouds portending ing ftorms of thunder and fhowers.

304. The form in which a Swarm hangs from a bough, is that of an inverted cone, big at the top, and tapering to the bottom; the point being only a fingle Bee; they adhere together in this manner, by hooking themfelves to each other by their feet. But at other times, when the plant or tree will not admit of their being thus fufpended; they fpread round the body of a tree or branch, (fig. 5.) or upon a hedge, bufh, fhrub, &c. in a variety of directions, often very inconvenient for hiving.

305. Low trees near an Apiary are very ufeful, for they attract the Swarms to fettle on them, which are thereby more eafily hived.

For

For Swarms will fometimes fix of their own accord near the Apiary, though no notice had been taken of their rifing. But fuch inftances are too precarious to be trufted to; and they will much oftener fly away without cluftering at all. A branch of a tree, or a hive, fixed upon a long pole, and lifted up among a Swarm, when in the air, has inticed them to fettle thereon.

306. No time fhould be loft to hive them as foon as cluftered; for the longer they hang, the more irritable they become, and the more unwilling they will be to hive. For when once fixed, they fend out fcouts to bring tidings of a proper habitation, and no fooner do thefe return, and touch the clufter, but there is a general fhake of the wings; after this, they prefently unknit and depart, unlefs they be immediately hived, and then it is a chance if they will ftay.

307. A large cloth or apron, and a hive floor or other board will be ufeful in the hiving; fpread the cloth upon the ground as nearly under the clufter as poffible; on that, place the floor, and a ftick about an inch thick laid acrofs; fo that when the hive is placed thereon, there may be ample room for the ftruggling multitude to enter the more freely and fooner in.

308. Or a Swarm may be fhook off a branch or fhrub, into a cloth, properly held under by an affiftant, and the cloth with the Bees therein, immediately laid on the ground, then placing a hive over the Bees, fupporting

supporting one edge, a little raifed, by a ftone, or fomething convenient, fo that no Bees be crufhed, and they will foon afcend up into the hive without any further operation, but that of fcreening them from the rays of the Sun.

309. If a Swarm hangs to a bough, or any thing that will admit of the hives fliding under them, firft cut off, in the moft gentle manner, any twigs that may be in the way; then with your left hand prefs the inverted hive upwards, to inclofe as much of the clufter as poffible, without difturbing the Bees, until with your right hand you give the bough a fudden and fmart fhake; this will caufe moft of the clufter to fall into the hive; among whom, in general, will be the Queen. Keep the hive in your arm as it is, until you have got to the board or cloth; (307) then gently turn it upfide down; one edge upon the board, and the other upon the ftick that lays acrofs; any Bees that have tumbled out, as well as thofe on the wing, hearing the buz in the hive, will foon join them. With a few twigs, difturb thofe that attempt to fettle again, and they will foon defift. But ufe no nettles, or water, which ferves only to inrage and injure the Bees.

310. Cover the hive with a cloth, boughs, or any thing proper to keep off the too piercing rays of the Sun; for otherwife the Bees finding their new habitation too hot, will be wife enough to quit it.

311. If

311. If it fhould happen to be more convenient to hold a cloth or large apron under
the Bees, than a hive to fhake them into,
let the former method be taken, and gathering up the cloth by the corners, very gently
and tenderly bring it down, and manage as
directod (307). To avoid repetitions ; *either* a
cloth or hive may be ufed, as fhall appear
moft convenient, in any of the operations
hereafter directed.   Let the hive remain
in this ftate until the evening, and then
(taking away the ftick) remove it to its
appointed place.   If taken away before, the
ftragglers will be loft.

But if it happens to be in a place inconvenient or improper to leave the Swarm
in until night, as foon as ever the Bees are
wholly got in, or nearly fo, it muft be
covered with a cloth, and taken to its def-
tined place at once : the ftragglers that are
left will return to the mother Stock.

312. It will alfo be proper to adopt this
method when a Swarm is fo very large as
to impoverifh the Stock ; for by taking the
hive away, as foon as a fufficient number
are got in, the reft (fometimes a great
number) will return to their former abode.

313. Should a Swarm fettle fo untowardly, that a hive cannot be conveniently held
under them, a light bafket will anfwer the
purpofe as well : the Bees being fhaken into
the bafket, fet it upon its bottom on the
ground, then a hive being placed over it,
they

they will quit the baſket, and fix in the hive.

314. Swarms often cluſter in trees much too high to be come at without the aſſiſtance of a ladder, ſteps, table, or the like, and ſometimes at the extremity of a ſmall bough, at too great a diſtance to be reached with the hive in your hand. In this caſe; after placing the hive in readineſs under the tree; and having prepared a ſharp knife, and a ſaw, aſcend the ladder, and gently cut away all the ſmall twigs and branches that ſurround the cluſter, and examine if the bough on which it hangs can be cut through with a knife; as this will diſturb the Bees much leſs than the action of a ſaw. Keep the branch ſteady with one hand while you ſever it with the other, or rather it ſhould be held by an aſſiſtant, and as ſoon as cut through, be brought gently down; taking great care that the Bees be not touched by any of the other branches. Then lay the bough with the Bees on it, very gently on the cloth or board, and ſet the hive over it. Before the evening the Bees will be fixed to the top of the hive, having quitted the bough, which may now be taken away, and the hive put in its intended place.

315. But ſhould it be impracticable, or hurtful to a tree, to cut off a branch, a baſket or hive may be tied bottom upwards upon a long fork, rake, or pole, and held under the Swarm while another perſon ſhakes the branch, either with his hands or ſome

K 2 other

other inftrument, fo as to get as many as poffible into the hive or baſket; after which, the remainder are to be diflodged by a long ſtick, with ſmall twigs tied to the end. Or they may be diflodged by twigs tied to the end of a long pole, until they ſettle more conveniently to be hived. At the ſame time the proper muſic, and fire arms, charged with powder only, muſt be in readineſs, left the Swarm take wing again, and now affronted with your treatment fly quite away.

It will be highly neceſſary in theſe trou-bleſome operations to defend your face and hands. (73, 76.)

(316. Another very difficult caſe is, when they ſettle at a great height, round a branch of a tree not flexible enough to be ſhaken; the moſt eaſy method of hiving them is, to ſet a hive upon a board or floor, whereon are two pieces of ſticks to raiſe the front edge of the hive about an inch, take this up a ladder (placed as cloſe to the Bees as poſſible) and reſt the board or its edge on the branch, as near the Bees as can be without hurting them. Then ſuſpend or faſten the hive with cords to the other branches of the tree, or ladder, in the ſafeſt and beſt manner that circumſtances will allow of. This done, with a ſpoon, gently take ſome of the Bees from the cluſter, and turn them out of the ſpoon at the door-way of the hive, this repeat ſeveral times, and they will crawl into the hive. This me-thod

thod may be continued as long as the other
Bees fhew no great refentment, or until you
have got about a quart into the hive. Leave
them a little while; the noife of thofe in
the hive will incite the others to march
therein alfo, and in about an hour the
whole Swarm will have entered. But if
inftead of this, they feem not difpofed to quit
the branch, take more of them away by the
fpoon, at intervals, until the others begin
to run into the hives themfelves.

By patiently proceeding thus, there is far
lefs danger, damage, and trouble, than by
thofe irritating and violent means generally employed in thefe cafes.

317. When Swarms hang too low to admit the paffing a hive underneath, a cloth may
be drawn under them, and a ftick laid
thereon; then fhake the Bees down, and
gradually withdraw the cloth far enough
to allow the placing the hive over it. If
there be any Bees already on the ground,
they will foon hear the noife of the multitude, and join them. If not, the hive fhould
be placed near them; or with a brufh or
wing, move the Bees nearer the hives,
as fhall appear moft convenient.

318. When they fettle in a hedge, fix
a hive over them, either upon forked fticks,
or any other contrivance. But firft fprinkle
the infide top of the hive with ale and fugar;
but *only* at the top, becaufe it is to that
part we want to entice them. Wait fome
time, and if this fhould not fucceed, intro-

duce

duce a hive *underneath* them, as far as
poffible, cutting away fuch fprigs and branches as may obftruct its paffage; then fhaking the bufh or hedge, caufe as many as
poffible to fall into the hive, and continue
fo to do until they are wearied of returning to the hedge, or have gradually joined
thofe in the hive, which they will do by
this management in a little time. Lay two
fticks acrofs the hive, and fet another over
it, and by night thofe that are upon the
ground, and on the outfide of the hive, will
be all gone in, and collected with the reft
now afcended in the upper hive, provided
the Queen be among them, otherwife fhe
muft be looked for among thofe upon the
ground or about the hive.

319. Should they clufter round the body,
or leading branches of a tree, apply the edge
of the hive clofe to the body, a little below
the fpread of the Bees, and where there
is the greateft bunch or clufter; gently prefs
the hive upwards, and with a fmall ftick,
force down as many Bees as you can into
the hive, but be fure not to hurt any
of them; then removing the hive to other
parts that have the largeft clufters, do the
fame there; it is very probable the Queen
will be among fome of thefe. The hive
muft now be placed as near as poffible to
the tree, and the reft of the Bees will join
their fellows, provided they are fo difturbed
as to prevent their fettling about the tree
again. As this is a very difficult cafe, the

Bees

Bees will be unavoidably irritated, and therefore the face and hands fhould be properly
fecured.

Though thefe methods will undoubtedly
fucceed, yet I have found the following
much eafier and fafer, when the fituation is
not too high.

320. Firſt, procure a fufficient number of
tables, ſtools, or caſks, that they may be ſet
on each other fo as to be of equal height
with the cluſter of Bees, or two ladders muſt
be fo placed as to admit a board from one
to the other, fufficient to hold a bee-hive.
This being done, hold the hive bottom upwards, and with a fpoon gently take up as
many as you can at a time, from the largeſt
cluſter, and put them carefully into the hive,
until there be a quart or more, if the Bees
will let you do it patiently; then turn the
hive upon its bottom on the board or floor,
already prepared; the edge of the hives next
the tree muſt be kept a little raifed, for the
eafier admiſſion of the conçourfe of Bees that
yet remain on the tree. When caſks or
tables are ufed, the ſtage formed by them
with the hive upon it, is to be gently moved
towards the tree, fo that the edge of the hive-
floor may touch the Bees; but if this fhould
be inconvenient, a thin piece of board may
be laid from the hive to the tree, as a bridge
for the Bees to pafs over; for the noife of
thofe in the hive, will attract the notice of
fuch as are on the tree, and you will prefently
fee them begin to diflodge and pafs the bridge

to

to their companions. This will be the sooner effected, if you gently stroke down those nearest the hive with a stick, or rather take from the largest cluster spoonfuls at a time, and put them upon the bridge near the entrance of the hive; for they will then go directly in, and when the greater number have entered, there is no danger but the rest will follow.

321. The usual way of brushing Bees into a hive enrages them most highly; this, however, is not all the mischief, for many are killed in the operation, and sometimes the Queen herself; in which case, the Swarm, even after having been hived, will fly away: nor will the Apiator himself be safe, unless very well defended. All these inconveniencies are avoided by the gentle method just recommended; and to a lover of Bees, is as agreeable an amusement as hunting or angling to others: I perform it without even a pair of gloves, unless in a bad day.

322. Authors direct, as a general rule, that Swarms should always remain near the place where they settled, until the evening, as otherwise those Bees that have not settled and are hovering about, not knowing where their companions are placed, will return to the old Stock, and will be treated with the same severity as strangers. In the many observations I have made, I can assert, that such consequence never followed, but that they were received as kindly as though they had never parted.

323. When

323. When Bees fettle in a hollow on the fide of a tree or ftub, clap the bottom of the hive fo clofe againft it, that not a Bee can efcape: let an affiftant hold it faft, and alfo tie a cloth round the edge, or with clay or the like ftop every opening: being thus well fe-cured, with a hammer or great ftone, beat round about the hollow, making the greateft noife you can, which in a fhort time will fo terrify the Bees, that for peace fake they will be induced to enter the hive: now and then ceafe the noife, and applying your ear to the hive, you will know by the buz when the greater part are in: you may then fet the hive down, and difturb thofe that remain in the hole with fmall twigs, which at length will fo weary them, as to make them enter the hive. Then ftop the hole with weeds, or any thing at hand, and your work is done.

324. Swarms will frequently make a hol-low tree their habitation. To diflodge them make a large hole with a chiffel, hatchet, or other fuitable inftrument, as near as poffible to the upper part of the hollow; for, if there be room enough, they will lie always above the hole they go in at: place the edge of the hive clofe to the hole, and forceably ftriking about that part of the tree where the Bees are, give them as much difturbance as poffible; alarmed and terrified at the ftrokes, they will prefently iffue out through the hole, and very likely fettle in the hive; but if not, on the branches of the tree, or on fome other place, that may be convenient for hiving them

them. After being hived, they should be placed near the tree they came from, to receive the stragglers.

325. But if they lie below the hole, they enter in at, make the opening beneath them; and take care that the upper hole, by which the Bees are to issue out, be the largest: sometimes however, all these methods prove ineffectual. We must then have recourse to fumigation; this is done by placing old rags, damp straw, or any thing that will make much smoke, underneath the Bees, and setting fire to it, at the same time disturbing them as much as possible by violently striking the tree; this will generally cause them to fly out and settle elsewhere.

326. The same method must be pursued if any Bees remain afterwards in the hollows, or places of lodgment, to force them out; and to prevent their return, the holes should be stopped with nettles or other weeds.

327. Should they settle under the roof, or in any vacancies of a house or other building, a continued noise, beating, or drumming against the part they are lodged in, will cause them to quit it; especially if the place of entrance be very much enlarged.

If this alarm should not succeed, plenty of smoke may be conveyed to them by means of a funnel, which will most likely drive them out. But where smoke cannot easily be introduced, water poured over them by a funnel, or squirted on them by a syringe, will so affect them that the combs and Bees may be
taken

taken away by the hands, which however ſhould be defended by gloves.

328. But in all theſe caſes it ſhould be obſerved, that the longer they have been ſettled, the greater will be the difficulty of diſlodging them, eſpecially if they have been ſome days, and have made combs; for they will then die, rather than relinquiſh them.

329. Therefore, where none of theſe operations take effect, the only way left (except that of deſtroying the Bees by the fumes of brimſtone) is, for the Apiator to be armed cap-a-pee (73). He may then boldly break an opening into the building or wall, ſufficient to put in his arm, and to take the combs away one by one; then having an empty hive or *two* ready, with ſeveral ſticks half an inch thick, place the combs in the hives, and between every two combs put two pieces of ſticks to keep them at a proper diſtance, ſo as not to cruſh the Bees that may be hanging upon them. If there be a comb containing young, it ſhould be placed in the middle. Then ſetting the hive as near as poſſible to the place of lodgment, the other Bees will be enticed to quit their old reſidence, and quietly enter this new habitation. If the next day they work kindly, all is well: otherwiſe drive the Bees out (372) and take away the combs and honey, eſpecially if it be at the latter end of the ſeaſon.

330. When Swarms come into a room, as ſoon as they are all nearly in, cloſe the windows and doors, that none may eſcape; let

them

them remain until they have cluftered, then cover them with the hive, and gently draw it along the wall or ceiling, to difengage them from it; afterwards take the hive, bottom upwards from the cieling, and fet it upon its bottom on the floor, with one edge a little raifed up by a ftick. Before night the reft of the Bees will go down and join their companions : they will do this the fooner if the room be fo darkened that they may *think* night is coming on.

331. When ftraggling Bees come into a room, if the upper fafh be pulled down, they will prefently go out again; but where windows are not fo conftructed, the Bees fhould be gently brufhed down to that part which does open, or otherwife they will beat themfelves to death againft the glafs, as they always afcend to the upper part, where the greateft light is.

332. In many buildings, as well as in hollow trees, there have been lodgements of Bees for a long fucceffion of years, without either hurt or profit to the owners. Swarms rifing from thefe might be watched and hived as other Swarms are; and were a hive with honey-combs in it, efpecially with a brood comb, fet in fwarming-time over the opening or paffage, by which they enter, it would be a means of enticing a Swarm to fettle there. A hive, fo prepared, and placed near them, will have the fame effect.

333. Stray Swarms are frequently feen in their flight over fields and commons : thefe may be enticed to fettle, by tinkling with a
key

key upon a fork, by whiftling, or by any other
fimilar noife.

In fuch cafes it will fometimes be a long
while before a hive can be procured, and in
the interim the Bees may reaffume their flight:
to prevent which, as foon as they are fettled,
throw your handkerchief over them, and tie
it by the corners fo as to inclofe them; then
cut off that part of the bough or fprig, to
which they hang, with as little difturbance as
poffible, and you may carry them in this
manner feveral miles with great eafe and
fafety. But fhould they fettle on the ground,
fpread your handkerchief, clofe by them, and
with a whifp of grafs or a fmall twig gently
fhove them upon the handkerchief; or if your
hat be laid over them, it is likely they will
afcend therein.

When you have procured a hive, and have
laid the branch acrofs a pail or pan, and two
other fticks acrofs, untie the handkerchief,
and fet the hive over the bough, refting upon
the crofs fticks; let it ftand until night, and
all the Bees will have entered into the hive:
but if you have them in a handkerchief, without any branch, lay the handkerchief on the
ground, untie it, and place the hive over it;
the Bees will foon afcend therein.

334. There have been many inftances of a
Swarm fettling upon a perfon's head (67).
In this cafe, if any refiftance be made, it may
be attended with fatal confequences; but if
you remain quiet and paffive, without giving
the Bees any affront or difturbance, not one
will offer to fting you.

335. As

335. As foon as you perceive a Swarm difpofed to fettle on you, take off your hat, and
carefully cover your head and face with your
handkerchief; but if this cannot be done, place
your hands hollow over your mouth, nofe, and
eyes, and then fuffer them to fettle upon you
quietly, calling at the fame time for affiftance :
or you may leifurely walk with the Bees upon
your head, with as much fafety and confidence
as Mr. Wildman himfelf, until you meet fome
one to affift you: let him take a prepared
hive, and hold it over your head, and the
Bees will very likely foon begin to afcend
therein; as foon as this is perceived the
hive muft be held a little higher, the better
to withdraw the Bees from the head; this
will be fooner effected if you go into a room
confiderably darkened. But fhould this method not fucceed, the Bees may be taken off
by a fpoonful at a time, and put into the hive,
until the greater part be taken off; then holding the edge of the hive fo as to touch thofe
that remain, they will foon crawl to thofe in
the hive : or, by giving your head a violent and
fudden fhake over a hive or table, the greater
part will fall off, probably the Queen, then
walking to fome diftance, thofe that remain,
miffing the Queen, will foon diflodge in
fearch of her; but, if inftead of this, they
remain quiet, and the other Bees return to
fettle on you, it is a fign you have ftill the
Queen about you ; whom, however, at the
next effort, you will probably fhake off; the

few

few then remaining, may eafily be taken off by a fpoon. Sometimes alfo a great fmoke made behind a perfon, fo as to blow over him, will readily diflodge them.

336. Should a Swarm attempt to fix up-on or enter another Stock, cover the hive im-mediately with a cloth, and fhut the door-way until they be fettled and quiet; then fet a hive over them, and in about a quarter of an hour open the Stock door-way, and by the four corners of the cloth lift the hive up and carry it to the place defigned for it. Early the next morning the hive may be taken up, and the cloth removed; but if they have already made a lodgment upon the hive, ftop up the door-way, and hold an empty hive, over the greateft clufter, and perhaps they will afcend; if not, take a fpoon, and gently put a quart or two of the Bees into the empty hive, then fet it over the reft, and they will follow; as foon as they appear to do fo, open the Stock door-way. The Swarm fhould be taken away as foon as they have done afcending.

337. When two Swarms rife together and fight, the throwing of duft or fand among them will generally appeafe the ftrife, and fe-parate them; or, they may be terrified into the ceffation of hoftilities by the explofion of a fowling-piece.

338. Should a Swarm fix very near the fpot where another had been hived a day or two before, it will be neceffary to place it four or five yards diftance, or elfe many of the firft hived Swarm returning to their alighting

alighting place, will repair to the new comers, and be killed. If a Swarm be too fmall,
the next that rifes, if not large, fhould by
all means be added to it, which will make
it a very good Stock.

339. It often happens, that two or three
Princefles go out with a Swarm, and fettle in fo
many clufters : when one clufter is very large,
and the others fmall, hive them all feparate -
ly; at dufk fpread a cloth upon the ground,
with a ftick acrofs, take the hives with the
fmaller clufters, beat the Bees out upon the
cloth, and then fet the hive with the large cluf-
erin it over them ; about two hours after this,
lift them, cloth and all, upon a proper ftand,
and before morning they will be united with
little or no flaughter; efpecially, if the fmall
clufters have been fprinkled over with ale and
fugar : let them remain in this fituation until
next night, when the cloth may be taken a-
way. Another method is, about an hour
after the fmall clufters are hived, to beat
them out upon a cloth, and take the Princefles from them (384), and immediately to
fet the hive with the large clufter over them ;
or they may be firft ftupified (389), and then
their Princefles taken from them; this will
produce a firm union without any contention.

340. But it is not *always* that the Swarm
feparates, although accompanied with two or
more young Queens, but will all fettle together: however, as foon as they are hived
great commotions and much flaughter will
enfue before the Bees can decide which
Princefs,

Princefs fhall reign. If the competition be nearly equal, and victory long in fufpence, all the Bees will quit the hive, in order to decide it more commodioufly in the open air : they will then either unite or feparate into diftinct Swarms : in this laft cafe to re-hive them all together, will be of no ufe, but may occafion the deftruction of the whole : they muft therefore be hived feparately, and treated as Cafts (366). But if they continue fighting in the hive until the next morning, it will be better perhaps to ftrike them all out of it ; and they will then either feparate or return to the mother Stock.

341. In thefe cafes open hives have a great advantage ; for by fetting another hive over them, and leaving the door-ways open, the Bees will feparate without quarrelling. The next night ftop the upper entrance, and the Queen that has the feweft partifans will be expelled without much ftrife.

342. It does not always happen that they quarrel directly, though there be two Prin_ ceffes ; for fometimes they continue undeter_ mined in their choice, two or three days ; but all this while they will be very reftlefs and confufed, nor attempt to work, until one be depofed and expelled, or flain.

343. All Swarms, if the weather be fair, will begin to work almoft as foon as hived ; but if the firft day be foul, fo as to prevent their going abroad, it difcourages them fo much, that on the fecond, though fine, they will fcarcely look out ; but when the third

I.   day

day proves unfair it fometimes makes them fo fulky as to choofe rather to die than to feek for food.

344. Butler fays they will live five or fix days without honey, and when nearly ftarved they ftring down, hanging by each others legs like ropes : this is a certain fign of approaching death, if not directly relieved (733).

345. When all the Swarms are gone, if any young Princeffes be left, they are generally killed two or three days after, and may be found dead about the hives ; though they are fometimes refpited until the execution of the Drones.

CHAPTER XII.

Of SWARMING BEES ARTIFICIALLY. *Of* CATCHING *the* QUEEN ; *and Method of* UNITING SWARMS *and* STOCKS.

346. IT has been already noticed of what great importance the Queen is to the ftrength, fupport, and perpetuity of every Stock or Swarm of Bees. A *truth* the antients were in fome degree acquainted with; but they fuppofed the principal Bee to be a *King*.

347. Xeno-

347. Xenophon, * who flourished about 2000 years ago, seems the most ancient writer who has taken notice of this peculiarity. His words are very remarkable: " There " is one particular Bee in every Swarm (or Stock) a leader of the rest, as one they willingly obey; where that remains, not one will *thence* depart; that removed, not one will stay behind, so strong is the affection they are inspired with to be governed by *it*."
He seems doubtful of the gender, by characterizing *it* in the neuter.

348. The immortal Virgil sweetly sung on this delightful subject above 1700 years fiuce. But with respect to any method of taming the Bees, or captivating the Queen, Virgil himself is silent. Columella, however, seems to have been acquanted with the secret, by directing one of the Queens to be killed in the union of Casts.

349. But the first account of captivating the Queen at will, is given us by father Labat; † who mentions, that he met with a man who seemed covered over with Bees, his cap particularly was so covered as to resemble those natural Swarms that settle on a tree: he was ordered to take it off; the Bees then placed themselves on his shoulder, his head, and his hands, without stinging him or any of the bye-standers.

L 2

350. In

---

* Cyropedia.
† Labat's Travels.

350. In like manner Swammerdam fecured the Mother Bee of a Swarm, by tying a fmall bit of thread to one of her legs, and then faftening it to a long pole, the whole Swarm immediately affembled round the end of the pole, to cover the Mother Bee, and might be carried wherever the bearer pleafed. Here we have the method of fixing Swarms; but from neither of thefe gentleman can we learn how to obtain the Queen.

351. Sir George Wheeler * indeed, lets us into the fecret, as told him by a Spanifh prieft, who faid, he had caught the Queen with a *fly-catch*, and then cutting her wings, had obliged her to remain at home; but it may be doubted whether this be not a genteel evafion rather than an explanation : a hive cannot be turned up, and a fly-catch thruft therein to intangle the Queen. And to watch her going out, which is very feldom, or her return, requires more than the leifure and patience even of a prieft.

352. It is furprifing that Butler, who knew how to ftupify the Bees with punk or mully puff, fhould not proceed one ftep further, and make ufe of it, in order to take the Queen, and manage the Bees at will: and it is ftill more furprifing, that the fagacious Reaumur, who appears to have read Butler, fhould not have taken the *hint* of the narcotic fume; but was conftrained to immerge the Bees in water, to obtain

---

* Wheeler's Journey into Greece.

obtain the Queen. The Rev. Mr. Thorley,* profited by the hint of Butler, and made ufe of it for the union of Stocks.

353. But Dr. Warder, § fo long ago as 1712, gives a particular detail of a method of performing this feemingly myfterious bufinefs with eafe and pleafure, and without fumigation or immerfion, as to Swarms or Cafts. Here he ftopped. For the information how to catch the Queen of a Stock we are obliged to the ingenuity of Mr. Thomas Wildman.

354. This gentleman's extraordinary performance with Bees, attraćted the notice of the curious few, as well as of the public; but however advantageous they may have been to himfelf, I fear they will be found of little utility to the world. Expećtations were raifed very high, and the moft fanguine hopes conceived of the great increafe of profit likely to arife from his mode of management.

355. Nor indeed fhould we have been difappointed, had the method of *Artificial Swarming*, which he defcribes page (133), ¶ *(allowing for a few alterations)* been found as practicable as it was expećted to be. His words are, " If an old hive is fo full of Bees, that " they reft in the night under the board, and

L 3 " fhew

---

* Thorley's Enquiry. &c.
§ The True Amazons.
¶ Management of Bees, 2d Edition.

" fhew no difpofition, to fwarm, * turn. the
" hive bottom up, give it fome flight ftrokes
" on the fides, fo as to alarm the Bees; they,
" will immediately run to the extremities
" of their combs : if you look attentively to
" the middle of the hive, you will there
" perceive the Queen among the foremoft,†
" feize her between the fore-finger and
" thumb, and confine her in your hand,
" until moft. part of the Bees take wing ‡ ;
" let her then go, § the Bees will foon join
" her, and fettle on fome branch of a
" tree. Put them into an empty hive ; put
" the old Stock in its place, ‖ that the Bees
" which had been out in the fields might
" enter in at their return ; and having re-
" mained an hour or fo, it is then put on an-
" other ftand near, or next their own : the
" hive having now what may be called a
" Swarm in it, is then to be placed on the
" ftand of the old Stock, and if the Bees in
" both work regularly, carrying loads, all is
" well. This backwardnefs to fwarm may
" be

---

* This may be the cafe, and yet not be in a proper
condition to fwarm for two or three weeks after, for want
of Drones or a Princefs.

† I never found it fo.

‡ Some may, but the main body will remain even
though no young Queen be left in the hive.

§ Rather cut her wings, and fix her on fomething in
fight of the Swarm, and which fhall be at the fame time
moft convenient for hiving them.

‖ Rather at the fartheft part of the Apiary or there
will be abundance of miftakes and Quarrels.

" be owing to their want of a Queen to lead.
" them forth; and the old Queen is loth to
" go until a young one is bred;* yet if a royal
" cell contains a young Queen, the Bees in
" both hives will thrive; as thofe in an old
" Stock will go on in expectation of the
" young Queen's coming forth."

356. " This feparation fhould not in *pru-*
" *dence* be attempted, unlefs you have a
" Queen in referve;† for if the Bees in the
" old Stock, when placed on their ftand are
" in an uproar, there is no Queen, nor prof-
" pect of a Queen among them; and in this
" cafe their own Queen fhould be reftored to
" them, and the referved Queen be put to
" the Swarm; or the Bees in the empty
" hive, which fhould then be carried to the
" diftance of half a mile, ‡ and remain there
" for a few days, until they have made fome
" works, and may then be brought back to
" their former ftation.

" Care fhould be taken that the number of
" Bees feparated from the old Stock, be fuffi-
' ient in number to make a Swarm; on this
" account it is *perhaps* better to ufe the fol-
" lowing method.§   A fufficient number of

L 4   Bees

---

* Confequently this operation will be labour loft.

† Aye! but Mr. Wildman has not informed us where
or how to obtain this fpare Queen. I doubt we may ruin
fome other Stocks in obtaining one.

‡ This muft certainly be very inconvenient, troublefome, and hazardous.

§ There is no occafion for *perhaps*, for moft *furely* it
cannot be done by the former.

" Bees fhould be taken out of the Stock, in.
" the manner that fhall be hereafter directed,.
" and put in an empty hive.* The eye will
" here judge of their numbers, when one
" half, or a fufficient number; is got into.
" the empty hive, it fhould be carried to
" fome diftance. The filence in either hive
" will foon indicate where the Queen is.
" It would be eligible that their own Queen.
" remained in the old Stock ; but if fhe
" does not, the referved Queen may be put.
" to them, and they fhould be immediately
" reftored to their former ftand, and the
" Bees or Swarm taken off, be carried to
" half a mile, as before."

357. I have only made a few curfory remarks,
by way of annotations, as the principle upon
which the whole is founded, is repugnant to
the experiments I have repeatedly made, on
purpofe to afcertain its validity. Not that
there can be any doubt, however, but that
Mr. Wildman, among the multitude of hives
he had turned up in his peregrinations,
may have had an opportunity of fwarming
Bees in the manner defcribed. But as I have
often turned up hives, in order to feize the
Queen, not only by myfelf but in prefence of
gentlemen, fufficiently converfant with Bee-
Majefty eafily to diftinguifh her, without
ever obtaining by this means the defired prof-
pect,

---

* So that this *following method* is a method to be taught
us hereafter ; and which we fhall hereafter particularly
remark upon.

pect. I cannot but conclude Mr. Wildman to be in an error. Besides, it is generally known that, on a hive being tapped, or any disturbance made, the Queen always retires for security to the inmost recesses of the hive, leaving her numerous guard to defend the outworks.

358. Therefore to clear this point up, a public experiment is necessary. Let Mr. Thomas Wildman go in the proper season into any judicious and practical Bee-Master's Apiary, and in his presence, and that of several others, equally conversant with the subject, take a Stock of Bees up and make them swarm upon his plan. This would, if successful, decide the point greatly to Mr. Wildman's honour.

359. I am particularly urgent upon this head, because the method, if practicable, may be easily performed, and without giving much disturbance to the Bees, and would therefore save a very tedious attendance in Swarming-time. Mr. Wildman also, in page 199, confidently repeats the same method of catching the Queen. Now if he can seize her majesty so easily, why pursue that other more difficult method of *driving*, which he is known to practice to obtain her? But even this favourite operation cannot be performed without being well armed: for every Apiator knows, and must have experienced, often to his smart, that in turning up a hive, the Bees, filled with ire, and armed with poisoned weapons, will attack him by hundreds, and make it very hot work, and
even

even dangerous to ſtand peeping after the Queen. Of this circumſtance Mr. Wildman ought ſurely to have apprized his pupils.

360. However from·this firſt inſtance it appears, that Mr. Wildman has no ſecret power over the Bees, to cauſe them to come out of their hives at the word of command, as many people have erroneouſly imagined; for at page 198 he diſclaims all pretenſions to any ſuch power, and acknowledges the whole to be a manual operation, ſimply that of *driving* the Bees into an empty hive, and then catching the Queen.

361. But notwithſtanding this declaration, the *truth* obliges me to obſerve, that he has led the public into the above error, by expreſsly aſſerting in his hand-bill (which I have ſeen, and have by me) that " the-fourth Swarm " he will *command·out of the hive.*" As this is ſo repugnant to what he has given us in his book, the practitioners in·the art will not be ſatisfied unleſs they have a direct proof in this inſtance, as in that·before recited (358).

362 His method of driving is much the ſame as has been practiced for more than two centuries paſt. Butler deſcribes it, and before him Lawſon, Markham, and otheis, as well as a variety of authors ſince: therefore not to ſwell theſe pages unneceſſarily, I ſhall only give thoſe methods which I have.found moſt convenient and eligible, and in ſuch a manner that all the operations ſhall follow each other in proper order, and without interrup-

tion;

tion; after which we shall take the liberty of making, such strictures and observations as we judge and hope may be of general utility.

363. But by way of introduction to the rest, we shall insert Dr. Warder's * account of his captivating a Queen from a Swarm, as containing many interesting and amusing particulars.

364. He tells us, " That to satisfy his curiosity, he was resolved to risk the loss of a Swarm; therefore about half an hour before sun-rise he took a Swarm of Bees that had been hived the morning before, to some distance from the stand, and striking pretty strongly the edge of the hive upon the ground, the Swarm fell out in a lump upon the grass. As soon as they were a little quiet, he stirred among them with a little stick, to find the Queen; at length he discovered her, and quickly taking her, he cut off her wings to disable her from flying, and put her into a little box with holes: the Bees left on the grass were soon sensible of their loss, spread themselves every way in search of their Queen, with a piteous and discontented note; in about an hour they rose, and flew to the place where they had pitched the day before, and divided in little parties to look for her along the hedge: he then laid the box with the Queen in it near one of these little companies, and they immediately began to gather

---

* The True Amazons, 1712.

gather from all parts, and encompafs her all round with joyful founds, well known to thofe who are ufed to Bees.

365. "The experiment was often repeated, placing the Queen fometimes on one fide, and fometimes on the other; by which means he could march or counter-march them in any direction he chofe. It is very remarkable that though honey was offered the Queen while prifoner in the box, fhe would tafte none while deprived of her family; nor did the Bees fhew lefs affection for their Queen, they never would leave her, though kept five days and nights without food, at which period they all died martyrs to their loyalty; the Queen furviving them but a few hours."

To Unite *two or more* Swarms *or* Cafts.

366 AFTER having a fmall Swarm or Caft, in two or three days or a week you may have fome others, all of which are to be hived feparately: about ten o'clock at night fpread a cloth on the ground, near the firft Caft, and lay a hive floor on the cloth, with a ftick acrofs, then take the hive which hath the fecond Caft, turn it up, fprinkle fome fugar'd ale among the Bees, and then ftrike the edge of the hive with fome force on the ftick, which will probably caufe all the Bees fall out in a lump; but if not, repeat the ftrokes until they do. The firft Caft muft be immediately fet over them, and in about an hour thofe on the cloth will have crawled

up,

up, and become one family. If any hang
about the outſide of the hive, with a ſtick
or feather ſtrike them off very gently upon
the cloth, and when all are in, ſet the hive
in its place : about five in the morning lift
up the hive, floor and all, and withdraw the
cloth, if there be any Bees on it, ſpread it
over the hive, and the ſtragglers will ſoon
enter therein : by crawling among each other
all night, they become familiar and reconciled.

367. In the ſame manner a third or fourth
may be added, until ſufficiently numerous to
form a ſtrong Stock for the next year ; but
this muſt be done time enough for the Bees
to lay up a ſufficient ſtore for the winter.

368. If this be done in the day-time, the
Bees of both Caſts or Swarms will immediately proceed to fighting, or fly away ; but being done in the night, it cauſes very little com-
motion, and very few Bees, ſometimes none,
are ſlain, except indeed the invading Queen,
who is generally diſpatched or expelled before morning ; being often found on the
ground, ſurrounded by two or three hundred
of her faithful ſubjects, who will ſtarve themſelves rather than abandon their beloved So-
vereign : a ſad and ſorrowful ſcene, to prevent which ſhe muſt be taken from them by
a ſmall ſtick, and then her ſubject Bees being
placed near the entrance of the hive, will
preſently join the reſt.

369. In hives or boxes that have openings in the the tops, this operation may more

eaſily

eafily be executed, by raifing the firft Caft and fetting the fecond or any other fubfequent ones, under it, let it remain double until the next night, by which time they will be all in the upper hive, then lift it gently up, and take the under one away.

370. To prevent any affray, fome have propofed to take away the Queen of the Caft when the Bees are knocked out, according to Dr. Warder's method, (364), and then to kill her. This, no doubt will certainly prevent flaughter; but it is very troublefome, and takes up more time than country people can or will fpare from their other occupations; therefore, as the damage arifing from the preceeding mode is but trifling, it would feem preferable for common ufe; efpecially if a little fugared ale is fprinkled over them, before they are incorporated. Cafts in the fame manner may be returned to the mother Stock, to prevent their being too much impoverifhed; which caufes many to fail before the next feafon. Thefe operations need no other defence than a pair of gloves.

371. Happy for Sovereigns of the human race, that the people are frequently facrificed for their good; and the prince but very feldom for the people's.

To DRIVE *or* SWARM BEES *Artificially, nearly upon Mr.* WILDMAN's *Second Plan.*＊

372. When a Stock feems very full of Bees, and difcovers the ufual fymptoms of being ready to fwarm ; efpecially if there appear many Drones, and thefe begin to lie out ; it will be neceffary to perform this operation : therefore about the middle of a calm and hot day (if fuch offers), remove the Stock upon a cloth (laid ready upon the ground) and immediately taking it up by the four corners, carry it into fome out-houfe, or the like, where but little light is admitted. Or it will be more eligible to have a ftraw hive made on purpofe in the form of a bafket, viz. narrower at bottom than at top ; it fhould be wide enough to admit any common ftraw hive a little way within it, as far as three rounds of the ftraw. Set this clofe to the Stock, and inftantly lift up the Stock and fet it thereon ; no Bee can then come out upon you ; and when taken into the houfe, the whole may be turned upfide down, viz. the Stock at bottom, and the empty hive upon it ; by thefe means the inconvenience of many Bees flying out upon you is prevented, which muft always be the cafe when a cloth is ufed. But a far better method than either of thefe may be feen (382). But in either way the hives are to be fupported by the frame

＊ Management of Bees, page 193.

frame of a chair, a bucket, or any other conve‑
nient fupport; and if a cloth is ufed, an empty
hive fhould then be ready, nimbly take the cloth
off, and place the empty hive on; if it does
not join clofe, tie the cloth fo faft round as to
prevent any Bees from efcaping: with one
hand fupport the hives fteady upon each other,
while you keep ftriking with the other hand
about three parts round the full hive (for the
part againft which you ftand muft not be ftruck)
from top to bottom as nimbly as poffible.

373. By this noife and difturbance the
Bees will be affrighted, and begin to afcend
into the upper hive, where there is more
quiet. After beating a few minutes, put
your ear from time to time to the top of the
hive, and by the buz you will difcover when
any confiderable number is afcended up; until
this happens continue the beating; fometimes
it will be half an hour, though generally only a
quarter before this be accomplifhed. If the
Queen fhould happen to be foon difgufted fhe
will quickly rife, and the reft will prefently
follow with a great noife.

374. If notwithftanding this, they do not.
rife, take a fmall ftick in each hand, and beat,
round the hive fmartly; the Bees by this time
whether afcended or not, will be fufficiently
tamed, fo that you may raife the upper hive,
refting on its edge next you, a little to‑
wards the light. If they be moftly got up,
take the hive intirely off; but if not, hold it
upon its edge between your fide and left arm,
and repeat the drumming againft the part
                                        where

where they have chiefly cluftered (for the
method muft be varied according as you fee
the Bees affeded) until you have got a fufficiency to form a good Swarm : then fet it
dowr. by you upon a cloth or floor, and return the Stock to its place again. If the
Bees of both hives are prefently after quiet, and
work kindly, it indicates that there is a Queen
in each, and all will be well ; at night the
Swarm may be taken and fet in the place defigned for it, which fhould be as far from the
ftock as poffible : but fhould the Stock appear tumultuous and reftlefs, it fhews there is
neither an old nor a young Queen. · The Swarm
muft therefore be taken and fet over, or by the
fide of it, the hive being raifed by a ftick,
and the Bees, as well as the Queen, will return
to the old hive again ; otherwife your Stock
will be intirely ruined.

375. If the Swarm has no Queen, it
will foon quit the hive, and return home
without further trouble. It will be proper
to put an empty hive in the place of the
Stock, to amufe the returning Bees, during
the operation.

376. Thus we have a *fecond* method of
forming a Swarm artificially, but without
any regard to catching the Queen.

377. But by another procefs (befides the before-mentioned) Mr. Wildman gives us a
flight notion of the matter under the article of
joining a poor Stock with a rich, page 143.
" For this purpofe carry a poor and a rich
" hive, into a room a little before night,'

M   " then

" then *force* the Bees out of both hives in-
" to two feparate hives," as before directed,
(372) " Shake upon a cloth, the Bees out of
" a hive that contains the feweft; fearch
" for the Queen," (*how, in what manner?*)
" and as foon as you have fecured her, with
" a fufficient retinue, bring the other hive
" which contains the greater number, and
" place it on the cloth on which the other
" Bees are, with a fupport on one fide, and
" with a fpoon fhovel the Bees under it.
" They will foon afcend, and while under
" this impreffion of fear, will unite peace-
" ably with the other Bees; whereas had they
" been united to the Bees of the richer hive,
" while in poffeffion of their caftle, many
" of the new comers muft have paid with
" their lives for their intrufion."

378. By this means it is true we have all
the Bees together; but he has forgot to in-
form us, what further is to be done with them,

However, we may guefs at it from his
further directions for uniting, page 223.
" The beft method of uniting Bees at this
" feafon (autumn) is to take the Bees out
" of both hives, as already directed, then
" to ftrike the Bees of one of the hives
" upon a cloth, take away their Queen, *and*
" immediately place over them, the hive
" in which the Bees taken out of the other
" hive are. When united and quiet, *the*
" *hive with honey*, in which they are to re-
" main, *is put over them*, and they will foon
" afcend into it, This method requires too
much

much leifure and patience to be generally
followed.

My METHOD *is* :

379. Near the clofe of the evening, when
the Bees, wearied with the toilfome tafk
of the day, are retired to their "golden
" flumbers," I innocently invade their foft
repofe, by removing the weak hive into a
proper place, with little light, and drive
them (372) into an empty hive.

But here it muft be obferved, that the
Bees will not be induced to quit the fooner,
by the loudnefs of the noife, fo much as by
the quicknefs of the ftrokes, and the concuf-
fions of the hive ; for which reafon Bees quit
a ftraw fooner than a box hive, wood fuffering much lefs compreffion than ftraw. Now
fome Bees will always linger behind, however long you may drum (374) ; therefore,
when the main body is out, thofe that rife
upon the edges of the combs by beating,
may be brufhed or blown off by a bellows
as they rife ; but if many ftill remain, cut
through the briar bindings, near the bottom,
loofen the combs from the fides, and alfo the
fpleets ; you may then lift up the rounds of
ftraw, leaving the combs ftanding, and blow
the Bees out from between the combs with a
pair of bellows : they will not refent this fo
much, as being forced out by a brufh or
feather, nor will it injure them fo much.
In a box or hive of our conftruction, the
combs are to be feparated from the fides,

M 2   which

which being lifted up, leave the combs ſtanding, as fixed to the bars.

380. As ſoon as it is fully evening, having all the Bees in an empty hive or box,
which ſhould be of the ſame dimenſions as
that of the rich Stock, (otherwiſe ſticks
muſt be laid acroſs it and treated (372); turn
the hive upſide down, ſprinkle the Bees
with ſugar and ale, ſet them upon a ſtool
cloſe to the floor of the rich Stock, which
immediately lift off, and ſet upon the poor
one; being thus doubled, place them where
the rich Stock ſtood.

381. The ſprinkling renders the Bees not
offenſive to the others, for by crawling among
them it makes them ſmell all alike; and being
done at night, they aſcend gradually, and as
it were imperceptibly among the others. I
have frequently done it without a ſingle Bee
being ſlain. Let them ſtand thus four or five
nights, having firſt ſtopped up the bottom
door-way: after this time, you may at night
take off the upper hive, and if all the Bees
be out of the under one, or nearly ſo, take
it away; ſhould a few remain, turn
the hive on its ſide, with its open part to
the door-way of the Stock, and they will
have joined the reſt by morning; if not,
ſtrike them out upon a board or cloth, and
ſet them to the Stock, and they will then
enter without difficulty: but if only a few
of the Bees ſhould have quitted the under
hive, double them again, and let them remain
a week longer. This performance may be
done

done eafily and fafely with only a pair of gloves; though I generally do it without.

382. In order to unite the Bees of a common hive in Autumn with another Stock, by means of one of my conftructed ftraw hives, it will be neceffary to meafure the common hive bottom, to know whether it will ftand within the compafs of one of my wooden tops; if it will not, a wooden top fimilar to mine, but wider, muft be made on purpofe. Near the clofe of the evening take one of the wooden tops, with the fliders therein, and place it upon fome fupport clofe behind the Stock, which muft immediately be lifted thereon, and the door-way ftopped; then take it to an out-houfe darkened, and turn it upfide down upon a chair frame, tub, or the like; be careful in the turning to keep your left-hand fteady upon the board, to prevent its flipping, and with your right-hand turn the hive. It will be proper for young beginners to tie the board down firft. Be mindful alfo, that you turn the fide in which the fliders *enter*, upwards, as they may otherwife flip out, and permit the Bees to efcape, and vent their fury on you. As foon as turned upfide down, fet one of my ftraw hives (with its top and ftraw cover faftened on) over it, then with-draw the fliders, tie a cloth round the join-ing, and drive the Bees (372). This being done, fet them upon a hive floor, and let them remain there until night, when being removed to the Stock you wifh to join them with, thruft the fliders in at top, fprinkle

M 3 them

them with fugar'd ale, and ftop the door-
way; then take the ftraw cover off, and immediately lifting the Stock up, put it over them,
and either then, or the next night, fet them
thus *doubled* upon their proper ftand.   But a
ftill greater fecurity will be to raife the Stock
you would drive upon the wooden top, with its
fliders in, the night before the removal, at which
time the door-way muft be ftopped, leaving
only a fmall chafm for air; this prevents the
poffibility of a fingle Bee's hurting the operator; fo that a child, had it ftrength fufficient, might do it with eafe.   This mode I
efteem the moft perfect of any, and capable
of being brought into the moft general ufe.

.383. I now proceed to give a minute
and *certain* method of finding and captivating the Queen; fince, (as I have already
obferved) Mr. Wildman's firft method has
often failed us.

384. Having drove the Bees out of a Stock
into an empty hive (372), let a clean and fpa-
cious board or table be in readinefs, as alfo a
fpoon and two or three pieces of ftick, about
half an inch thick. Set the empty hive on the
table or board, with its edge refting on thefe
fticks, and near the further end of the table;
then inverting the hive that has the Bees in
it, fet it upon a ftool clofe to the table, and
take up a fpoonful of Bees at a time, firft
from the largeft clufter, and turn them leifurely out upon the table, but fo as not to
hurt or crufh them.   They will prefently
fpread fo that you may eafily fee if the Queen
                                                      be

be among them ; be as quick with your eyes
as poffible, and if not in that fpoonful, ftrike
the Bees under the empty hive ; then proceed
with another fpoonful in the fame manner,
until you obferve the Queen, whom you muft
immediately feize between your finger and
thumb, and put into a fmall box with holes
in it, with fome of the woi kers for company. But if after fpooning all out, you fhould
have miffed her, look upon the ground, as fhe
may have fallen down, and you may have
trod on her. If fhe be not found, you muft
repeat the operation, for among fuch a multitude, it will be very eafy to over-look her.
If it is a Stock that has been drove to take
away the young Princeffes, in order to prevent
fwarming, according to Mr. Wildman, the
whole of the Bees muft nicely be examined,
becaufe there may be three, four, or more
Princeffes ; all of which are to be taken a-
way. What Bees are fcattered about may be
taken up by the fpoon, and returned to the
reft ; or if the window be fet open, they
will fly to their ufual abode ; or if an empty
hive be fet near them, and a room darkened,
they will prefently-affemble in the hive.

385. It fhould always be carefully obferved,
that in turning up and holding a hive in order to
drive the Bees the *edges* of the combs fhould be
next you, otherwife the flat fides of the combs
will be inclined to each other, and being very
heavy the ftrokes will loofen them, and they
will fall againft each other, and crufh many of
the Bees to death, perchance the Queen herfelf, and thus ru n the Stock.

386. It

386. It is very poffible for a Stock to be taken up at the eirtical moment, when the Queen is gone out for air or recreation, therefore on driving no Queen will be found; but fhe may return afterwards, or even before the operation of driving is finifhed. This circumftance fometimes occafions the experiment to prove fallacious.

387. A lefs tedious method of forcing a Swarm is, to fet the Stock in its proper place after having drove a fufficiency of Bees into a hive; and let thefe remain: if both are quiet and work, they have each a Queen; if not, beat the Swarm out by the fide of the Stock, or fet it upfide down with its edge even with the rifing board, and they will rejoin the Stock. Try again fome days after.

388. But the following is a much readier and eafier way, by means of hives or boxes conftructed upon my plan. In the morning thruft in the fliders to the Stock you would Swarm, take off the cover, and fet over it an empty hive, with its door-way ftopped; withdraw the fliders, and let them thus remain until about mid-day; then fetting a ftool, or the like, near the back of the Stock, lift it thereon, immediately ftopping the door-way with a rag; carry it to fome diftance, and with two fticks drum or beat againft it, until by your ear you find there are a competent number in the upper hive, or if a box, you may fee by the window. Again put the in fliders, let them ftand about half an hour, when, if both are quiet, the Stock fhould be taken to its ufual place, and

and the Swarm remain until night. But if you have not fucceeded, put the Swarm over the Stock again, and try fix or eight days after.

389. But if Bees muft be *drove* to form an *artificial Swarm,* I fhall prefer the Rev. Mr. Thorly's method, which he recommends for *uniting;* but which, with little variation, is much better adapted to our prefent purpofe.

390. This is done by a narcotic fumigation, produced from the *fungus maximus,* or larger mufhroom, varioufly known by the name of burt, punkfift, frogcheefe, puffballs, or mully-puffs. Thefe are of various fizes, and fome as large as a man's head : they are not fit for the purpofe until ripe, at which time they turn brown, and are light; but if fo ripe as to have the infide turned to powder, they are ufelefs.

391. They may be found about autumn, at the time that mufhrooms are; and generally on commons and dry grounds. They are to be dried gradually by the fire, or fqueezed flat, and put into a paper bag, and then into a flow oven, after the bread is drawn, letting them continue all night. When they will eafily catch and retain fire, they are fit for ufe.

392. With a pair of fciffars cut a piece of the punk, as large as a hen's egg (better at firft to have too much than too little) and fix it to the end of a fmall ftick, flit for that pur-pofe, and fharpened at the other end, which is to be ftuck into the infide top of an inverted empty hive, fo that the flit end of the ftick may reach as high as the middle : the hive is then to be put into a pail or bucket near the Stock you want to fwarm.

393. This

393. This done, fet fire to the punk with a candle, and immediately place the Stock of Bees over it, tying a cloth (which you muft have in readinefs) róund the joinings, fo that no fmoke may come forth. In a few minutes time you may hear them drop like hail into the empty hive. When the major part are down, and you hear very few fall, beat the top of the hive gently with your hand, to get as many more out as you can; then loofing the cloth lift the hive on a table or broad board, and knocking the hive againft it feveral times many more will tumble out, perhaps the Queen among them; as fhe often falls one of the laft. If fhe be not there, fearch for her among the main body in the other hive, putting them out upon the table; for the Bees will be quite fenfelefs, and you may handle them as you pleafe.

They will continue fo but a fhort time, therefore, having taken all the Queens out, put as many Bees and a Queen as will be fufficient to form a good Swarm into an empty hive, ftop up the door-way, and place it as the greateft diftance; put the reft and another Queen into the Stock, which fet in its place again. The next morning unftop the door of the Swarm, and deftroy the fuperfluous Queens; which will effectually prevent the Stock from cafting.

394. But as all thefe proceffes of *forcing* a Swarm is like forcing a man and his family to quit both houfes and treafure, which can fcarcely ever be done without a great deal of trouble; permit me to accommodate matters,

ters, and propose a more gentle method of leading them imperceptibly to do what you would
have them, without any violence. Not that it
shall always be *more certain* than any of the
foregoing, but as it can be performed with the
greatest facility, and is at the same time void of
all danger or damage, both to the Operator and
to the Bees, should it not succeed, no harm is
done, and but a trifle of time lost.

395. To do this with common hives, have
ready an empty one, and two pieces of wood,
about two inches broad, and long enough to
lay across the hive that is to be moved; if
one end of each of these pieces be cut circular, they will be better adapted to extend to
the edge of the hive. Have also in readiness a
bucket, pail, or pan; or what is still better,
an old hive with the top cut off. On either of
these place the Stock hive, that is full of Bees,
and ready for swarming, upside down; and
immediately set the empty hive over them;
then lift them thus doubled on the stand a-
gain. This must be done soon after dark, and
with a pair of gloves on.

The next evening, the Bees being then
quiet and reconciled, the joinings must be
closed with tempered clay, or other plaister-
ing, leaving only the usual door-way, to
which a resting board must also be fixed.

396. This little disturbance, if there be
a perfect Swarm ready; that is, a competent
number of Bees with a Queen and Drones;
will cause them in a day or two either to
rise and swarm, or ascend into the upper
hive,

-hive, and there remain a feparate Swarm: both working cordially together and going in and out at the fame door-way. Thus they are to remain until a little before the ufual time of taking honey.

397. They are then to be feparated at *night*, (605) carrying the upper hive to a ftand at the greateft diftance. If the next day either of the Stocks feem tumultuous and difcontented, that hive muft be raifed about half an inch : for being without a Queen, they will otherwife return to the other hive. Near the clofe of the evening take it to fome out-houfe, drum out the Bees that remain, and take the honey and wax for your pains. On the contrary, if when feparated the Bees of both hives are peaceable, and work as ufual, you may preferve either the Swarm or Stock according as they are for goodnefs.

398. This bufinefs, however, may be conducted with ftill more eafe and certainty, by ufing hives or boxes of my conftruction. Firft, having thruft in the fliders over the Stock (in the day-time) take off the cover, then fet on the empty hive, and withdraw the fliders ; let both door-ways be open. This fhould be done as foon as the Stock becomes populous. When you find both hives are well filled (467, 586) in the middle of the day put in the fliders ; and if the Bees both above and below work as before, it is a fign that there is a feparate Swarm in the upper hive, which at night fhould be taken off, and placed as far from the Stock as it conveniently

ly

ly can be; then faften on the cover of the Stock, and withdraw the fliders.

·399. But fhould either hive fhew difcontent, and there appear a great throng or croud about the door-way of the hive, it indicates that there is no Queen in the upper; and therefore the fliders muft be taken out, and the hives remain as they are, until more favourable fymptoms appear, when the experiment may be again repeated. However, a careful eye muft be kept over them, for after this alarm, though they may not choofe to feparate and afcend into the upper hive, yet they may all of a fudden take it into their heads to fwarm out, either on that day or the next.

400. As the whole of this operation is exceedingly eafy and fimple, a child may perform it; and fhould it not happen to fucceed, there is nothing to regret, nor any thing loft.

401. Regard muft be had to this circumftance of a feparate Swarm, whenever you feparate double hives; for if the Bees, after fome time fpent in driving, do not feem at all inclined to relinquifh their hive, it is moft probable the top one is a feparate Swarm. Therefore, if fuch a one is wanted to be kept, leave off driving, and fet it in fome diftant place, and if that day or the next they work peaceably, and there be no extraordinary croud at the door-way of the old Stock, there is no doubt of its being a diftinct Swarm.

402. It is a very eafy matter to fave the Bees of Stocks in common hives, without cruelly deftroying them, and may be done thus.

thus. Nearly at the clofe of the evening take the Stock whofe honey you want, drive the Bees out (372), fprinkle them with ale and fugar, and then fet them under the Stock to which you would unite them. Let both hives thus remain until the cold weather fets in; then early in the morning, or in the evening, lift the upper hive off, and fet it upon a loofe floor, clofe by; when if the greater part of the Bees have not quitted the under hive, turn it up on its fide; with its open part as near the door-way of the Stock as poffible, and the Bees will gradually quit their unftored hive, and unite with the full one. However, let me here obferve, that this bufinefs may be much more conveniently done, by means of my open top hives, into which the Bees may be drove, and the Stock fet over them, with lefs trouble than by any other method whatever (382).

403. Having thus given a detail of the manual operations, it will now be requifite to make fuch obfervations, as may, perhaps, be of fome fervice in the *application.*

404. Driving of Bees is a very antient practice, but on accouut of its feldom fucceeding has never come into general ufe. Butler obferves that it was practifed in Greece, Sicilly, Italy, &c. under three diftinct confiderations, viz. of exfection, or cutting off part of the combs, in Spring and Autumn, and of driving at Midfummer: all which he efteems unprofitable or pernicious, at leaft in our climate, whatever it might be in thofe plentiful warmer countries. Nor from Butler's

time

time to this have we any better reasons for approving of it, either for the purposes abovementioned, or for that of Artificial Swarming.

405. We will first attend to what Mr. Wildman himself urges upon the subject. He acknowledges there is danger of killing the Queen in the operation ; and consequently (I will add) the loss of the Stock. With respect to obtaining the Queen, he says, in page 198, " There is an art necessary to perform it, " namely, Practice, which I cannot convey " to them : nor can be speedily attained ; yet, " until this art be attained, *the destruction of* " *many hives of Bees must be the consequence;* " *as every one will find on their first attempt to* " *perform it.*" To which let me add, *for ever after*. Nay, I will put it home to Mr. Wildman's own bosom, whether, notwithstanding his frequent practice of *driving*, he himself does not often ruin a Stock of Bees by the operation ? for the Queen is often lost upon the ground, or crushed to death between the edges of the hive, or smothered with the running out of the honey. Many of the commoners are also killed or lost, the combs are loosened, the eggs shaken out, and many of the embryos spoiled by the repeated concussions, and perhaps so chilled for want of their usual warmth during the operation ; that the whole or greatest part prove abortive.

406. For by experiments made on my own Stocks, I am fully convinced, that however

ever well the procefs may have been performed, Stocks feldom thrive after it. Whether this be owing to the caufe juft recited, or to the diftrefs and terror the Bees fuffer from the violence, cannot with certainty be determined; but fo it is, the Bees never work kindly after it. Neither do I fpeak this of my own Bees only, for the fame ill fuccefs attended all of this neighbourhood fo treated, that have fallen under my notice; and this in fo great a degree, that inftead of benefiting the publick, it has more firmly riveted the people to their old burning cuftom; fo that they now abhor the very idea of further improvements.

407. But fuppofing the method had *fo far* been eligible, there are ftill greater objections againft it, as being attended with a great deal of trouble and time; and when done, may probably prove to be labour loft: for as there are no *certain* figns to indicate the precife time of a Stock's being ready to fwarm, the operation may confequently be attempted before there are Drones or Queens ready; in which cafe it muft be repeated, perhaps feveral times: a fport I believe few country-people will be brought to delight in, unlefs the Bees, like flys, had no ftings; and there was nothing to fear, nor more to do, than to turn up the hive, and feize the Queen, as Mr. Wildman directs, at page 199.

408. We may further object, that although the operatton fhould prove fuccefsful, and a complete Swarm be obtained thereby; yet the *chief* benefit for which the practice is

defigned

defigned (viz. to fave the trouble of watching
the rifing of the Swarms) is not anfwered; becaufe the births of the Princeffes are very uncertain both with refpect to time and numbers. Although you take out all the royal
brood cells which you perceive at the time of
driving, yet there may be fome you can
neither fee nor come at, or others may be
built afterwards. Swarms may therefore afterwards rife with fome of the Princeffes,
without being perceived (as no watch will be
kept) and may not only be loft, but what is
ftill worfe, the Stock will thereby be fo impoverifhed, as moft probably to perifh before
the next year's honey gathering.

409. From the whole I think we may
fafely infer, that it will be much better to
lull them afleep by a dofe of Thorley's fopo-
riferous fume (389), from which no damage
can arife either to the Queen or the other
Bees; tho' how far the brood may be injured
I cannot fay. This operation will not take more
time than the other, and a fmall quantity of
fume does the bufinefs. I have tried the
fume arifing from many forts of gum refin,
and other drugs, none of which would either
kill or ftupify the Bees, except the fume of
fulphur.

This however is certain and total deftruction
if there is fufficient of it to pervade the whole
hive for a few minutes; but in a lefs quantity,
many of the Bees will recover when expofed to
the air again, while others perhaps may efcape
being affected at all, and be able as foon as

N   the

the hive is lifted up, to revenge the death of their friends. Gunpowder in half an ounce made damp, and managed as directed for wasps (671), will have the same effect on Bees: but the combs and Bees are greatly discoloured thereby; therefore of the two a sulphur rag is preferable.

410. But to return and make short of the matter, I can see no good reason for forcing of Swarms at all : let me ask what are the advantages? If to keep the Bees conftantly and wholly at work, this may be done by doubling, that is, adding an empty hive to them as foon as they have occafion (480, 484). If to fave the expence and trouble of watching them in fwarming-time be the object? this I acknowledge would be of fome advantage, could the operation be eafily done, and terminated fuccefsfully; but this we have fhewn is not the cafe. The expence of hiring a child to watch cannot exceed ten fhillings in any year, in moft perhaps not half; what perfon who has a dozen or more hives would grudge fo trifling a fum? and where there are fewer Stocks, and out of the view of the family, can it be prudent to rifk the deftruction of fome of thefe few Stocks by the operation, for the fake of fo fmall a faving, when the prefervation of a fingle Swarm will amply repay it?

411. Befides, in a large Apiary, it will be a very arduous tafk to drive a great many Stocks; and fome of them moft likely two or three times over. To this may be added, " the very great rifque of deftroying the Queen,

" Queen, which is of the utmoſt importance,
" for the leaſt injury done to her brings im-
" mediate deſtruction to the hive." * How
can it be thought that country people .can
ſpare thoſe hours of attention; can ſupport
that anxiety and care; and acquire that dex-
terity, to be gained only by a courſe of many
years experience;‡ which are Mr. Wildman's
inſtruments of witchcraft in theſe operations;
unleſs, like him, they had nothing elſe to do?

412. We have eſtimated the expence of
watching at ten ſhillings, but ought we not
to balance againſt this the labour and trouble
of driving in the Artificial way? I believe
no one would do that buſineſs under ſixpence a time, and eſtimating this only once
to a Stock, will take off one half; but as it
may be required to be repeated two or three
times, it may ariſe to as much, if not more,
than watching; not to mention that after all
this expence there is a great chance of loſing
after-ſwarms: for, relying upon what has been
done, no attention will be given to prevent
it. The moſt plauſible argument in favour
of this practice is, that it is neceſſary when
Stocks will not ſwarm in due time; but
what then? If they be doubled, no harm
can poſſibly ariſe; they certainly beſt know
their own condition, and there may be many
impediments to ſwarming beyond the reach
of our infpection. What good will coercion
do?

---

* *T. Wildman on the Management of Bees,* 199.
‡ *Ibid.* 201.

do ? Had we not better *lead* them gently, according to their own propensities, than to risk their ruin and our own reversionary profit, by irritating them by our violence ? Inlarge but their habitations, and so far from being indolent, they will labour with the most anxious and unremitting assiduity to replenish their hives, as far as nature's bounty can supply, and make you a present profit of a hive or two of virgin honey; and the next year a large and early Swarm: thus amply recompencing your forbearance and care.

413. After all, both from Mr. Wildman's own acknowledgment, as well as from what we have related of the matter, it appears that the danger and difficulty, must render the practice wholly unfit to be generally followed; and though it is now ten years since it has been introduced, but a very few persons have adopted it, and several of these have relinquished it from its unsuccessfulness.

414. Now although we hold driving to be very pernicious to *Stocks* when done for the purpose of *swarming* them; yet we do not mean that it is so when performed for the sake of uniting (366) or of separating hives, which will be treated of hereafter (607); provided that Stock *only* which is to be taken be drove; for *any Stock that is designed to stand*, should by no means be meddled with, except to raise or to double it; and the less disturbance the Bees have the better.

415. However, if any one should choose to swarm the Bees by force, let him always
carefully

carefully observe that it muft never be attempted until they give very ftrong figns of being ready for the feparation. A calm ftill day muft alfo be chofen; for turbulent weather difcommodes them in their work, and makes them angry and revengeful. The middle of the day, when they are moftly abroad, is likewife to be preferred. For if fwarmed, when the greater part are at home, there will be a large Swarm it is true; but the Stock will thereby be too much reduced; and the brood fuffering for want of its ufual warmth and attendance, will alfo fail, fo that before the next fummer, the Stock itfelf will perifh, or be too poor to do any effential fervice.

416. Before any perfon attempts to perform this operation, he ought to be well acquainted with the appearance of a Queen Bee. If he has not this piece of knowledge he muft acquire it, either by fearching for one among fuch of his neighbours Bees as have been fuffocated, or by applying to fome experienced perfon to fhew him one. For unlefs the Apiator can diftinguifh her at the firft glance, it is a hundred to one but fhe eludes the fearch, when he attempts the performance; and which happens fometimes to the moft experienced, even at a time, when there are two or three Queens in the Stock. Therefore when the Queen is not found, the Bees muft be all fpooned (376) over again. And if fhe be not then found, the old Queen has fecreted herfelf

among

among the combs, and will not quit her. poſt, however long you may drum. (379).

417. Or perhaps, at the critical moment that a Stock is taken, the Queen may be gone out to recreate and air herſelf, and conſequently you muſt miſs her in the hive.

418. That ſhe does ſo, I once, and only once, had ocular demonſtration. One of my Stocks, at the latter end of the ſummer, had ſuch a prodigious number of Drones, that they conſumed, almoſt all the honey, as faſt as the labourers procured it. This I thought ſhameful, and therefore, was determined to kill great part of theſe luxurious cormorants, as faſt as they appeared at the the door-way. At this time, there was a large number of workers at the door, drumming with their wings, and uttering joyful ſounds. Unluckily attempting with my finger to cruſh a returning Drone, as I thought, though it proved to be the Queen I hurt her, though not mortally, ere I perceived my miſtake. She ſtaggered, and was unable to walk. The concourſe of Bees that were at the door ſaw her diſtreſs, and were in the utmoſt conſternation; they licked her with their tongues, and uſed all the little endearments they could to reſtore her. This continued ſome minutes. But being ſtill diſabled, a number of Bees got under her, and carried her upon their backs into the hive.

420. I was not without my fears for the event, as ſuppoſing ſhe would die with the injury: However, the next day, the Be s
worked

worked with the fame alacrity as ufual; confequently the Queen recovered.

421. From this inftance I conjecture, that
the Queen often makes an excurfion in fine
weather, accompanied with a great retinue.
At this time alfo numbers eroud the door,
drumming with their wings, and the whole
hive feems full of joy. I had obferved this
circumftance many times before; but never-
fufpected the reafon of it until then; and
no doubt others have obferved the fame.
My own avocations are too numerous
to fpare the neceffary time for fuch minute
and clofe inveftigations as to afcertain whether it be upon the above account or not,
that the Bees appear in that unufual manner. Perhaps fome ingenious Bee virtuofo,
who is bleft with fufficient leifure to make
the neceffary obfervations, will be able to
clear up this point.

422. But to return to our fubject. When
a fufficiency of Bees to form a Swarm are
driven out of a Stock, obferve whether
there be any royal cells fealed up; if there
are, fet the Stock in its place again, tho'
there fhould be no Queen; for as there
foon will be one, the Bees in that expectation will go on with their works. And
the Swarm may be fet in fome other place;
without the trouble of turning them out,
to fearch for a Queen: unlefs you want a
fpare Queen for any particular purpofe, either
of ufe or curiofity.

423. But if it appears that there is no royal
brood, fet the Stock in its place, and minutely

examine

examine all the drove Bees, and take out all
the Queens. If only two are found, put
one to the old Stock, and the other to the
Swarm, fhould there be more than two,
felect the two largeft; the others may be
referved, with a few Drones, in a little box
with holes, laying a little honey on the top
for their fubfiftence; or if they be put in a glafs
veffel, and watched, you may perhapsbe entertained with the confummation of the royal
nuptial. A moft furprizingly rare fight! We
cannot, however, difmifs this fubject without
fhewing how to fix a Swarm to any place you
wifh.

424. Let it be remarked, and it is very wonderful, that fuch wild, ferocious, and revengeful infects as Bees, fhall by a few minutes confinement, and fmartly beating upon their hive,
be divefted of all their courage and ferocity; and
become fo tame, as to fuffer themfelves to be
taken up in the hand, without difcovering the
leaft refentment, unlefs you hurt them. For
when they have been taken off the ftand,
carried to fome diftance, confined by means
of a cloth or another hive placed over them,
and the hive has been brifkly drummed
upon for a fhort fpace, their panic and terror is fo great, that you may do as you
pleafe with them. In confequence of
which, the Queen is then to be fearched
for, and when found, is to be put into a
little box which you fhould have ready for
that purpofe. Then take her into a clofe
room, cut off one of her wings, which will
prevent

prevent her efcaping, tie the fore part of her body round with a filk thread, fo as not to injure her; or rather put her into a very fmall bag of crape, catgut, or other like open materials; pin it to your hat, cap, or any thing elfe you would choofe,, and lay it down clofe to the Swarm. The Bees will foon gather round her, and remain there until they die, if you do not remove them.

425. Thus feveral Swarms, driven out of as many diftinct Stocks, and confined with their refpective Queens, may be fixed upon different parts; as one upon the head, one upon the fhoulders, and another upon the chin; by tying a fmall bandage with the Queen faftened to it, to each particular part. Or, by the fame device may be fixed to a pole, and carried where-ever you pleafe. By a ftrong fhake of the head, they may immediately be diflodged therefrom if the Queen has been placed there without confinement, having only a wing clipped. Or they may be taken off with a fpoon. If a Queen be taken away and concealed from a Swarm, near a window that is open, the Bees will prefently fly into the air; but by placing the Queen again in their view they will prefently return. This will appear to have been done by a word of-command, to perfons unacquainted with the fecret.

426. But thefe are merely tricks, that tend more to deftroy, than improve Bees; and is befides fo very diftrefsful a fcene, that no true lover of thefe very ufeful infects can

practice

practice it without regret, and therefore I, fhall inlarge no further upon it.

427. Though I have faid Bees by driving are made very tractable, yet, let me apprize you, that however nimbly the introductory part, viz. that of taking the hive off the ftand, and fetting it on another, or on a cloth, may be done, fome Bees will inevitable efcape, and be apt to fting you. Therefore a young beginner fhould always put on a fafe-guard, efpecially if he has not been familiar with the Bees before. I generally do it with only a pair of thick leather gloves on.

428. Before I clofe this chapter, I cannot refrain from addreffing myfelf to thofe who will not be perfuaded to their own good, but will obftinately purfue the old deftructive method of fuffocating their Bees; imagining that " by deftroying them they may have " the greater increafe," a notion as void of fenfe, as it is of truth, unlefs we could verify Virgil's mode of raifing Bees from a dead carcafe. We fhould think it the higheft abfurdity and cruelty in a king to fay, in order to multiply my people, I will find means every year, to have many thoufands of them cut off.

Let my intreaties prevail on fuch to practice the method I have propofed (395, 402). It is not more expenfive, and requires but little trouble; who that has a fpark of common fenfe, or common humanity would grudge

grudge that, for the preſervation of ſo many
thouſands of uſeful and induſtrious inſects?.
Was the *Supreme Being*; to treat us as the
country people treat their Bees, how wretch-.
ed would be the ſtate of human nature !

429. Dames and good women, I conjure
you by all that is good and praiſe-wortby,
not to deſtroy your Bees, leſt you yourſelves
ſuffer in . ſome future ſituations. After
having read this book, you cannot plead
ignorance, but muſt for ever remain inex-
cuſable.

CHAP.TER XIII.

*Particular Inſtructions how to manage Glaſſes
of various Figures, and in different Arrangements, as well for Entertainment as
Emolument.*

430. THE inimitable works of theſe
wonderful .inſects have in all
ages engaged the attention, not only of the
naturaliſt and philoſopher, but alſo of every
perſon endowed with the leaſt ſpark of
genius, or .ſpirit of enquiry. To gratify ſo
laudable a curioſity, we will now proceed
to exhibit to the inquiſitive, the ſeveral methods of . obtaining a more perfect inſpection
of their extraordinary works and œconomy.

431. But let it be premiſed, that the uſe
of glaſſes, is not wholly reſtricted to *amuſement*; they are of real uſe; by enabling

us to take honey from the Bees, when in its greateft perfection. The fafhion and arrangement of glaffes for the above pur- pofes depends, indeed, more upon fancy, than any precife rules. We fhall, however, defcribe fuch as we think the moft eligible.

432. That kind of glafs globe, which is made ufe of for ftreet lamps, will do as well as any, and is eafily procurable; the open part, we fhall call the bottom. It fhould hold about a peck; for, if bigger, it cannot in many fituations be filled in time. A ftick of a proper length, muft be placed upright in the middle of the globe, with holes near the upper part, to receive two other fmall crofs fticks, to keep it fteady; that the Bees may the better fix their combs therein. In fome places, globes may be had with a hole at the top, on purpofe to receive the ftick, which is to be faftened over the top by a fmall peg. If the infide of the globe be previoufly rubbed with wax, fo as to roughen it, the Bees will be greatly affifted in crawling up.

433. The floor on which it is to ftand, muft have a bevil or flant cut out, three inches wide, and defcending from the middle to the edge, which muft be left very thin; by this means, when the globe is fet on, there will be a free paffage for the Bees, at this part under the edge of the glafs; directly under which, the deepening fhould not be above three-eighths of an inch.

434. The

434. The firft large Swarm that rifes, is to beput into this globe inftead of a hive. There fhould be Bees enough nearly to fill it ; but if not, add a Caft (366) to them afterwards. For if your fituation fhould not be a very plentiful one, or the fummer fhould prove unfavourable, a fmall quantity of Bees will not be able to fill the globe, and a box befide, which they fhould do ; for they cannot be kept in the glafs, through the winter, without perifhing. The globe is then to be fet in a Bee-houfe, and a cloth or fome other convenient covering muft be placed over the glafs, to keep the light from the Bees; for otherwife, *that*, and the novelty of their habitation, will be fo difguftful to them, that they will be apt to quit it.

A piece of empty honey-comb, (if virgin the better) placed previoufly in the glafs, (493) will the fooner reconcile them to it ; and if in two or three days afterwards, they have begun to work ; there will be no danger of their deferting it.

435. When they have nearly filled the globe, or feem to want more room, raife the glafs upon another hive or box (480). In about four or five weeks after, if the feafon has been favourable, the brood will be all in the under hive or box ; and the globe, filled with honey and wax, may be taken off for the owner's profit.

436. But after the firft week of July, whether they have filled the globe or not, they muft be raifed on a box, that they may begin

to

to work therein for their winter ſtore. About
a month after, take the globe off at night,
and the next morning turn it up, and
tap the ſides with your fingers, until the Bees
have quitted, and left it to your diſpoſal. If
they do not readily come out by tapping,
blow now and then among them with a bellows, which will haſten their exit.

437. Another method is, by ſetting a
globe *over* a ſtrong Stock, as ſoon as honey
gathering commences (480, 484). But as
the bottom of the globe being circular, will
not extend over the openings of the box or
hive; therefore, before you ſet it on, place in
the ſliders, then ſetting the globe on, lay pieces
of tea cheſt lead (that from the bohea cheſts,
as being thickeſt, will be beſt) tin, tile, or
clay over the openings, which may extend
beyond the circle of the bottom of the globe,
at the ſame time raiſing the edge of the
globe in front near half an inch by two
pieces of ſtick, at three inches diſtance from
each other, for a door-way for the Bees; the
reſt of the raiſed part, ſtop with clay, or
cow dung. Then withdrawing the ſliders,
the Bees will aſcend, but the ſooner if a
piece or two of a comb be previouſly fixed
in it (434). The door-way of the Stock
muſt alſo be ſtopped, in order to compel
them to paſs out only from the middle. The
bottom door way muſt however be opened three
or four days after they have begun to work in
the globe, and then the middle, or globe
door-way muſt be ſtopped up, that the Queen
may

'may be prevented ·from depofiting any of her eggs in that. By this means, the globe will be filled with *intire* virgin honey and wax, and fhould be taken off as foon as it is fo (480).

438. But the moft minute, as well as the moft comprehenfive view of the Bees and their operations, is to be obtained by caufing a Swarm to work in feveral diftinct glaffes without any hive at all. For this purpofe, procure feven three-pint glafs veffels of any form you pleafe. Glaffes, however, in the form of a flower beaker, (fig. 13.) without top or bottom, and not above eight inches high, will not only make the beft appearance, but will likewife fupport fuch pieces of empty combs, as are to be placed in the upper part, to a great nicety, without any other contrivance than circular pieces of plain glafs cut out fo as to cover the tops ; or, if another range of glaffes are defired to be fet over thefe; pieces of rattan or mahogany wood may be fubftituted, either with circular holes, or flits, as moft agreeable. (The beaker form I would recommend as the moft eligible for all glaffes that are to be fet over Beehives, or boxes, to thofe perfons who purchafe Bee glaffes on purpofe).

439. A board or frame muft then be prepared of the proper dimenfions for thefe glaffes to ftand on, with their mouths, or open ends downward. The circles made by the glaffes being marked, 'four or five circular holes, each about three quarters of an inch diame-

ter

ter, or ſlits half an inch wide, are to be made
within each circle, over which the glaſſes
are to ſtand. This board or frame muſt be
raiſed an inch, by nailing a broad hoop round
it; or if ſquare, by nailing on fillets of wood,
obſerving to cut out a proper paſſage for the
Bees in the front fillet. The whole apparatus ſhould alſo have a bottom, or floor to
ſtand on.

440. A portion of fine virgin comb muſt
be placed in each glaſs, ſo as to extend from
one ſide to the other. Small ſlips of combs on
each ſide of the other, will preſerve it from
falling when the Bees firſt aſcend, and when
the work is compleated, appear the hand-
ſomer.

441. The apparatus being thus in readineſs, and every glaſs ſet in its place, let the
firſt large early Swarm you have, be hived as
uſual; but if not a large one, add a Caſt
afterwards (366). As ſoon as the Swarm is
hived, take them to ſome out-houſe, catch
the Queen (384), cut off one of her wings,
(as otherwiſe ſhe will not ſtay) and put her
into one of the glaſſes, (turned with its mouth
upwards); and with a ſpoon, as ſoon as poſſible, put in as many Bees to her as you
conveniently can, and then turn it down
upon its place over the board. The reſt of
the Swarm is by ſpoonfuls at a time to be
forced under the board; which, if raiſed a
little, will admit them the more eaſily, and
they will ſoon aſcend into the glaſſes. At
night, ſet the ~~glaſſes~~ *board* down cloſe to the floor
again,

again, and put the whole into the Bee-houfe; or if defigned to ftand in a room in the dwelling-houfe, the direction of (135) is to be obferved.

442. When the glaffes appear nearly full, or the Bees feem to want room, they are to be raifed on a box hive. But, as the dimenfions of the frame, on which the glaffes ftand, may be too large for the top of the box, to obviate this difficulty, four pieces of wood muft be nailed, or dove-tailed toge-ther, fo as to leave an opening of the fame diameter as the top of the box. But the pieces muft be fufficiently broad to reft upon, and likewife extend beyond the edges of the box, far enough for the frame to ftand upon. Lay this fquare on the box, and in the even-ing, lift up the frame and glaffes, from the floor, and fet them upon the fquare, that has been previoufly laid over the box.

443. If the frame will not readily part from the floor, by reafon of combs fixed thereto, they muft be previoufly loofened, by a long and very thin knife; or a fheet of tin thruft under it. The next morning, the paffage or door-way of the frame muft be flopped, to oblige the Bees to pafs only through that of the box.

444. As faft as the brood are hatched, and the vacant cells filled with honey, the glaffes are to be fucceffively taken off, by fliding a piece of tin under each; then nimbly taking the glafs to fome diftance, turn it up, and tap about the fides with your fin-

O   gers,

gers, and in a little time, the Bees will quit it, without offering you any injury.

445. But ſhould they not be filled in time (615, &c.) they muſt nevertheleſs be taken off, one or two in a day, that the Bees may be compelled to begin their works in the box. If any of the glaſſes ſhould have a conſiderable brood in them, cut out as much of the combs as have honey in them as you can, and fix thoſe parts that have brood in them into the glaſſes again, until they are hatched. Or the. whole may be kept to work without a box until honey-gathering be over. In this caſe, as faſt as any glaſſes appear full of honey, and without brood, they ſhould be taken off, and empty ones put in their place; but as ſoon as honey fails, *every* glaſs that is full, and without brood, muſt be taken away at night, and the others are to be ſet over another Stock.

446. When all the glaſſes are off, put in the ſliders of the box, and draw it a little away from the front, raiſing the frame about half an inch; at night you may ſafely take it off; perhaps there may be many Bees in it, and it may alſo be full of combs; ſet it upon its edge by the ſide of the box, and by morning the Bees will have left it; if not, drive them out. Let it be obſerved, however, that little pieces of tin, tea-cheſt lead, tile, or wood ſhould be ready, to cover the holes with when the glaſſes are taken off.

447. By this proceſs the Bees being compelled to work in *ſeven* diviſions, thereby afford the moſt conſpicuous *view* of all their

operations,

operations, and in a far fuperior degree than when in larger bodies; for then being very much crowded by numbers, and, inclofed by combs, little fatisfaction can be obtained, and the inquifitive mind muft be greatly difappointed. Not that this contrivance, or indeed any other of boxes with fliding frames, drawers, or furrounded with glafs windows can poffibly give a view of the *Queen* as often as the owner pleafes, or as Mr. Wildman feems to pro-mife; for if there be but a *fingle comb* in a divifion, the Queen will *not be feen* but when fhe depofits an egg; at all other times fhe is furrounded and veiled from our fight by her numerous retinue.

448. Upon the above plan, a pyramid of glafies may be fo arranged as to form a beautiful encampment of thefe wonderful infect warriors. Boards muft likewife be provided, of fuitable dimenfions, to lay between each range of glaffes, and correfponding holes made in them; that the Bees may pafs freely through, from the lower to the upper.

449. Another way is to have a glafs circle or hoop, without either top or bottom; over this a board perforated with proper holes is to be placed, on which another glafs of lefs dimenfions may be put, and ftill fmaller glaffes round that: indeed there are many other contrivances of this kind, that an ingenious fancy may devife, and to which we can fix no limits: the whole, as may be fuppofed, from the expence attending them, are defigned

O 2

only

only as elegant exhibitions. for perſons of fortune.

450. However, it muſt be remarked, that
the number of the Bees is to be in proportion to the number and bulk. of the glaſſes,
and alſo to the height of the aſcent; for glaſſes
more than one ſtory high two good Swarms
will be required, making together about half a
buſhel. Nor muſt the. exceſſive labour it will
coſt theſe induſtrious inſects in theſe ſlippery te-
nements be forgotten ; and therefore to ſhorten
their. taſk, no glaſſes ſhould be above ſeven
or eight inches high ; otherwiſe, multitudes
will die of the toil, nor will the Stock be
worth any thing the next year.

451. With reſpect to taking off the glaſſes;
this is to be performed in the ſame manner as
the preceding. The whole ſhould be taken
off the firſt week in July, and drove together
in an empty box, when the Bees having
time enough before them, will be enabled
to fill it. Or if left until autumn, the
Queen muſt be taken from them ; and if very
numerous, the Bees muſt. be divided, and
united to other Stocks.

452. We now deſcend to deſcribe a more
humble, though much more uſeful plan, viz.
that of ſetting only one range of glaſſes upon
a box or hive ; by which we may be enabled
to draw the honey from the Bees at the critical time, when the moſt aromatic flowers, that
yield the fineſt honey, are in perfection.

453. There are glaſſes. to be had in
London, blown purpoſely of ſeveral ſizes ;
theſe

thefe are globular in the upper part, but
contract towards the bottom. This figure I
fuppofe is adapted to fecure the combs from
falling out, and at the fame time to form a
more pleafing fpectacle. As to the firft
intention, it is perfectly needlefs in fuch
fmall veffels, as the Bees will fix their combs
fo as to require no fuch fupport; while the
globular contracted form of the glafs gives the
combs an inconvenient fhape, and renders them
incapable of being taken out, without being
previoufly cut. Common tumblers are preferable to thefe, but the beaker form (fig. 13) as
before obferved, is by far the moft convenient.

454. Nor ought any of thefe to be lefs than
half a pint, for I have often obferved, that
in fmaller veffels the Bees wafte a great deal of
time and labour, by not having fufficient room
to work in, crouding too much upon each other,
fo that many, when they are got therein, are
obliged to return back again with their loads.

455. Before the glaffes are fet on a box-
hive, or the cover taken off, the fliders muft be
put in. Then having in readinefs pieces of tea-
cheft lead, adapted to cover any openings that
might appear, fet on the glaffes, and having covered all the crevices with the lead, keep it tight
by fmall ftones or pieces of lead thereon; but
where lead cannot be eafily come at (though
every confiderable tea-dealer can furnifh it)
pieces of tin will do. All being now fecured, fo that no Bee can get out at the top,
withdraw the fliders, and cover the glaffes
with a cloth or the like. But where glaffes

O 3

are

are fet on a ftraw hive, and not in a houfe; the circular part of another ftraw hive, without a top, is to be placed as a circle round the glaffes, and a pan to cover the whole; both of which may be lifted up at pleafure, and the glaffes viewed with as much eafe and fafety (ftanding at the back of the hive) as with boxes in a houfe. It is beft to fet the glaffes on near the clofe of the evening.

460. Each of the glaffes muft have a piece of empty comb, placed acrofs the top; without this inticement it will be a long while before the Bees will afcend to work in them, and oftentimes not at all; but with this, they will begin the very day. Every year, portions of fine comb fhould be referved for this purpofe, carefully wrapped up in paper, and placed where they may be kept dry, and no moth get at them.

461. As foon as the glaffes are filled with combs, and thefe with honey, (which you may know by the cells being nearly all fealed or covered over with wax) they are to be taken off, and empty ones placed in their ftead. The nice point now confifts in determining the quantity that can fafely be taken away; for otherwife you may take fo much and fo long, as to leave the Bees no time to ftore their hive fufficiently to fupport them through the dreary feafon of winter. Regard here is to be had to the ftrength of your Stock, and the goodnefs of the feafon. In fituations where Stocks ufually afford a hive of honey (befide their own) about that quantity may be

drawn

drawn from them. Where profit only is intended, confection glaffes of two quarts each
will be beft: a fingle glafs may be fet on firft;
if they feem eager in filling it, it indicates
plenty of pafturage, and you may then venture to fet on more. Alfo, when there are
honey dews, they fhould be fully fupplied
with glaffes. When they feem too much
crowded in the bottom hive, it fhews they
have not room enough in the top, and more
or larger veffels muft be furnifhed them, elfe
they will either lie out or fwarm. About the
middle of July the honey in general begins to
fail; therefore the glaffes muft be all taken
off; likewife whenever the Bees flacken their
work in them; the fame method muft be
purfued; for if kept on longer, *they will begin to* feed on the honey that is in the glaffes.
When combs that have honey in them, are
put into glaffes the Bees will eagerly afcend,
and carry away all the honey, and then under
a foolifh miftake begin to work, and refill the
cells again.

462. Obferve alfo, that no glaffes are to be
fet on a Stock that is intended to fwarm; nor
over any that you purpofe to take; as it will
prevent the Bees from filling an under hive.

463. Some feafons are fo unfavourable for
honey, that no Stocks will bear drawing,
without being too much impoverifhed thereby; befides which, attention muft be paid to
fuch Stocks as being much more numerous in
Bees than others, will fill feveral glaffes;
while others fhall not be able to fill one. No

O 4

dif-diſcriminating rules can be given for every caſe, ſomething muſt be left to diſcretion, and to obſervation formed upon practice. Bees will much readier fill glaſſes ſet over them, than by the ſide or collateral.

.464. Inſtead of glaſſes, either where theſe are not to be had, or where curioſity is not the motive, old cracked mugs or pans may be ſubſtituted, and will ſufficiently anſwer the purpoſe.

465. By this method we acquire more perfectly, with more eaſe, and without running any riſque, all the advantages intended by the frequent ſhifting of hives, ſo much extolled by ſome authors ; and this moreover without giving any diſturbance, or doing any injury to the Bees. At the ſame time you are enabled to indulge in the pleaſing contemplations, and to examine at leiſure with what aſſiduity and ſagacity theſe our diminitive ſervants effect works of ſo much wiſdom and utility.

CHAPTER XIV.

The METHOD *and* TIME *of* RAISING *or* DOUBLING HIVES *and* STOCKS.

466. IT has already been obſerved (282) that Stocks ſhould be double hived when they begin to lie out. We now add, that

that they are likewife to be fo when you wifh any particular Stock -not to fwarm; as alfo, when they fhew figns of being too much crouded, and want an enlargement of their habitation. Laftly, Stocks that have not fwarmed by a certain time, muft be fupplied with an additional hive.

467. By the term *Raifing* Stocks, is generally meant the operation of fettng an empty hive under a full one, or upon lifts or ekeings. While by that of *Doubling*, we mean the adding an empty hive to a full one, by placing it under, or at its fide.

468. Before we proceed further, it will be highly proper to be able to judge of the fullnefs of a hive, in order to its being doubled, efpecially of fuch as are without windows. This may be tolerably well afcertained, by attentively obferving in the day-time the croud going in and out of the hive. If the croud be conftantly greater than formerly, the number of the Bees has moft affuredly been confiderably increafed. Some fhare, however, of experience is here abfolutely neceffary, as that alone can enable us to determine with the requifite precifion: therefore, as another, and indeed by no means an inconfiderable help, ftrike the fides of the hive with your fift in the evening; and if it be full of Bees you will hear a great buz all through the hive; but if partially filled, the buz will feem to come moftly from the middle. The hive alfo, if full of combs and honey, will feel tight

tight and folid to the ftroke; whereas if there be only a few combs, it will feem hollow, both in found, and to the touch.

469. When numbers of Bees are obferved to play idly about the entrance of the hive, while others keep drumming with their wings; and if at the fame time the hive feels heavy; it is a certain fign that the Bees want more room, either for themfelves or their honey; and the Stock muft therefore be immediately doubled. For it is likely they cannot fwarm, either for want of a Princefs or of Drones, and therefore being inactive at a time when there is moft honey to be got, the moft precious part of the feafon will be loft, in waiting longer for their fwarming. Nay, if the fituation and feafon be very good, a Swarm may ftill rife notwithftanding the doubling.

470. No Stock fhould be raifed*, until replenifhed with Bees; which in fome years is not until the latter end of June or middle of July; and fhould they then continue fcanty and feel light, fuch muft *not* be doubled at all, unlefs you firft add a Swarm or Caft to ftrengthen them.

The greater the number of Bees in the fpring, and the heavier the hives, from the number of combs, the fooner the Stocks will want doubling. This may be done in fuch cafe in May, or if the fpring be very early in April.

471. Such

---

* *We fhall ufe the terms* Doubling *or* Raifing *as fynonimous, when applicable to the collateral or ftory method.*

471. Such Swarms of the preceding year as are populous and weighty, will be the fitteft to fet glaffes or fmall veffels on inftead of doubling; for thefe will be good Stocks for the next year.

472. It has employed much time and ingenious contrivance to prevent the Queen's breeding in the old hive or box, after a frefh empty one has been added to it. But in fome feafons fhe *will* do this whatever methods may be taken, either in the collateral method, or that of raifing. This I have feveral years experienced; but efpecially in the year 1779, I obferved that of old Stocks which had been raifed three ftories, and all of which were well filled, the *two* uppermoft hives had broods in them when taken even in the autumn.

473. From hence I infer, that next to glaffes or fmall veffels, the fureft way of obtaining the greateft number of *intire virgin hives,* will be to place empty hives. *over half* of thofe Stocks which were laft year's Swarms, and are now in proper condition, while the other half may be *raifed,* or ftand to fwarm. By this management thefe Stocks will work themfelves down into the *under hives,* and thus form frefh Stocks for next year, and are then to have empty hives placed *over* them in their turn; while the others are at the fame time to be raifed, as being then of two years ftanding. Thus they are to be changed alternately, year after year, furnifhing a large quantity of fine honey and wax, and at the

at the fame time alfo preventing any of your
hives ftanding more than two years; longer
than which no Stocks fhould be fuffered at
any rate to continue in one hive; for after
that period the combs become black and
filthy; many of the cells choaked up with old
and ufelefs farina; and the whole hive peftered
with moths and other infects, often to the
intire deftruction of the Stock. To prevent miftakes, the ftands fhould be all num-
bered, and a regifter kept of the age of each
Stock.

474. Never let any of the Stocks want
room, for that will teach the Bees to be idle.
They fometimes require enlargement very fuddenly; for by a large delivery of young in the
fpace of a few hours, the hive will become
too much crowded; which will probably occafion a fudden and unexpected Swarm to
rife.

475. The Stocks of the laft feafon that

may remain *fingle* until the Swarm be out;
for if raifed before, it may prevent fwarming,
or, elfe retard it until too late. But fhould
any of the Bees lie out more than three or
four days (281), rouze them from their beginning inactivity by raifing them.

476. But if you have Stocks enough already, and therefore do not want Swarms, fet
an empty hive under them as foon as ever
they either feem crowded, work brifkly, or
the weather be enticing.

477. The

477.. The fame thing muft alfo be done to all Stocks that are two years old and upwards; for they will by thefe means be frequently prevented from fwarming; and confequently there will be the greater chance of their quiting their old tenement and filling the new under one in time.

478. The raifing of Bees has been directed by Mr. Wildman, and other writers, to be done in the day-time: this I have found a very troublefome and difagreeable tafk, and not to be executed without receiving fome ftings, unlefs properly covered. Boxes with fliders that ftand in houfes, are however to be excepted, becaufe the Bees do not fee the aggreffor before the operation is over.

479. But to do it with ftraw hives without giving offence to the Bees, and with the greateft cafe to the operator, the evening, when it is but juft light enough to fee how to place your inftruments, is a much properer time; or a clear ftar or moon-light night will be ftill better. It may be done however late at night by the light of a candle and lantern, brought no nearer than is abfolutely neceffary, which is better than in the clofe of the evening; for the later this bufinefs is executed, the more quiet and fleepy are the Bees, and, before they are much alarmed, the operation will be over.

480. The method of doing it is this; fet clofe to the Stock a ftool, chair-frame, or the like, fo that it may ftand firm; have ready an empty hive

hive with its cover off, and alfo a hive floor. Lift up the Stock, floor and all, very gently, put it upon the ftool, and place the empty hive and floor upon the ftand; the Stock muft then be lifted up from its floor, and fet over the empty hive. The floor with the loofe Bees on it, muft be placed and fupported, fo that the edge may touch the door-way of the Stock, or at leaft the edge of its floor. Many Bees will oftentimes be left on it; but they will join their companions before morning. However, if there be any danger of rain, they muft be fecured therefrom by a proper covering. A pair of gloves is all the defence necef-fary for this operation.

481. Where hives have not a *moveable floor*, this operation will be more trouble-fome to perform, and fome of the Bees will be killed, by fetting the empty hive over the loofe ones that remain on the ftand after the Stock is lifted off, and fet upon the ftool. When the empty hive is in its place, the Stock is then again to be lifted up, and put upon it. Thus for want of the advantage of a moveable floor, the Stock undergoes a double removal and difturbance.

482. Early in the morning, examine if you have fet the hives right; the upper door way upon a line with the bottom one. If there be any openings, flip pieces of tin or tea-cheft lead over them, and plaifter them and the joinings with clay, or any other proper fubftance.

483. But

483. But obferve this *general rule*, do no more at the time of any operation than is abfolutely neceffary. It is always beft if the Bees infult you, to go from them for a little

By this gentle mode of proceeding, you will accomplifh it with eafe and fafety, and without any breach of friendfhip.

484. When an empty hive is to be fet *over* a Stock, you have only to fhove in the fliders of the latter, take off the cover, then fet the empty hive over, and withdraw the fliders. This may be done with very little rifk in the day time; but at night there is no hazard of receiving even a fingle fting.

485. As the variation in joining collateral boxes, confifts only in introducing the fliders into the fides inftead of the tops, there needs no farther explanation. Whenever a hive or box be fet *under* another, keep both door-ways open for fome days : this eafes the Bees of the unneceffary labour of climbing up the empty hive with their burdens, perhaps for weeks, before the upper one is fo full as to induce them to work in the under. But fhould they not in two or three days work out at both door-ways, fhut the upper one, by which means, they will become acquainted with the bottom entrance. In a few days after, open the upper one, and they will continue to pafs out of both; and if they are then nearly in want of room, or if there be plenty of honey to gather, it will compel them to work in the under hive;

and

and they will do this the ſooner, in proportion to the eaſe with which they can
either aſcend or deſcend. And not only
much time and fatigue will be ſaved by this
management, but the hives will be alſo much
ſooner filled. A conſideration which ought
to be of great weight with the owner. Nor
is this all: for by adding a hive early,
with the middle door-way *open,* the Bees
are in no wiſe hindered, and whenever ſo
diſpoſed, will deſcend without any care or
attendance of the Apiator.

486. Here it may be proper to obſerve,
that if a good Stock or Swarm be purchaſed
about ſwarming-time, it ſhould be ſet on
an empty box or hive, ready placed with
its door-way ſhut, nutil the Bees be well acquainted with their new ſituation.

487. In collateral boxes, both door-ways
may be left open when firſt doubled; which
ſhould be early. The Queen, having then
room enough in one box, will not be tempted
to move into the other, until more combs are
wanted, for her continually increaſing family. Therefore, about the middle of the
honey harveſt, or the firſt week in July;
due regard, however, being had to the nature of the ſeaſon; ſtop up the door-way
of that box, which is intended to be taken
for the honey. The Queen will ccaſe, in
general, to depoſit her eggs therein, and the
Bees will have ſufficient time to fill the
brood-cells with honey, as faſt as they become empty.

488. The

488. The ingenious Madam Vicat, a Swifs lady, who has favoured the world with fome fenfible remarks; and alfo an experienced writer, under the fignature of a *Lover of Bees,** which may be found in the appendix to Mr. Wildman's treatife; have from their experiments concluded, that Bees will not afcend to work in an *upper hive,* unlefs late in the feafon, and when they have neither fwarmed, nor have any hopes of a Princefs.. Want of room will then oblige them to afcend, but if a Princefs be bred, they will rather fwarm than do it.

489. Thefe obfervations are in general true; and while the Bees are confined to the paffage of the bottom hive *only,* and with fo few, and fuch limited openings, as they feem to have been in the experiments made by connoiffeurs, the fame refult will almoft always be obferved. But with more inlarged, and better difpofed communications, and with a *proper management of the door-ways,* in the manner above defcribed, the Bees will act differently, induced by the great facility with which they can accomplifh their defigns.

490. Glafs, in particular, is very difagreeable to Bees, and fo unlike any habitations they are ufed to, that nothing but neceffity,

P or

---

* *Whofe method of fetting one box* before another; *had been tried before Worlidge's time, and was found unfuccefsful.*

or the ftrong temptation of a comb, pre
vioufly placed in it, will intice them to buil
therein.

491. Neither muft it be concluded, be
caufe fome Stocks cannot by any manage
ment whatever be induced to work in a
upper hive, that therefore it is from averfiol
For they may have a fufficiency of rool
already. To which may be alfo added, tha
fome years, and fome fituations, may be 1
bad, as not to yield a fupply fufficient to fi
two boxes: or the Bees may not be ful
ficiently numerous to perform fo much worl
Under fuch circumftances as thefe, it wi
be in vain to expect the Bees to work, eithe
in an under or upper box: and therefol
the failure cannot with any propriety c
fhadow of reafoning, be attributed to th
fcheme or mode of management; unlefs yo
can fuppofe the author pretends to inftrue
you how to command the feafons alfo!

492. The better to elucidate this poin
permit me to recite an experiment, which
have frequently repeated. This confifte
in placing an empty box hive over one with
Stock in it, after previoufly fixing in fome piec
combs, filled with honey, by way of decoy
The Bees always afcended immediately, ar
with the greateft avidity eat up or carrie
away all the honey, under a fuppofition, th
it was placed there for that very purpol
or might be foon taken away again. B
finding afterwards, that the combs remaine
they began to refill the cells; and gradual
add(

added others until they had filled the
box. While in other boxes without decoys,
they have only raifed fome combs, upwards
between the bars, without conftructing any
at the top, or filling the box.

493. Some years ago I had a *fmall* box,
the top of which had the ufual number of
holes. In May the Bees feeming to want
room, another box was fet over it, and
the lower door-ways ftopped. The Bees on
this entered in at the upper paffage, and went
through the holes into the under box without
difcovering the leaft inclination to work in
the upper one, although at the fame time
there was fuch plenty of honey pafture as
occafioned them to caft out a great number
of their brood to make room for their honey.
Provoked at this, I took the empty box off,
(a perilous tafk with fuch boxes) and inverting
the full one, fet the empty one over it, bottom
to bottom, without any bars between. This
at once hit their fancy ; they prefently not
only extended their combs upwards, but alfo
began combs at the top of the upper box,
working them downwards, fo that the upper
and under combs met, though not in right
lines ; the whole forming a curious and gro-
tefque appearance. Nor have I ever fince
found that by fetting boxes over others that
had holes in them, after the common manner,
or communicated with each other by partial
openings only, the Bees could be induced to
work in the additional box.

P 2   494. But

494. But where bars have been ufed, if the feafon has been good, they have feldom difappointed me. It may be proper here to relate a remarkable inftance of two Swarms, each of which when hived, being too numerous for one of my ftraw hives, many of the Bees were forced to lie out. Empty hives were then fet over each of the Swarms; and during the fummer they half filled thefe with the pureft honey and wax.

495. Thefe examples prove inconteftibly the propriety and advantages of bars, over any other conftructions; the reafon feems to be this, the openings between the bars coincide fo well with thofe between the combs, that the Bees meeting with no obftacle to their afcent, are deceived into a notion that the two boxes are but one; and therefore carry on their works without hefitation. Happy for us, if many of the falfe notions among men proved as beneficial.

496. Bees that are kept in common ftraw hives, are often obliged to be idle for want of room, greatly to the owner's difadvantage. To remedy this, fuch Stocks as are weighty and feem full of Bees, and that have not fwarmed by the middle of July, or by the time the black-berries begin to blow (for feafons and fituations muft be allowed for) efpecially if the weather has been fine; fuch Stocks I fay fhould be turned upfide down, and empty hives placed over them (493). The Bees being in this unnatural pofition, will more readily go into the empty hive, than if they had

been

been ſet over it in the common way. This
will generally be the caſe; but it muſt be allowed that ſometimes neither one way nor
the other will ſucceed. Therefore after they
have been doubled a few days, it will be
proper to try how matters ſtand, by ſtrik-
ing the upper hive with your fiſt in the
evening, when the Bees are all at home. If
a large quantity of them have fixed themſelves
in it, you will hear a conſiderable buz; but
if this be not the caſe, fix in another empty
hive a comb with honey in it; and at night
take the other empty hive off, and place this in
its ſtead: inticed by the honey-comb, they will
ſoon aſcend and begin to work.

497. Another way is to turn an empty
hive upſide down, and near the bottom
cut an opening ſufficient to form a proper
door-way, to which fix an alighting-board;
lay the uſual bars acroſs the top, and at night
ſet the full hive over it; and either then, or
early the next morning, block up the other
door-ways, and plaſter the joining all round,
ſo that no Bee can come out, but at the new
bottom entrance. This will anſwer better, as
being more agreeable to their uſual ſtile of
building; but after they have ſtood thus
a few days, in order to ſhorten the toil of the
Bees crawling up the empty hive, open a
middle door-way; and if they then work at
both paſſages, it is a ſure indication that they
have begun to make combs in the under hive.
By this management they are continually kept
employed to their maſter's advantage; and

P 3

not only fo, but when the hives come to b
feparated, the bottom one may probably contain a Swarm, and be referved as a Stock for
next year (398).

498. Who that poffeffes but a fmall portion
of humanity, and has the example of thefe
induftrious creatures continually before his
eyes, will not pluck from his bofom the
hand of flothfulnefs, and perform this kind
office, as well to encreafe his own ftore,
as at the fame time to fave the innocent
and deferving infects from the murdering
match!

499. A lefs advantageous method is purfued by fome country-people; thefe ufe what
they call an *ekeing* or *lift*; confifting of three
or four rounds of another hive, the edges of
which are made even, and fewed down with
packthread. The full hive is raifed on thefe,
to give them more room. This practice is attended with many inconveniences, and often
proves infufficient for the intended purpofe;
and therefore it is beft to raife them at once,
as before directed (480), efpecially as it may
be equally, if not more eafily performed.
When it is obferved that the Bees in the fpring
feafon do not carry in farina, it is to be
apprehended that the Queen is dead. If fo, as
foon as their honey is confumed, and often before if honey pafture be commenced, they will
relinquifh their own hive, taking with them
what honey may be left, and unite with fome
of the other Stocks, occafioning thereby an
unufual

unufual cronding at the door-way of fuch
Stock, as though invaded by robbing
Bees ; or as if they were going to fwarm.
When fuch circumftances appear, the *Queen-
lefs* Stock fhould at night be fet over fome
other (480, 484).

500. To thofe who have glafs windows in
their hives or boxes, it may be of fome ufe
to know, that when Bees begin to work in a
hive, they conftruct the rudiments of feveral
combs at once: and to accomplifh this with
the greateft cafe and expedition, a part of the
Bees are formed into as many diftinct ranges,
hanging down from the top like fo many
chains, by which thofe that are to fafhion
the combs, afcend and defcend. If the number
of Bees be very great, they hang clofe and
thick, like fo many curtains ; but if not many
in number, few only can be fpared for this
purpofe ; therefore they then form chains of
fingle Bees, linked to each other by the claws,
the bottom Bee keeping the whole link fteady
by clinging faft to the floor; but this being a
hard tafk, it holds it but a few minutes, and
then it gives place to another. In the evening they draw up to the top in a clofe clufter,
to take their neceffary repofe.

501. When therefore a Swarm has been
hived, or a Stock doubled, and the Bees hang
down as above defcribed, it is a fure fign that
they have begun to form fome combs therein ;
or if it be a doubled Stock that has not fwarmed; there is no danger that it will; if honey-
pafture be plentiful, until the additional hive

be

be nearly filled. In ftraw hives that have no windows, by gently lifting them up behind, a peep may be had without danger.

502. There have been inftances of fuch very hot fummers as to melt the honey, and foften the combs fo much as to ruin the Stocks. The fummer of 1779, had in fome places this effect: in fuch cafes fhelter the hives as much as poffible, by mats, bags, long ftraw, or branches of trees, and alfo raife the hives half an inch or more, to admit the air. In bee houfes fet all the doors open, and frequently water the ground about the hives.

503. In all extenfive Apiaries, it will be ufeful to keep two or three Stocks in boxes, as ferving for indexes or ftandards, indicating the ftate or fuccefs of all the other Stocks. The windows affording a proper and fufficient infpection for acquiring fuch information.

CHAPTER XV.

Of the PASTURAGE *or* FLOWERS *proper for* BEES; *with a Catalogue of them, and Obfervations thereon; alfo, of the proper Number of* STOCKS *requifite for different Situations.*

504. HOwever fkilfully Bees may be managed, the profits arifing therefrom muft in a great meafure depend upon the

goodnefs

goodness of the situation for pasturage; or in other words, upon the quantity of such flowers as will yield the greatest plenty of fine honey, and of farina for the sustenance of the brood.

505. Bees under very indifferent management, where a profusion of food can be speedily acquired, will succeed *better* than others under the most *skillful*, can possibly do, where bee-flowers are soon exhausted, or are inconsiderable in quantity, or at too great a distance.

506. On the other hand, in a bad situation, and with bad management, they will produce but a trifling advantage; and should a few untoward seasons succeed each other, they will be reduced to nothing. To these united causes is owing that scantiness of Bees observable almost in every county of this kingdom, some particular heaths and commons excepted. For as these are generally skirted by woods, and as woods, heaths, and commons hardly ever suffer from the ravages of the unsparing scythe, the Bee-flowers are left untouched. Particularly favourable are such commons as are thickly covered with mole-hills, on which the wild thyme spreads its aromatic sweets ; but pleasing to the Bees alone ; to sheep and other cattle unsavory, and by them unheeded.

507. Where heath or broom abound the collections of honey are very large ; these plants continuing very long and late in bloom,

often

often to November; but though the *quan-tity* of honey be very confiderable, yet its *quality* is very ordinary; perhaps there is none worfe, except that acquired from buckwheat, which alfo furnifhes a profufion.

508, Honey collected from gardens, is in England generally fuperior to any other; as thefe afford more aromatic and fweeter flowers than either fields or woods; but then the quantity is very fmall compared to the other.

509. It is an error, however, to fuppofe that the Bees gather from all fweet flowers, indifcriminately: fo far from it, they are very nice in their choice, and entirely reject thofe we moft efteem. The choiceft productions of the flower gardens, as rofes, pinks, hyacinths, auriculas, fweet-williams, ftocks, honey-fuckles, jeffamines, and many others of gorgeous and varied hues, as well as highly fragrant odours, are all as ufelefs pageants to our Bees, unworthy their leaft regard: while flowers of little or no apparent beauty, and fo minute as to appear to us fcarce worthy of notice, furnifh to them the choiceft ftores, and the richeft repafts.

510. But where a choice is denied them, like the poor among mankind, they are com-pelled to feed on coarfer diet: nay, inftances are upon record of their collecting from noxious plants, highly prejudicial to health. The large wild Bees indeed collect from all forts of flowers; but their honey is defpi-cable.

511. The

511. The following catalogue of flowers, contains those *only* that I have observed the Bees to visit with any considerable attention. They are arranged according to the succession of blowing, except that several blow at the same time, and many of them vary according to the time of sowing or planting.

512. Winter Aconite, Laurustinus, Snow Drops*, Hazel, Crocuses*, Sallows, Oziers, Primroses, Violets, Standard Almonds, single Wall-Flowers*, Apricots, Peaches; Nectarines, Plumbs, Cherries, Pears, Turneps*, all the class of Brasica or Cabbages, Coleworts, * &c. Gooseberries, Dwarf Almonds, Rosemary,** Apples, Strawberries, Tulips, May or White Thorn, Heath,* Gofs, or Furze, Star of Bethlehem, Borage**, Rasberries*, Laburnum, Columbine, Barberries, Beans*, Syringoes, Sweet Briar, Mustard, Tares*, Clover, Spiked Star of Bethlehem, Cucumbers, Greek Valerian, Bladder Sena, French Willows*, Thyme**, White Poppies, Mignonette**, Blackberries, Lime Tree, Hysop*, Garden ~~Fennel~~*, Nasturtium, Ladies Fingers*, Cats Tails, Sainfoin, Buckwheat*, Maples, Alders, Sweet Scabius, Sunflowers, Spanish Broom, Starwort, Michaelmas Daifies, Winter Savory, Paffion Flower, Jacob's Beard, and the larger Ivy.

513. Thofe articles marked with a * are fuch as produce the greateft quantity of honey or farina; and thofe with ** fuch as afford honey of the higheft perfection.

514. If

514. If this last was deposited by the Bees in cells by itself, it would be in the highest request and of great value; but as honey from inferior flowers is collected at the same time, both sorts are mingled together, and form an aggregate in quality, proportionate to that diversity: therefore, glasses set over boxes or hives, at the critical time, that is, when the choicest flowers bloom, seem the most eligible method of collecting the most of it as perfect as it can be obtained.

515. Of the flowers here enumerated some furnish farina, and others honey; and some both. Farina is gathered very *early* in the spring, as soon as the Bees begin to breed, and is continued to be collected until autumn; whereas in general the honey-harvest does not begin until late in the spring, and is over early in the autumn or before.

516. Farina is that simple dust or flour found on the stamina of flowers, and varies in colour according to the bloom from which it is collected; but in general it is yellow. This the Bees brush off, and form into little balls, and fix into little cavities of their legs, and carry into their hives, to feed the brood with, while in the maggot state. This is commonly thought to be wax, but it is not so; nor has it any of the properties of wax; neither can it by any art that we are acquainted with be converted into a waxy substance. After many repeated boilings it will not assimilate either with the wax or the
water.

water. Besides, was it wax a Swarm would collect most of it when they were first put into a
hive; the reverse of which is evident, for
then they are seen to carry hardly any; whereas in the spring, when a Stock can want no
wax, they are seen to carry in the largest
quantity of farina.

517. The country-people have given it the
appellation of *Bee-bread*; they might rather
call it brood-bread; for there is no proof from
any of the observations that have been made
respecting this substance, that the Bees feed
upon it themselves. It is most probable that
the Bees swallow this substance, and concoct it
in their own stomachs in some degree, and then
feed the Bee-maggots therewith. Its proper
name is *farina*; and to prevent injurious mis-
conceptions of it in practice, we shall constantly call it by that name.

518. The winter aconite is the first blossom that furnishes this farina; the snow-drop
and crocus follow: after these the fallows,
especially the white sallow, which will be
cloathed with blossoms so replete with this
yellow dust, that the Bees will cluster so
thick upon them, as might induce one to
think a Swarm was going to settle there.
Many of these near an Apiary, must be greatly
serviceable, as will also plenty of crocusses and
snow-drops; as also *single* wall-flowers.

The whole class of cabbages, savoys, broc-
coli, &c. if let run to seed, or to sprouts,
will afford very seasonable supply, when the
bloom of other plants becomes scarce. Turneps,

neps are useful.   Almonds afford a moderate quantity of farina; gooseberries yield more, and rasberries exceed both.

519. The fruit trees afford honey of a good quality, so do beans, but not in great quantity : vetches or tares, and buckwheat yield it in great plenty; so does clover, but the white forms the best honey. Heath and broom furnish very large quantities, when hardly any other flowers are left.   Spanish broom is much extolled by Bradley; but if the Bees can find honey in other flowers, this will be wholly neglected. Rosemary blows early and holds long, and is perhaps the first aromatic plant that supplies the Bees with honey, and that of a fine quality.

520. But the two most favourite Bee-plants for honey are lemon-thyme, and borage. Lemon-thyme continues to bloom a considerable while, and furnishes a most delicious honey, for colour and fluidity like mountain-wine. Large quantities of it may be planted for edgings, as well in the kitchen garden and pleasure ground, as in the flower division.   It takes up but little room, if properly trimmed once a year.

521. This elegant plant forms a pleasing ever-green edging all the year; but when in bloom the slight purple hue of its flower, contrasted with its green and yellowish foliage, attracts the eye, while the organ of smell is regaled, and the senses enlivened by its aromatic odours.   At the same time the jocund Bees humming their joyful songs, rove from

flower

flower to flower through every walk, and excite the moſt pleaſing ſenſation in a mind bleſſed with ſympathetic ſenſibility.

522. But of all plants *Borage* ſeems moſt devoted to the ſervice of the Bees, both on account of its *long* continuance in bloom, and the excellent quality of its honey. It well deſerves the ſignificant epithet of *Bee-Flower*.

523. It may be managed ſo as to flower from early ſpring to November, if no froſt of conſequence ſhould intervene. It affords plenty of ſeeds, and if theſe be ſown at different periods in any ſoil, the plants may be raiſed ſo as to be in ſucceſſive bloom as long as the weather will permit the Bees to collect their honey. From this plant they will gather at all times, even when the atmoſphere is ſo wet or cold as to deprive all other flowers of their honeyed ſweets. But theſe plants ſhould be confined to a particular ſpot; for ſhedding their ſeed very faſt, when once in the ground it will be difficult to exterminate them. Thoſe ſown by hand, or ſelf-ſown, when come up muſt be thinned by an hoe in the ſame manner as turneps, to make them blow the the ſtronger.

524. Mignonette is another Bee-flower, but as I was not acquainted with it, as ſuch, until this year, I cannot determine as to the quality of its honey: the Bees ſeem as fond of it as of borage, and will gather from it as long. It may alſo be continued in bloom until the latter end of November, by ſowing it at
different

different times ; therefore, if the compafs of ground allotted for the Bee ftands be fown with this or borage, and proper path-ways made, it would be of fingular benefit to the Bees, and afford no fmall pleafure to the fpectator; efpecially if an edging of lemon-thyme be added, and the extreme circumference planted with rofemary.

525. I have been lately informed of a flower which grows on the borders of Hertfordfhire and Cambridgefhire, about Barkway and Royfton, and is there called *Cats-tails.* It is found once in three years, according to the labouring-people; from whom I have received this intelligence, in very great plenty, and furnifhes a prodigious quantity of honey, tho' a very troublefome weed to the farmer. This plant, however, is not confined to thofe parts, for I have fince heard of it in the fields about this part of the country, though too late for me to profit by the information. The beft defcription I can procure of it at prefent is, that from the root many round ftalks arife, which afcend higher than the corn: thefe ftalks are rough, hairy, and in a fmall degree prickly, and befet with brownifh fpots from top to bottom. The leaves are narrow like wall-flowers, and are placed fingle one above another at fmall diftances on each fide of the ftalks, and are of a pale green. The ftalks are furnifhed with branches all the way up, which are about two inches in length, and clofely fet with flower-buds; thefe decreafing gradually towards the end refemble a cat's

tail

tail. The flower-buds, at their first appearance, are of a purplish colour, but afterwards,
when expanded, of a pale purple or blue;
and are nearly funnel-shaped, with a purple
thrum. It blows in June, and, I suppose, is
annual. From its producing so large a quantity of flowers in succession, it would seem to
be a valuable plant for the Bees.

526. Perhaps, there may be a variety of
green-house plants very acceptable to Bees;
but as thefe are confined to gentlemens
feats, we pass them over as not being of general use.

527. There are feveral flowers mentioned
by fome authors, which are omitted in my
catalogue; because I could not perceive the
domeftic Bees take any notice of them; notwithftanding fome of them derive their ap-
pellations from the Bees, as mellilot, apium,
honey-wort, meliffa or haulm, &c.

528. Lavender and baulm, though apparently excellent Bee-flowers, were to my fur-
prife generally neglected, or vifited but very
fparingly by the Bees.

529. The autumnal ftar-wort, or Michaelmas daify, are ferviceable Bee-flowers. That
fpecies, however, ftiled by Millar* the Italian
blue, and which he tells us is the Amellus of
Virgil,

---

* *Gardener's Folio Dictionary, Cistus.*

Q

Virgil, does not seem to anfwer to Virgil's defcription : .·

> " The flower itfelf is glorious to behold,
> " And fhines on altars like refulgent gold."
> DRYDEN's VIRGIL.

An honour much too glorious for fo mean a flower.

The root boiled in generous wine is what Virgil prefcribes to reftore fick Bees. I believe it has no fuch virtue; but as the falernian wine elevated Virgil to fing immortal fongs, it may probably have a cordial effect on the Bees. Good Englifh ale, a liquor Virgil never tafted, will however prove more falutary.

It is very likely that a difference of climates, as well as of feafons, may occafion a very confiderable difference in the nature and difpofition of flowers for yielding honey.

For it may be remarked, that though in fome years the Bees will collect from fweetbriars, May, or white thorn, Greek valerian, honefty, or lunaria, and fome others; yet in other feafons they will not be feen to touch them. This may arife from the peculiarity of the weather, as to heat or cold, moift or dry, at the blooming-time of the above flowers. In a very wet or very dry feafon, flowers yield no honey. If the former happens while the beft flowers are blowing, the Bees muft collect from very inferior ones, as their choice is then limitted. They will be nearly in the fame dilemma when there is a long fucceffion

of

of very hot weather: for though the honey collected at the first opening of the blossoms is excellent, yet the heat causes these to dry and fall off so soon that the quantity is very small.

530. Instances are very common of less honey being collected (in some situations) than was sufficient to support any Stock through the winter: much less to afford any surplus to the owner (571).

531. The cistus labdanum hath its leaves covered with a clammy kind of gum, from whence I was induced to hope it might furnish the Bees with *Wax*; but they never applied to it for that purpose; the flowers indeed they sometimes gathered from, though but seldom. Nor could I ever observe them to collect any thing from laurels, pines, or firs; though some writers have asserted that they collect their wax from those trees.

532. The great Boerhaave mentions their gathering wax from the rosemary leaves. I have many of these plants about my Apiary, and have frequently and attentively observed them, but never saw the Bees take any thing from the *leaves*; the *flowers* indeed they were greatly enamoured with, and enriched themselves with their nectar. How, where, or from what they collect the valuable article of wax, seems yet a mystery. I am inclined to think that they suck it from flowers into their stomachs, as they do the honey, and carry it thus into their hives, and then apply it to the

intended

tended use, warm and pliable as it comes from that organ. For in places where considerable quantities of white poppies bloom, the combs made at that time are remarkably *white*, and extensive combs will be formed in a much shorter time than usual; nor is this remark wholly my own, several Apiators having noticed the same.

533. When there are large fields of white clover, near an Apiary, and the bloom not cut off, the hives will be filled in a short time.

534. Large woods near a Bee-ground are of very great service: not only on account of the plenty of farina they afford, but also of the honey dews; for there being a great number of trees so near each other, a large quantity of that article is necessarily gathered in a much shorter time than it could be from the same number of trees scattered through the distance of perhaps several miles.

That the nearer and more plentiful all the honey pasture is, the more journies the Bees can make in a day, and consequently collect a larger quantity, is a proposition that seems self-evident.

535. It has been said, that Bees will fly three miles for pasture; be it so; you will not dispute, however, that if they had but three rods or three yards, they would fill your hives much sooner. If Bees will usually fly so far for provender, how comes it to pass that so many Stocks perish for want, when it has been well known that at half a mile distance they might have collected honey in plenty?

or

or how is it that poor Stocks on being removed, not more than that diftance, have
prefently become rich, and filled their hives?
I queftion whether they ever traverfe for food
in fpring or autumn more than a ~~quarter~~ of a
mile.

536. In Egypt and other eaftern nations,
it has been a practice to remove Stocks of
Bees in waggons or in boats from one place to
another, even to a very great diftance. As
faft as the flowers fail in one encampment
they proceed to another, through the whole
feafon. Something of this nature has been
attempted in France, where, perhaps, it may
have proved fuccefsful; but from the inftability of the Englifh climate, the advantage
arifing from fuch a fcheme here would not be
adequate to the expence.

537. Whether it would be eligible to cul-
tivate a field or large fpot of ground, with
plants purpofely for Bees, is at prefent doubtful, becaufe all the neighbouring Bees, and
numberlefs other infects, would become equal
fharers of the provifion; but notwithftanding
this; if the increafe of honey fhould prove confiderably greater than it would otherwife have
been, and of more or even equal value with any
crop that might have been raifed on the ground,
it would be a very eligible practice for many
farmers to adopt; not only as a valuable change
to many pieces of ground, but for the improvement of fuch as would otherwife from
their natural poverty be good for little, and
yet might produce a rich crop of Bee-flowers,

Q 3 viz.

viz. Borage, buckwheat, sainfoin, tares, and white clover. Buckwheat is often sown to be afterwards plowed in as manure ; but by this management it would be made of double advantage; as might also white clover, by letting it stand for seed, which is valuable and chiefly imported from Holland. Sainfoin and tares may likewise be cultivated for the same purpose, and with a similar advantage; whereby there will be a two-fold crop, one of honey, from the flowers (which must not be cut) and another from the seed.

538. It is referred to the judgment of the experienced, whether the value of the honey and seed would not be more than adequate to that of mowing a particular field or two for fodder. How far this scheme may be generally practicable, I will not determine ; but at any rate it cannot be an unprofitable step to appropriate, in large extensive gardens; some poor or mean spots for the cultivation of Bee-plants ; for though other Bees will undoubtedly participate, yet from the greater vicinity of the flowers to the Apiary, your own Bees will collect by far the greater share of honey, &c. being enabled by their taking shorter journies, to make much quicker returns ; and therefore, though you cannot reap the whole advantage, you will certainly benefit considerably more than if no such provision had been made. Moreover, if the neighbouring Bee-gardens be equally well furnished ; the advantage will be mutual, and the

Stocks,

Stocks of the whole circuit abundantly improved.

539. One plant in particular, and to which few people have any dislike, deserves peculiar encouragement, as it affords in the fruit a very agreeable repast for themselves, and in the flowers for the Bees; I mean the *Strawberry*, of which I have many beds; they are raised high and laid oval: no pains are taken with them, but drawing out any weeds that may appear. These plants, though growing in a manner wild, afford as much fruit as those upon which much time and care have been bestowed.

540. One remarkable circumstance remains to be unfolded; which is, that of all the *fruits* raised by us, I know of none except the amber gooseberry, that the Bees will feed on, but of this, when left upon the bushes until dead ripe, they will devour the pulpy part in the same manner as wasps do.

541. When Stocks have had an extraordinary day of honey-gathering, they seem as it were to praise the Deity for his bounty, in a full and joyful chorus, easily distinguishable by attentive Apiators. The same may be observed when they have been so successful as to have filled their hives, great numbers having then no more work to do, are seen to frisk about full of sport and play before their city gates: but the idle and the epicure Drones undergo a sad reverse, a dismal fate; for they must now no longer partake of that delicious food

Q 4   which

which others have induftriously accumulated
with fo much toil and labour,

542. Water is abfolutely neceffary to Bees,
but as our climate is generally charged with
moifture and dews, there are perhaps but few
places that require any water to be fet on purpofe for them; except in a very dry feafon;
or if there be no pond near the Apiary. In
this cafe the public feeding troughs (760)
filled with water, will anfwer the purpofe; or
broad fhallow pans filled with fmall rough
ftones, and the water poured among them:
Thefe will enable the Bees to ftand and fip,
without danger of drowning, which otherwife
they would be liable to. Ponds covered with
duck-weed are very convenient to the Bees,
as thefe weeds will buoy them up fo as to enable them to fip with fafety.

543. Let us now endeavour to inveftigate
what number of Stocks may be kept, fo as to
give the moft profit, and from thence draw
fome inferences with refpect to the emolu-
ments accruing to the proprietor.

544. For this purpofe a review of what has
been faid by former writers on this fubject,
will furnifh us with fome ufeful information.

545. Rufden relates, " That on the 21ft of
" June 1677, a colony being weighed, it was
" fifty-five pounds, and on the 28th of June
" it weighed eighty-five pounds, which was
" an increafe of thirty pounds in feven days.
" But in the fame fpace of time a fingle Stock
" or Swarm can feldom increafe five pounds.
" The reafon is, the colony having but *one*
" brood

" brood, can fpare moft of the working Bees.
" But the Stock or Swarm having *each* of
" them a young brood, when the harveft of
" Honey-Dews comes, they being feparate,
" cannot fpare fo many labourers, in propor-
" tion as the colonies; nor have they a fuffi-
" ciency of vacant combs to put the honey
" in, the chief part being filled with brood.
" Neither are the colony Bees obliged to go
" abroad in bad weather; as are the Stocks
" or Swarms, whereby many are loft."

546. Rufden's boxes were ten inches high,
and fixteen inches over, on the outfide :
" One of thefe, (he fays) taken from a co-
" lony generally weighed fifty-fix pounds,
" while Stocks only weigh twenty-eight
" pounds." (Here he is certainly miftaken,
I have bought many farmers Stocks, that
have weighed forty-five pounds and upwards): but he fubjoins, " Or a Stock that
" has not fwarmed forty pounds. A colony
" alfo will have one fifth part more good
" honey : nor do they put their honey into
" thofe cells that have had brood in, as
" Stocks and Swarms are obliged to do."

547. " But fuppofing the Swarm left as a
" balance to the worth of the colony (which
" it doth not near do) then the Stock taken
" up will not weigh half that of the colony
" taken off, befides the fuperior goodnefs of
" the honey."

548. He obferves in another place, " That
" he took fome colonies off that year of fifty-
" feven pounds, fixty-one, and fixty-four
                                    " pounds

" pounds weight each, fo that colonies turn
" out more than doubly profitable, and have
" more virgin honey than three ftraw hives."
He ufed three boxes to each colony.*

549. The Reverend Mr. Thorley mentions,
that in fome fummers he has taken two boxes
from one colony, each weighing forty pounds,
and left ftore enough in the other for their
maintenance (his boxes were ten inches deep in
the infide, and the breadth twelve or fourteen
inches), difcounting therefore ten pounds, for
the weight of box and wax, there will be 6olb.
left for the proprietor, and the greater part
pure virgin honey.   This gentleman's fon in-
forms us, that in a good feafon he has had (at
Ball's Pond, near Newington-Green) a glafs
globe filled in thirty days, containing thirty-
eight pounds of fine honey.

550. Dr. Warder,† of Croydon, gives us
no calculation of the profits of his boxes ; but
to thofe who keep Stocks in the ufual way,
his advice is worthy of $_{r}e^{ma}$rk.   In order to
become a wealthy Apiator, he advifes, " to
" begin with ten good Stocks, at ten fhillings
" a Stock (though in fome counties they are
" much

---

* *The word Colony conveys no idea of a Stock of Bees, that
is kept from fwarming ; but quite the reverfe.   Much lefs can
we conceive that thereby is only meant a Stock raifed three
ftories high.   A Swarm might properly be called a Colony, had
they no fupreme head ; but the inftant they are fettled, they become an independent empire.*

† *True Amazons.*

" much cheaper). · The first year by doub-
" ling your Casts, you will be able to have
" about twenty-five good Stocks, and the next
" year about sixty, and the third year about
" one hundred and fifty, barring casualties,
" and they prove good years ; so that when
" you have raised this Stock, you are rich
" enough, if not over covetous. Should
" there come good weather, you may have
" about one hundred and sixty Stocks to
" take, which, at five shillings a Stock, good
" and bad, comes to forty pounds ; a good
reward for the pains taken with them.

551. Here the woman with her basket of
eggs, spontaneously intrudes upon the mind.
This spceulation seems the result of the Doctor's calculations in his study ; for it is much
to be questioned whether such a rapid increase
has ever been found in England.

552. However, I think we may safely remark upon the whole, that the situations in
which these several gentlemen made these very
great profits, must have been of the extraordinary kind ; and withal but few or no Apiaries
in the vicinity to participate in the pasturage.

553. The professor Wildman has given us
no estimates of this kind, and therefore I may
proceed to say something of my own Apiary,
which could never furnish near such a quantity
of honey as above related ; nor will my situation support more than eighteen Stocks, and
some years not even twelve.

554. It must be a very good year, and a
very good Stock, to afford me a box of twenty-
five

five pounds. Nor will the run of Stocks in this neighbourhood yield upon an average above sixteen pounds of honey each.

555. If by raising your Stocks you are so lucky as to keep them from swarming, the number of Bees in each will consequently be very great; and should it prove a favourable season for honey-gathering, a great quantity will be collected in a few days; for as according to the old adage, "Many hands make light "work," so two pecks of Bees in one hive, will procure twice the quantity of honey than if the same number of Bees had been divided into two hives. The more Bees together the greater their prosperity.

556. That colonies, or in other words, Story Stocks well conducted, will yield far greater advantage in every respect than common hives, in similar situations, must be readily acknowledged by every judicious person who shall have tried both.

557. But neither Warder nor Rusden have given us any directions for discovering what situations are favourable for this prodigious increase; nor made any allowance for the many deductions that must be made for the loss of Stocks in the winter and spring; nor for those years in which little honey can be obtained; nor for the unavoidable swarming of colonies, notwithstanding every precaution.

558. I am not conversant with heath countries; but it seems improbable, that any of them can possibly allow of such a rapid and prodigiously great increase as Warder supposes. Our climate is too change-able

able and unfavourable for it. And if we have one good year in three for Bees, it is as much, as upon an average, we can boast of. The mildest of our seasons are checquered with too much variety to be very proper for this nice business: so that it may be safely questioned whether Russia's much severer clime, be not more propitious.

559. In Spring and Summer it frequently happens that the day cloathed in the brightest splendor, and with its genial warmth gladdening the hearts of men and Bees, shall suddenly become cold, wet, and gloomy. In such inauspicious weather the Bees, compelled to stay at home, will quickly consume as much honey as they had laboured for in the preceding fine days. Should these unfavourable transitions be frequent during the honey harvest; especially at the time of the Honey Dews falling, farewel plenty! Want! consuming Want, throughout the winter, will be the portion of these useful and industrious insects; and will inevitably destroy them in the Spring, unless timely relieved by the fostering hand of charity (733, 752).

560. The Reverend Mr. White observes, that the village in which he dwelt, though a large one, would only supply ten colonies; and yet his boxes were less than a peck measure.

This village was surrounded with beautiful meadows and fine gardens. Whereas, in the adjoining county of Cambridge abounding with extensive barren heaths, which allow scarcely any flowers to spring up and blossom; there is such a profusion of honey, that he had seen 70 or 80 hives in one farmers yard, even

just

just after the burning-time. And this, notwithstanding the inundations of the fens, the
farmers plough, or the numerous flocks, that
graze on those almost barren heaths. To which
we may add, that the same circumstances are
observable in Hampshire and Wiltshire.

561. The village from which I write has a
great affinity to that described by Mr. White:
and yet, about a mile from hence, upon the en-
virons of a very extensive common, and skirted
with ample woods, Bees thrive amazingly.

562. Marshy grounds are very unfavourable to Bees. I have known some that did
not thrive on such, but on being removed
about a mile to a higher and drier situation,
soon became strong and well replenished.

563. Should several neighbours vie with
each other, who shall keep the most hives,
it will impoverish the Stocks of all.

But although this may happen to be the
case in some few places; yet England is in
general very thinly stocked with Bees. Should
every farmer and cottager, however, keep a
few, all the honey and wax the flowers
could possibly yield, would be as regularly
collected as the apples of the orchard, or the
wheat of the fields; and prove a great advantage to themselves, and the kingdom in general.

564. Most of the cottagers throughout the
island, with a very small portion of trouble, and
at a very little expence, as has been shewn, provided their Bees be managed properly might
half maintain their families by the profits.
Many of these labouring people keep poultry: which, though requiring both much

attention

attention and expence, prove but little advantage to themfelves, and of great detriment to
the farmers. Bees, however, few of them will
keep, tho' demanding much lefs attendance,
much lefs expence, and yet, when properly
managed, will yield twenty times the profit.
How prepofteroufly abfurd is fuch conduct!

565. Though in fome fituations very great
profits cannot be made: yet in all a profit
may be obtained fufficiently adequate to the
time and expence beftowed on thefe induftrious fervants, by their no lefs induftrious
and humane mafters and protectors.

566. From the principles laid down, we
may infer, that the number of Stocks of Bees
muft be limited according to the nature of
the fituation: and that a place or diftrict may
be over-ftocked in the fame manner as pafture for fheep. For if twenty of thefe be
confined to a pafturage that will fupport but
ten, what elfe but poverty, leannefs, and even
death can be expected. So, if an Apiator
keeps twenty Stocks of Bees, though he finds
year after year, many die in winter for want,
and the reft but fcantily provided; it muft be
folly, not to take the *hint*, and reduce them
in future to half the number.

CHAPTER XVI.

Of HONEY DEWS.

567. THE Honey Dew is not a liquid
depofited by the air on the leaves
of plants, as is generally fuppofed: For then,
like other dews or fogs, it would fall on,

and

and adhere to all forts of plants indifcriminately, whereas, it is found only on a
few particular plants; and on them but
partially, for the young leaves afford none.

568. The oak, maple, fycamore, hazle,
and bramble, are, as far as I can find, the
only plants on which it is found. Neither
is it difcovered like other dews, early in the
morning: But fome hours after the fun has
fhone with its greateft fplendor, that is about
ten or eleven o'clock; and continues, more or
fewer hours, in proportion to that fplendor.
For cloudy, dull days are incompatible with
Honey Dews. This fubftance is as tranfparent
and as fweet as honey, and is in fact, perfect
honey, attracted through the pores of the
leaves, by a peculiar fultry heat; particularly
when reflected through clouds. Sometimes
it is found on the leaves in the form of little
drops or globules. But at other times being
more diluted, by the greater moifture of the
atmofphere, it covers the leaves, as though
they were fpread with a fine fyrup.

570. The time in which thefe Honey Dews
are generally found, is from the begining of
June to the middle of July. But it will vary
in proportion as the weather is wet or dry;
which will occafion them to be either fooner
or later. The hotteft and drieft fummers,
produce the largeft and moft frequent Honey
Dews. In cold and wet feafons, few or
none of them are to be feen. When the
year is backward in its fruit, it betokens that
the Honey Dews will be late alfo; fometimes,
even fo late as the middle of harveft.

571. Butle

571. Butler has a remarkable obfervation upon this fubject; Honey Dews he fays, were in the year 1617 produced two months after the ufual time. There having been a long. continuance of wet weather, no Honey Dews were found until the latter end of Auguft; which proved exceedingly hot. But the quantities were fmall and of little fervice. For the Stocks when taken, proved light: and moft of the Stocks and Swarms that were kept, died, for want, before the end of winter; excepting only in the heath countries; were the heath being then in full flower, afforded the Bees that plenty of honey which could not be obtained from the Honey Dews.

572. Whenever a Honey Dew is found, the Bees are fo extremely eager to fetch it, that they quit all other work, that their returns may be the. quicker and more numerous; and left a gloomy change fhould deprive them of the precious prize. No harveft fwain, dreading impending ftorms, can be more anxious, or expeditious, in haftening the houfing of his crops than thefe aërial tribes in this their delightful office; fo much fo, that thronging in too great numbers at the door-way, they joftle and tumble each other down. And fmarting woe to thofe who fhall thoughtlefsly ftand in their way at this important crifis. Their joy on thefe occafions, is expreffed in fuch inceffant and loud notes, as to be heard at a great diftance. By thefe tokens it may

R   be

be known there is a Honey Dew, without
feeing the trees from which they gather it.

573. ʼThe Bees of fuch Apiaries as are
far diftant from thofe plants that produce
Honey Dews, cannot collect near the quantity
that thofe can that are near. Gardens in particular, feldom furnifh plants of this fort.

574. A very furprifing fource of honey
was obferved by the Abbé Boffier in France.
This he tells us, the Bees collected from the
excrement of a fmall infect called a Puceron,
vulgarly a loufe, infefting the bark of fome
particular trees; fuch as holm-oak and the
lime. In the middle of fummer they furnifh the moft of this excrementitious fweet:
In the Autum (tho' that is the time the Bees
have moft need of it) but little, and of inferior quality to honey gathered from flowers.

575. As I was ignorant whether any thing
of this kind had ever been noticed in England,
and as there are both oak and lime trees on my
premifes, I have from year to year, very attentively obferved them; but could never
perceive any fuch appearances as defcribed
by the Abbé; I muft therefore leave this
matter to be afcertained by fome one who
fhall be more fuccefsfully inquifitive.

C H A P.

CHAPTER XVII.

The Method of Separating DOUBLE HIVES *or* BOXES; *and of taking the* HONEY-COMBS, *and* HIVES *in general; with many Observations and Precautions relating to* STOCKS *during the Summer.*

576. HAVING accommodated the Bees with the most convenient and proper necessaries for the growth and preservation of their families, and increase of their treasure, it is but reasonable that as a requital for this trouble and expence, we participate with them in the profit; therefore to shew how to obtain this to the greatest advantage, is our present task.

577. Stocks that have emitted Swarms, in general will not afford an extra box or hive of honey that summer; nor can it be expected from Swarms; unless in both cases the Bees be very numerous (a peck at least), or the seasons and situations very good.

578. The prosperity of a Stock depends much upon the Drones: for if these be deficient in number, or not born until late in the summer, the increase of your Bees will be

proportionably

proportionably limited : on the contrary, if
they be too numerous (418, 580) they will
devour the honey fo faft that the Workers
can hardly keep a *fingle* hive fupplied, much
lefs fill an additional one (830).

579. When the Drones have been too few
in a Stock, I have watched their coming out
from other Stocks that feemed to have too
many ; and taken fome of them away with
my finger and thumb. I have put a dozen
or two of thefe, having previoufly cut off one
of their wings, or wetted them, to prevent
their flight, to a dronelefs Stock, where they
were kindly entertained. The Stock prefently afterwards was greatly improved.

580. On the contrary, when they are too
numerous, they may be deftroyed by the finger laid on them as they rife from the refting-
board (582). Great difcretion however is neceffary, left too many be killed ; for this will
prevent a proper increafe of young ; and alfo
the Queen's being fufficiently impregnated to
produce a brood the next fpring.

581. When their numbers are moderate,
the working Bees themfelves will deftroy
them the latter end of July or beginning of
Auguft ; according as the feafon may have
been : for about this time honey-gathering
failing, and the Queen having no further occafion for their fervices, a general maffacre is
ordered ; though fometimes this is not executed all at once, but gradually. Heaps of flain
may be feen before fome hives, while before
others very few, the reft being expelled.
                                                This

This only protracts their fate a few days, when famine, inexorable famine, terminates their exiftence.   At this fatal period the Workers keep guard . at the door - way, that none may re-enter their once blifsful habitat ons.

582. Sometimes it happens, though the inftances are but few, that the Drones are fo very numerous that either the other Bees would not, or could not attempt any violence againft them ; in confequence of which fo much honey is devoured in autumn as to impoverifh the Stock, and occafion its deftruction.

583. To remedy this evil, when the other Stocks kill their Drones, quietly place yourfelf by the fide of the door-way, in the middle of a fine day, and crufh every Drone with your finger as they pafs out or in.   By this means a great number may be killed in a fhort time ; but it muft be done without flurry or hurting any of the Workers ; for fhould this be done, though by chance, it will enrage them fo much that it will be beft to leave them a while, and to refume the tafk an hour or two afterwards.   Or a piece of wood may be fixed before the door-way, and a part of its bottom edge cut out deep enough to admit the Workers, but not the Drones : thofe that happen then to be out muft remain fo.   In the evening, the working Bees being all within the hives, the Drones that are without fide may be eafily deftroyed.   The board muft then be taken away, and re-fixed in the course of the next day, and in the evening

the

the fame operation is to be repeated. Two or three times will probably be fufficient to deftroy the whole; or, at leaft, fo leffen their numbers as to give the working Bees a great fuperiority, and encourage them to deftroy the now ufelefs Drones.

584. But in general the killing a few by the hand, will excite the Workers to finifh the cruel but neceffary bufinefs. Sometimes the feparating of double hives will have the fame effect; the difturbance putting them in a paffion, they will vent it upon the defencelefs Drones.

585. Thofe Stocks that foonest expel their Drones, will increafe greatly in honey, and be the boldeft and ftrongeft in defending themfelves againft all their enemies : and alfo generally produce the earlieft Swarms.

586. It being now time to reap the reward of all our care and patience, it becomes neceffary to give fuch information as will enable the Apiator to know when a ftraw-hive is full, and fit to be taken. To judge of this, ftrike in the evening with your fingers all round upon the hive ; if at the firft or fecond ftroke a great noife is made, and continued for a confiderable time, you may be fure it is full of Bees; and if upon ftriking all round the hive, and near the bottom, it feels folid to your ftrokes, you may conclude is it alfo full of honey : on the contrary, if it founds hollow, it is not full, and muft remain longer, or even until honey-gathering be over. When the Bees on ftriking make but little noife, and

that

that only for a short time, it shews there are
but few : nevertheless if it has signs of being
full of honey, it should undoubtedly be taken;
for if permitted to stand, it may be assaulted
by robbers in the autumn, or the Bees may
perish by cold in the winter.

587. When a box is placed under another,
and some combs are made therein, the Queen
commonly ceases to lay her eggs in the upper,
and begins to deposit them in the under box;
about three weeks after which time the upper
story will be destitute of brood. It is not
however to be then taken, because time must
be given for the Bees to fill the vacant cells
with honey; and also, nearly to fill the under
box for their winter store : otherwise, the upper full one being taken away, should the
honey harvest presently fail, the Stock will be
left unprovided, and must perish through famine before the next season.

588. But the Queen will continue often to
lay both in an under and upper box or hive;
being very unwilling to leave her old familiarized apartment. When hives therefore are
taken with brood in them, great circumspec-
tion must be used in separating those parts
of the combs that have brood; these must
be put into an empty hive, and placed over
or under the Stock, as may appear most
convenient. In boxes or hives with windows, it may be known in which of them
the Queen is, by introducing the sliders as
soon as an additional one becomes full. Leave
them an hour or two, in which time, if

R 4 either

either of the boxes have not a Queen, the Bees of that Box will be in the utmoſt hurry and confuſion : but if there happens to be a Queen in each, the Bees of both boxes will be quiet, and the additional one may be taken off and kept as a Swarm. If there be only one Queen, and ſhe in the old bottom hive, ſtop up the door-way, and withdraw the ſliders, which will induce her to aſcend, and make the upper one her reſidence; but for greater certainty ſtop the bottom door-way, when a box is firſt ſet on; this will not give the Bees any extraordiuary labour; for their way will be as ſhort down into the box, as up by the door-way. If after all ſhe is ſtill in the old box at taking-time, drive the Bees into an empty hive, and ſetting the door-way of that againſt the door-way of the virgin box, they will unite without further trouble.

590. I have taken at the latter end of Auguſt, both the under and upper hives of a Stock that had been raiſed three ſtories, which yet had brood and farina in both, the upper and under door-way being left open; and the ſame in other years, though the upper door-way was cloſed up. Therefore ſuch large ſtraw hives as have been raiſed, had better be left until the uſual time of taking, as then there will be the leſs riſk of their having brood.

591. The ſeparation of hives or boxes, when ſtored with honey-combs, is the moſt difficult part in the management of Bees. This has given me no little perplexity for

ſeveral

feveral years; as I. endeavoured to find out
a method, not only of performing this very
difficult operation with eafe, but alfo with
little or .no additional expence. After a variety of experiments, however, I was fuccefsful enough to hit upon three methods of
operating, all of them fufficiently practicable,
and which I here offer to my reader's choice.

592. The implements ufed in the firft
method are, a double tin-plate made fixteen
inches long and fixteen broad, by having
a flip neatly foldered on, and as even and
fmooth as poffible; one end of it fhould
be turned over a wire that it may not hurt
the hand, when fhoved between the hives.
Or milled iron, of the thicknefs of the
tin, may do. Alfo, two faws, of about
four or five inches wide, which are elaf-
tic, and at the fame time of a proper fubftance
for our purpofe, without cafting. A cloth
to throw over the hive, an empty hive; and
alfo a chair-frame, pail, tub, or the like;
fhould all be in readinefs.

593. If it be a hive or box that is to be
·taken off, juft after dark, ftop all the door-
ways and thruft in the fliders to the under
hive; then fhove the tin-plate between the
upper and lower hive, as gently as poffible,
and if it is not in a: houfe, keep your left
hand in the front, to prevent the hives from
fliding out of their place. Thruft the faws
under the plate, one on each fide, until the
edges are even with thofe of the tin. Lift
up the whole together, at the fame time extending

tending your fingers as much as poffible under the faws, to keep them clofe up to the
tin both before and behind in order to prevent its cafting, or being hollow: which it
will do without the faws, and thereby would
let the enraged Bees out, in great numbers,
greatly to your and their prejudice, all which
the faws prevent.

594. As foon as it is taken off, fet it
leifurely upon a board or hive floor, and
take it to fome out-houfe; then turn it upfide down, upon a pail, &c. floors tin and
faws altogether, without loofening them in
the turning; take off the board with one
hand, at the fame inftant extending your
other hand over the faws and tin to keep
them clofe down, until you have placed an
empty hive with the door-way previoufly
ftopped over it. Keep them fteady while
you withdraw the faws, then holding your
left hand firm upon the hive with the other
drum about four or five minutes, then take
away the tin, and drum again until you hear
by the buz that the greater part are afcended.
There is fome nicety in the management of
the faws, but a little practice will make it
very eafy: and what is more, not a Bee can
come out to hurt you. Tho' on perufal this
may feem tedious and difficult, yet I have
felt more difficulty in giving this defcription
than in the performance itfelf.

595. If there be any brood in the combs,
thefe are to be cut out, and fo placed in an
empty hive, which has bars or openings, that
when

when the hive is inverted the combs may lean
flanting againſt the ſides, and not flat againſt
each other. The hive is then to be placed
over the Stock. If there be any fragments
of combs or honey upon the top of the
Stock, they muſt be ſcraped off firſt, and
then the ſliders withdrawn. But when there
is no occaſion to ſet a hive over the Stock the
cover is to be faſtened on before the ſliders
are taken out.

596. When a hive is taken off, it ſhould
not be carried near the dwelling-houſe, for
the next day the Bees will come in great
numbers to ſearch for their ſtolen treaſure,
and be very troubleſome viſitors; many of
them will be alſo loſt in the purſuit.

597. This operation may be performed
in the day-time; but the Bees that are returning home, ſeeing the diſturbance, will
become cloſe enquirers of what is doing; as
will alſo thoſe of the other ſtands, ſo that
one or two Stocks will be the moſt any one
can poſſibly manage without being armed
cap-a-pée. Boxes in a houſe, may however
be taken by day-light without much in-
conveniency.

598. In order to render the ſaws unneceſſary, plates both of iron and pewter have been
tried; but to preſerve their evenneſs or level
when uſed, they were obliged to be made
ſo thick, that on introducing them between
the hives, the Bees were greatly more eu-
raged, and at the ſame time had ample opportunity of iſſuing out upon the Apiator.
The

The tin-plate, being fo thin, readily cuts its way and feparates the combs with greater nicety and with lefs umbrage, than can be done by a knife or any other inftrument; at the fame time confining the Bees as it paffes.

599. If a bar three inches wide be fixed in the middle of the bottoms of the hives, correfponding to the middle bar of the tops; it will render the tin-plate unneceffary; for the faws, when thruft in at the fides, will reach to the bar, and thereby clofe the whole bottom up. But that end of the bar that is to be next the door-way, muft be fpread dove-tail ways, and be bevilled down to a feather edge, otherwife it will ftop up the door-way.

600. My fecond mode of feparation is performed by a thin wainfcot board; which muft not be thicker than a quarter of an inch. It is to be of the fame dimenfions as the tin-plate (592). At one end a thin fharp piece of iron or flip of tin is to be let in, and faftened down, but muft extend or projeĉt about half an inch beyond the board. To this muft be added a piece of coarfe linen, eight inches wide, and fufficiently long to go round any hive or box you ufe, and leave about fix inches over: At one end of this cloth, and near the edge, a wire hook is to be fixed, in order to faften it and keep it tight when extended round the hive. This is the whole of the apparatus.

601. When about to ufe it in taking off or feparating a hive or box, let the cloth be

previoufly

previoufly made pretty damp; then ftopping
up the door-ways of the Stock you would
feparate, draw the *edge* of the cloth round
the fkirt of the hive, within one or two
rounds of its bottom, and fasten it tight
with the hook. The intention of wetting the
cloth is, that whenever the hive be lifted up
it may drop evenly down. An affiftant is
then to lift the hive up, (firft giving it a little twift, to loofen the combs from the under hive) juft high enough to admit the
boards being flipped under it. In doing which
great care muft be taken, not to flide it
againft or to intangle the cloth, but to pafs
freely under it, the bottom edge of the cloth,
hanging upon the board as it paffes. By
this means, though the hive be lifted fo high
that the Bees might eafily efcape, yet the
cloth, like a hanging curtain, falls upon the
board fo clofe all round, as to prevent their
paffing. The chief nicety of the operation
is in the firft introduction of the board : Be
careful therefore to lift up the cloth a little
and clap the end of the board to the joining, where it is to be introduced; fet down
the cloth upon it; the affiftant is then to
proceed as above directed. As foon as taken
off it is to be treated in the fame manner (594).

602. But it would be better if this
board be made fo as to receive a brafs-
wire net-work about ten inches fquare, with
the mefh not wide enough for a Bee to pafs
through it, and let into a rabbett, and tacked

thereto

thereto with flips of tin to keep it faft and
fo as not to rife above the level; it will then
be very convenient for the infpection of fuch
hives as have no windows; for by fetting
the board upon the frame of a chair, or
ftool, by the fide of the ftock, then ftopping
up the door-way of the hive, and lifting it,
off upon the board, you may eafily peep underneath and infpect it as long as you pleafe
with the greateft fafety. Or you may turn
it upfide down, to infpect it. After you
have fatisfied your curiofity, the door-way
is to be unftopped, and at night the Stock
placed on the ftand again. Or, it may be
lifted thereon as foon as you have done.

603. It may likewife ferve for the fame
purpofe in afcertaining the ftrength of Swarms,
and in purchafing Stocks or Swarms. So that
confidering the very trifling expence of this
whole apparatus, its fimplicity and extenfive
ufefulnefs, together with its great durability,
when taken proper care of, it may perhaps
with juftice be efteemed the beft adapted for
performing the feparation by day-light, and
as perfect as the defign will poffibly admit of.

604. But thofe who do not choofe to be
at this expence, may have cloth of fufficient
dimenfions to draw over a hive, with a circle
of about ten inches cut out of the middle;
and any kind of net or open work, that will
not permit the Bees to pafs through, fewed
therein; this will anfwer every purpofe, except *feparation.*

605. The

605. The laſt proceſs we ſhall particularize ſurpaſſes even the foregoing, both in the facility of the execution, and as requiring no expence for inſtruments.

In order to ſeparate an upper hive, on the preceding night cloſe up the door-way with a rag; and then run a thin long knife between the hives, as far as you can, ſo as to looſen the combs from the under hive. This indeed will ſomewhat irritate the Bees; but their anger will ſubſide before the next night; and the operation will be greatly facilitated by it. The next night lay a cloth upon the ground before the Stock you want to ſeparate, and ſtop up the door-way with a rag; then have a board or looſe floor ready placed by the ſide of the Stock; and, after thruſting in the ſliders, give the hive a little twiſt, lift it up, and ſet it upon the board or floor. Immediately with a knife or piece of tin, ſcrape from off the bars ſuch Bees and pieces of comb, as may be thereon, towards the front of the hive; ſo that they may fall on the cloth. By this management the looſe Bees will be preſerved. The cover is then to be put on as quick as poſſible, and the ſliders taken out; and the hive that is taken off, to be removed to an outhouſe. In the ſame manner treat as many more as you want to ſeparate; ſetting them in rows, or marking them firſt, that you may readily know to which Stocks they reſpectively belong.

606. In

606. In the morning, take the firſt and drive them into an empty hive; and as ſoon as this is done, ſtrike them out again upon a cloth placed before the hive they belong to; one end of the cloth being alſo tacked up to the reſting-board, by which they will crawl up, and re-join their companions. Then proceed to the ſecond in the ſame manner, and ſo of the reſidue.

607. But if the operation be performed in fine ſettled weather, inſtead of removing them into an out-houſe, turn them upon their ſides, (upon chairs or the like) with their bottoms or open ends to touch the reſting-boards of the Stocks; and before morning moſt of the Bees will have deſerted their own hive and got to the main Stock, without driving. Thoſe that have not, muſt have a cloth thrown over them, and be taken to a conſiderable diſtance, or to an out-houſe and drove (372). It will be neceſſary to obſerve the rules relating to the probability of there being ſeparate Swarms among them (401.)

608. Here I would remark that after ſeparation, the Bees are ſo terrified, that when turned out, they will readily paſs into another empty hive and there remain ſeveral days, until their terror is abated, though no Queen be with them. Nor will Bees quit a hive ſtored with honey or brood when ſeparated, unleſs by force; or by being left ſeveral days, in which time much of their honey will be conſumed by them; or by
neigh-

neighbouring Bees, Wafps, &c. fo that force or ftupefaction is the only eligible method.

As thofe Bees which efcape during the operation, will clufter together about the place where it is performed, they fhould be gently brufhed off as often as they fettle: but if this be not done, they will return home either the fame or the next night.

609. If *under* hives are to be taken, lift off the whole together, and fet them on a proper fupport clofe by. Then placing a frefh floor on the ftand, lift up the upper hive, and fet it thereon. The hive left, muft be managed as thofe before-mentioned (607).

610. Should a Stock be fo full of Bees, after having been feparated, as to lie out, fet an empty hive over them until the latter end of September; at which time great part of the brood having quitted their cells, and the nights being alfo cool, they will all readily go into the under hive; the empty one fhould then be taken off.

611. It muft be very obvious to perfons converfant with Bees, that nothing fo much enrages them, as being robbed of their well-earned treafure; confequently to attempt it at a time when they are moft vigorous and irritable, even in the face of the fun; muft be attended with much more difficulty and danger than when they are furprifed in the chill of the night, and under the mafk of darknefs, and when they

S   are

are incapable of feeing the invader. The
finefs alfo is generally over in this
before they are recovered from their con
nation.

612. Collateral boxes are feparated ·
more eafe than ftory boxes, as having bars
fliders to each ; whereby the Bees are fo
fined that not one can come out. But if a
bottom frame be made to the ftory b
with bars fimilar to thofe of the top (1
there will be no pre-eminency in this p·
on either fide ; for in both ways, unlefs
great care be taken to cement the join.
the moth will certainly breed between,
endanger the Stock.

613. It is poffible that by fome
management, or accident in feparating.
Queen may be killed ; (though I have fe:
met with fuch a mifchance). This
be difcovered by the tumult of the Stock
In fuch a cafe it will be heft to *unite*
to fome weak Stock, if it happens not
later than the middle of July, that they
have time to replenifh the hive. But o
wife, unite them to a well furnifhed
for the winter.

614. I have tried to take honey in a
lar method *to* that of the Greeks, as r·
by Sir George Wheeler. This on re
feems indeed very fimple and eafy ; but
ever fhall make the attempt will cer
find it both extremely troublefome and
gerous; and indeed not to be done,

Compleatly armed.   But inftead of any of
hefe methods, that of ftupefaction, before-
mentioned (389) may be ufed ; as the Apiator fhall find moft eligible and agreeable to
his own ideas.

615. Whoever would wifh to make the
moft of their Bees, fhould never let them
be in want of room ; for whenever additional hives fcem full of honey and crouded
with Bees, they muft be taken off, and
others, or glaffes, fet on, as long as there is
plenty of honey pafture, that no part of the
honey harveft may be loft. Whenever Bees
croud about the door-way, and feem idle
(after fwarming-time is over), it is a fure
fign they want enlargement.

616. In common hives this advantage is
intirely loft, efpecially, where the fituation
is very good, and the feafon favourable ; for
when the hive is once filled, the Bees can
do no more ; and therefore, take their pleafure and are very joyous. Many country
people, have not even the fagacity to raife
them by an ekeing or lift, (499). Nor indeed
can thofe cots that have fhelves one above
another, admit of it, if they had the inclination. So ill contrived are thofe receptacles
for Bees.

617. It is of great confequence to know,
or obferve, when the Bees have done honey
gathering ; for that muft be the general time
of taking up hives in the common way, as
alfo from all thofe that yet remain doubled,

on the improved plan.   For as foo⌐
the flowers decay, or ceafe to yield ⌐
lufcious fweets, the Bees will begin to
on their hive honey; and particularly t
in the doubled ones on that hive w
they do not intend to be their winter f⌐
And fhould there be many Drones left at
time, a great deal of honey will be confu
in a very few days.   No gormandizers
turtle or venifon feaft, can be more vorac
than the Drones are at this time.

618.   About the beginning of Augu
the ufual time of failure, efpecially if a ⌐
deal of rain happens to fall then.   Bu
our feafons vary, fo will the time for
⚫eafing of this bufinefs.   The fummer o⌐
year 1779 being hot and dry, the flo
were exhaufted long before the ufual per
therefore Stocks fhould have been ta
near a month fooner than moft of them ⱱ
(the heath countries excepted).   This wa⌐
reafon that   many Apiators had not
the honey they expected; becaufe they
let their Stocks ftand until great part
eaten.   For the Bees will confume ⌐
honey in the firft five or fix weeks
collecting is over,   than during the ⱱ
winter; unlefs it prove very mild.

In fome former years I have perceive⌐
Bees begin to eat the honey out of the
combs in my boxes, and out of the glaffes
were over them, as early as the 25th of
The country people are greatly deceiv⌐

this matter; for feeing the Bees continually carrying in a yellow fubftance upon their legs, they unjuftly conclude their ftore is increafing, whereas it is quite the reverfe; this fubftance being only to feed the young; and as thefe are continually increafing until October, fo much the more honey will be confumed, without the leaft advantage to the owner. For thefe very young Bees, as well as the old, are all to be fuffocated together; however late the time of taking may be. A practice as abfurd as it is unprofitable!

619. Through the windows of box hives may be readily feen, when the Bees begin to empty the cells of their honey; which will be a profitable advice with regard to all the reft, if the Apiator be provident enough to attend to it. But it is more particularly important to thofe that deftroy their Bees. For the longer the Stocks ftand in thefe circumftances the greater will be the diminution of the honey; not only by the old Bees, but alfo by the continual hatching of the young; which continues even fo late as October. But in the double mode, the detriment is perhaps not great; as all the young Bees are faved; whether taken up early or late (588).

620. The following rules and precautions fhould be obferved in taking up the Stocks in autumn.

621. Take up all that are more than two years old, for the combs after that time will

become

become black and foul, by being the re-
ceptacle of feveral repeated broods. Great
part of them are alfo crammed with ftale
and ufelefs farina, which altogether caufes a
hive to feel heavy, which when taken yields
but little honey, of a very bad quality; and
fo fmall a portion of wax as hardly to anfwer
the extraction. Old hives are alfo very fubject to the moths, which deftroy many Stocks
every year. The Bees of fuch Stocks may be
drove and added to other Stocks; or drove
into one of thofe hives you have taken of the
prefent year, that is properly filled with
honey.

622. In thefe particulars the double method has alfo a great fuperiority; for by fo
frequently fhifting the hives, the combs are
never old and black, nor ftuffed with ftale
farina and other impurities; confequently
yielding more wax and honey, and of a purer
quality. For the impurities being interfperfed
among fo great a number of cells, it is next
to impoffible to procure the honey without
fome mixture of fuch heterogeneous matter.

623. Take up all Stocks that are light, and
that are neither full of Bees or honey.

624. The greater the number of Bees in a
hive, the larger muft be the quantity of honey
to fupport them until next feafon; confequently a hive full of Bees, and but little
honey, muft be *taken*; or both Bees and honey
will be loft.

625. Stocks in autumn that are full comb-
ed down to the floors, fhould be taken: one

fuch is worth three or four others, nor will they
be fo proper to ftand; for, being quite full of
honey, in the fpring there will not be vacant
cells enough to depofit the brood in; and therefore though the Stock in fpring may be rich in
fweets, yet it will be but poor in Bees, and
confequently not likely to fwarm that feafon;
or if it fhould, the Swarm will be late and
inconfiderable. In our double method no fuch
inconvenience can arife; becaufe another hive
can be furnifhed them in the fpring as foon as
they feem to want it.

626. When a wet fummer makes honey
fcarce, keep the beft Stocks: but after a dry
and plentiful one, a moderate Stock will prove
beft for ftore.

627. No Stocks fhould be left, unlefs three
parts full of honey, as near as you can guefs.
The Bees of thofe Stocks, which have not
quantity, fhould be incorporated with others
that are well provided.

628. To judge of the weight and fullnefs
of hives, obferve the directions (586);
this may alfo be fufficiently well judged of,
by poifing them in your hand; by which
method, after a little expererience, you will be
enabled to make a proper eftimate. A me-
morandum may likewife be made of the
weight of an empty hive or box, floors and
all; by which means the weight of a Swarm
or Stock may at any time be known to a great
nicety; firft ftopping up the door-way to keep
the Bees in, and then weighing the hive.

S 4   629. Several

629. Several weak Stocks fhould be uni
into one, and placed in a good hive of hon
which will both fave the Bees, and form
excellent Stock for the next year; for w
Stocks generally perifh in the fpring. Thou
I have known inftances of weak Stocks fitu
ed near a large common, fkirted by woods,
with few others Bees in the neighbourho
that have profpered; and the enfuing fpr
proving early and favourable, have fent
large Swarms; however, it is by no me
prudent to truft to fuch contingencies.

630. It may be taken for a general rule, t
the more fcanty your pafturage, or the poc
your fituation, fo much the more popul
and richer, fhould the Stocks be that are
for the next year. Cafts in general are ne
worth keeping; but fhould be united at
(366): however, if inadvertently any
ftanding in autumn; they are to be drove
and incorporated with other Stocks; but
their combs are virgin, and great part emp
they fhould be carefully preferved as de
combs for your glaffes next year. Thefe fho
be wrapped up in paper, and depofited in fc
dark but dry place; otherwife the moth
get to them, and eat up the wax. Or fc
of the hives may be preferved, being clo
ftopped up, and taken care of as above-m
tioned. Thefe will excellently ferve for
ditions to your old Stocks the next year;
the Bees finding fo much ready-made fu
ture, will more certainly quit their old h
tations.

631.

631. If a bee-keeper refides in fuch a fituation for pafturage, as to admit of keeping a
large number of Stocks, and is defirous of fo
doing, he muft obferve to leave ftanding all
thofe each year, that are *proper* for it, until
there be the number wanted.

632. In the double methpd not only *this*
fhould be attended to, but *alfo*, not to raife
or double your hives until they fwarm, or at
leaft not before it be too late for them to
fwarm with fuccefs; or in cafe of much lying-
out.   From hence it naturally follows that the
profits muft be very limited, until the defired
increafe be made; but when that point is
once obtained, there will foon be ample intereft for all the trouble and forbearance.

633. If Stocks are left double until autumn,
the Bees will gradually afcend into the upper
box or hive, as faft as they confume the honey
of the lower one, and in proportion as the
weather grows cooler.   At this time no Bees
will guard the door-way, and therefore either
the box muft be taken, or the lower entrance
ftopped up, and the upper one opened ; otherwife wafps or robbing Bees will invade and
ruin the Stock.   From the fame principles
the Bees of a common ftraw hive, that have
been fet over a Stock inverted or turned upfide down, will *defcend* therein at the ap- ·
proach of cold, provided there be but one
Queen in both.

634. Bees greatly decreafe in autumn and
winter.   A great many that were bred in the
fpring or in the preceeding autumn, die of age;

others of hard labour, cold, and a varie
accidents ; fo that hives which were very
of Bees in the latter end of fummer, by No\
ber appear very vacant; nor will they ceaf(
minifhing, till a frefh brood begins to re
nifh the deferted cells.　This fhould fee
convincing demonftration of the *neceffit*
faving the .Stock Bees, when the hone
taken, inftead of fuffocating them.　For t
hives contain as many young Bees as thofe
preferve ; and when both united toget
form a very populous Stock for the fpr
even after the inevitable decreafe, by a nai
old age.　Some prejudiced people, how(
will always fhut their eyes againft the cle
light !

　635.　Weak Stocks may at any tim
ftrengthened by Cafts, or by holding a l
mouth'd bottle to the entrance of a very
pulous Stock, when gently ftriking the
numbers will be in a hurry to come out,
fo be catched therein.　As foon as you l
got a fufficiency, cover the mouth of
bottle with a paper, having air-holes in
at night fix the mouth of the bottle to
mouth of the hive you would replenifh, (
ing up all other openings ; the Bees will
quit the bottle to enjoy more comfortabl(
commodations ; or by fetting fome hon
combs upon a hive floor, and an empty
over them, great multitudes will be attr(
to feed : when there is a company adequa
your intention, ftop the door-way, and
confine them until night.　Take the hive g(

up, for the Bees will be collected at the top, fet them over or under the Stock you wifh to ftrengthen, and the next morning or evening take away the empty hive.

636. It is worthy of remark, that when by age or any accident a Queen dies, the Bees of that hive commonly quit it, and join themfelves to fome other Stock: but to make themfelves the more acceptable they gradually take the honey from their own hive, and carry it as a prefent to their new affociates. That fuch an accident has happened to a Stock may be known by a clear and uninterrupted humming of the Bees in the hive; by there being a great croud at the entrance (provided it is not fwarming-time); by their feeming melancholy and indolent; by their not carrying any farina; and appearing not to fight or quarrel.

637. Upon any fufpicions of this kind you may by attentively obferving, readily difcover to which of your Stocks they are carrying the treafure; for in this cafe the Bees of this Stock will be feen in an unufual hurry, and precipitately going in and out in great crouds. You may either permit them to continue carrying off the honey; or if the queenlefs Stock be your own, poife it in your hands, and if you judge there be honey enough left woith taking, at night remove it to an outhoufe, and if there be any Bees in it, drive them out into an empty hive, and fet it clofe to the Stock, mouth to mouth, and they will unite with the Stock before morning, otherwife you would lofe all the honey.

638. But

638. But if the hive be heavy, full of Bees, and perhaps a large brood, and if the Queen has not been long dead, it will be prudent to preferve it. This may be done if it be at a time, that fome of your Stocks can fpare a young Queen, or even a royal cell fealed up, which being put juft within the door-way will be received with the greateft pleafure, and will immediately encourage them to proceed to their work again. But otherwife, fet the hive over a weak Stock to incorporate with it.

639. All Stocks however do not defert their hives on this melancholy occafion ; but will continue to work, though very little, and with no fpirit; and will gradually decreafe, until at laft none are left; or perhaps before that period, will become a prey to robbers.

640. If a Queen dies, though feveral weeks after a fwarm is hived, they ufually defert their hive, and return to the mother Stock, tranfporting their honey with them.

641. As many country people, notwith-ftanding all that has been faid, or all the arguments that can be ufed, will yet remain obftinately blind to their own intereft, and annually deftroy their Bees ; therefore, that we may not be accufed of a fond partiality, we fubjoin the pernicious method.

642. Prepare a few rags dipped in melted brimftone ; thefe, at night, are to be fet on fire, and laid in a hole made in the ground near the bee-ftand. The Stock is then nimbly to be

taken

taken off and fet over the fuffocating fume, which in a very few minutes deftroys the lives and happinefs of thoufands. A few ftrokes of the hand, will caufe thofe that ftill hang among the combs to fall; which concludes the dreadful cataftophe!

Alas! ill-fated Bees! doomed to be victims of your own induftry!

643. The cruelty of this practice, the poet has adverted to, with fuch pathetic energy, that I feel myfelf conftrained to tranfcribe it.

644. " Ah fee where robb'd and murder'd, in that pit,
Lies the ftill heaving hive! at evening fnatched,
Beneath the cloud of guilt-concèaling night,
And fix'd o'er fulphur: while not dreaming ill,
The happy people, in their waxen cells,
Sat tending public cares, and planning fchemes
Of temperance, for winter poor; rejoiced
To mark, full flowing round, their copious ftores:
Sudden the dark oppreffive fteam afcends:
And us'd to milder fcents, the tender race,
By thoufands, tumble from their honey'd domes,
Convolv'd and agonizing in the duft.
And was it for this you roam'd the fpring,
Intent from flower to flower? for this you toil'd
Ceafelefs the burning fummer-heat's away?
For this in autumn fearch'd the blooming wafte,
Nor loft one funny gleam? for this fad fate?
O man! tyrannic lord! how long, how long,
Shall proftrate nature groan beneath your rage,

Awaiting renovation ? *When obliig'd,*
Muſt you deſtroy ; of their ambroſial food
Can you not borrow ; and in juſt return,
Afford them ſhelter from the wintry winds ;
Or, as the ſharp year pinches, with their own
Again regale them on ſome ſmiling day ?
See where the ſtony bottom of their town
Looks deſolate, and wild ; with here and there
A helpleſs number, who the ruin'd ſtate
Survive, lamenting weak, caſt out to death.
Thus a proud city, populous and rich,
Full of the works of peace, and high in joy,
At theatre or feaſt, or ſunk in ſleep,
(As late, PALERMO, was thy fate) is ſeiz'd
By ſome dread earthquake, and convulſive hurl'd
Sheer from the black foundation, ſtench involv'd,
Into a gulph of blue ſulphureous flame."

THOMSON's SEASONS.

645. But to countenance this yearly maſ-
ſacre, a very plauſible reaſon will be retorted
upon me. That as Bees live but a *year*, to
what purpoſe keep an old or laſt year's Stock
which will die of themſelves, tho' we do not
deſtroy them ? A hive of Bees may be compared to a city, whoſe inhabitants conſidered *ſingly* have a limited and ſhort duration,
but the City may continue populous, for a
thouſand generations. There is a continual
ſucceſſion of births, as well as of deaths.
So is it with the city of Bees, in which, at
the uſual taking-up-time, there are Bees in
every ſtage of life ; from infancy to mature
old

old age. And are in this refpect, upon
a par with any Swarm you have. The walls
of their city indeed, being made of ftraw,
foon decay, and their combs, after two years
become black and foul, and detrimental to
their future profperity, But the Bees as a
collective body, will perpetuate their focieties,
like every other clafs of creatures, as long
as the world endures.

646. But here it may be afked, if we
are never to deftroy the Bees, what is to be
done with them, when we have as many as
our fituation and pafturage will fupport?
Whenever you become fo fortunate, augment
each Stock, by re-uniting the Swarms again to
them (379). By which means your Stocks
will afford you a very great increafe of virgin
honey, or of glaffes of honey of high value.

647. When Stocks are fo populous as to
contain in each of them, as many as three
good Swarms, it is as many as will thrive
together in one hive; therefore if you have
ftill more Swarms, unite two or three of
thefe to form one Stock; and fhould you
have too many Swarms; either fell *them*, or
fome of your Stocks, or, obtain permiffion
to fet them in diftant gardens. For unfavourable feafons will come, accidents may
happen, and your home Stocks be diminifhed
and want a reinforcement.

648. Laftly, there is one way, fuper-
eminent in wifdom and beneficence; rather
than expofe your fuperfluous Stocks to a needlefs and barbarous burning, give them to

fome

fome of your poor, but deferving neighbours, who live at fuch a diftance as not to interfere with the pafturage of your own Stocks. So will the hungry be fed, and your own hearts exult in the pleafing joy of conferring a benefit on a deferving family, and faving the lives of thoufands of fuch induftrious infects.

CHAPTER XVIII.

Of Wafps, Mice, and other Deftroyers of BEES, *with the Means of Prevention.*

649. THE Bees, like many other worthy and induftrious people, are often plundered of their well earned wealth, circumvented in their honeft labours, and robbed of their peace by the idle, the vicious, and the envious.

Of this wicked fraternity, the Woodpecker or (as fome call it) the Tree-creeper ftands foremoft, feizing them without mercy, as they are gathering farina from off the fallows, in early fpring.

650. The Sparrow and that voracious and daring bird of fuperftition, the Robin Redbreaft, will peck them off the flowers, or even (as I have often feen) ftand upon their

refting

refting boards and feize them as they
iffue from their hives. Swallows catch the
Bees as they fly and carry them to their nefts.
Thefe birds fhould be deftroyed by the gun,
by limed twigs, or by giving a few pence to
children to take their nefts.

651. The moufe is a very formidable
enemy in the winter, deftroying a Stock
prefently; to which he is often tempted, by
the large and deep gafhes injudicioufly made
by country people in the edges of their hives;
by which he is admitted without obftruction or difficulty. But where this is not the
cafe, he will endeavour either to enlarge the
entrance, to make a frefh opening in the
fkirts, or fome other part, or make a lodge-
ment over the top, under the hackel, and
there form his neft; and by degrees gnaw
a way through into the center of the hive,
for the more ready fupport of himfelf and
young. Therefore where hackels are ufed
(pans are not fo liable to this inconvenience)
the tops and fkirts fhould be often examined.
The door-ways fhould alfo be leffened, by
pieces of wood, cut to proper dimenfions,
or by plaifter or clay, thereby rendering the
entrance too low for them, as well as flugs
or fnails to enter.

652. But if your Apiary be much infefted
by mice, traps fhould be fet; or a kitten,
reared and fed therein without being fuffered to come into the houfe, will at the
fame time keep the mice from your Stocks,
and the birds from your grounds, and there-

T   by

by not only preferve your Bees but alfo your garden feeds. The kitten, however, of any cat indifcriminately will not do. Cats, as well as men and monkies, have a diverfity of talents, adapted to different purpofes: therefore choofe one from a dam famous for birds and field mice, and let the kitten remain with her mother long enough to receive her inftructions, and to profit from her example. There are few quadrupeds but what give their offspring an education, fuitable to their fituation in life: whether all bipeds do fo, too, I pretend not to determine. Befides, the amorous parley of a congrefs of cats on a ftarry night will prove highly terrific to this whole fpecies of vermin.

653. When thofe flow movers, the flugs, blunder their way into a hive, it is by miftake and not by intention; (for their tafte is not fuited to relifh fuch fweets) and their company is as difagreeable to the Bees, as that of drunkards, or a debauchee, would be to a fociety of angels; however as thefe fimple infects do no harm, they will in time find their way out again. I have often feen them againft the windows of my boxes, but never found any, either dead or alive, when the boxes have been taken up.

654. Hornets in fpring, will watch the coming out of the Bees, and deftroy them. But as thefe fierce infects are few in number, and fcarce, unlefs they be nefted near the Apiary, they feldom do any great damage.

655. Wafps are extremely dangerous at
the

the latter end of fummer, and in autumn.
A Wafp is much ftronger than a Bee; fo much
fo that one will difengage himfelf from two
or three Bees, and probably with the death
of one or two of them. They are very bold,
and will frequently get into a hive in fpite
of all obftacles, and at the greateft hazard, but
are generally either killed or efcape loaded
with the choiceft .honey. But when the
weather grows fo cold that the Bees cannot
keep guard, numbers will then get in and
devour a great deal of honey, as well as
many of the Bees; and fhould the Stock be
weak, will totally deftroy it.

656. The winter's wet and cold generally
kill many of the Mother-Wafps, while in
their torpid ftate. If the fpring alfo be wet
and cold, it hinders their breeding, and
caufes the brood to be few and late. Should
the beginning of April be warm, and afterwards cold and ftormy, it will prevent their
coming out for food, and moft part of them
will be ftarved to death; freeing the Bees
from the danger of them that year. Nay a
continuance of wet, though without cold, fo
fpoils their nefts, that few Wafps will be feen
'till the middle of September. But a mild
winter, when fucceeded by a hot and dry fpring
and fummer, will fo favour their increafe,
almoft in every place, that, without diligent
attention, many Stocks will be ruined by
their depredations.

657. The heft time to prevent a great
ncreafe of their mifchievious infects is in the

fpring

fpring; by killing the Mother-Wafps, in March or April, when they firft make their appearance, among old timber and buildings, to collect fmall fhivers of the wood to form their nefts with. They alfo vifit the goofeberry and currant bufhes about that time. By deftroying *One* then, you in fact cut off a whole brood. For all the common Wafps, or Workers, die in the autumn, leaving only the females, to renew the fpecies the next year.

658. Phials of fugar and ale hung about the places of their haunts, will attract their notice, and allure them to their deftruction. But thefe muft not be placed among your Bees, for they alfo will then fip and die; therefore, wherever you fet the phials, they muft be well looked after, and if the Bees are obferved to vifit them, they muft be removed further off, or ftopt up, until honey gathering commences: at which time the Bees will be in no danger; at leaft not till the latter end of the fummer when as young Wafps beginning then to be very numerous, many perfons very imprudently place phials of fugar and ale among their bee-ftands, thereby inticing all the Wafps of the neighbourhood into their Apiaries. This however fhould be cautioufly avoided as above directed.

659. Perhaps a piece of liver, or fweet fruit put into the bottom of a long necked bottle, would be moft eligible; the Bees, not liking fuch entertainment, will then be in no danger.

670. It

670. If Wafps are feen to attempt any
Stock, efpecially in autumn, contract the
door-way by a piece of tea lead or tin, pierced
with holes, and faftened thereto, leaving
only about half an inch for the paffage of
the Bees. For a few in number can defend
a fmall pafs againft a mighty hoft. But
fhould the Bees feem remifs and not fufficiently courageous to do their duty, thruft a
fmall twig feveral times into their hive; this
will rouze and irritate them, fo as to make
them vent their fury upon the Wafps; and
the Apiator too if he does not make a
nimble retreat.

671. Wafps nefts fhould be fought out,
and as many deftroyed as poffible. For a trifle
boys will do it by way of diverfion. The
beft method of doing it, is to take half an
ounce of gunpowder, wet it juft fufficiently
to make it ftick together to burn without explofion, fimilar to what the boys call a wild-
fire. Put it into a paper, rolled up like a
quill, of about a finger's length : leaving one
end open. It muft be made up but a little
while before it be ufed, or it will grow too
dry. A little before night, or very early in
the morning, when the Wafps are all at home,
examine if there be any more paffages to
their nefts than one, and with a clump of
earth or fod, ftop them all up but one,
and have another fod in readinefs to ftop up
that alfo. Then with a match fet fire to the
end of the fquib, thruft it directly into the
hole or mouth of the neft, and immediately
ftop it up with the fod as clofe as poffible,

that

that none of the fume may efcape. In a few minutes the Wafps will be all fuffocated, but will recover again in a fhort time if expofed to the air; therefore for the greater certainty, the neft fhould be dug up with all expedition, and either burnt or buried. The neft may be dug up whole, as a natural curiofity worthy of notice. Some nefts may be very extenfive, and will therefore require double the quantity of gunpowder. If two ounces be ufed, and all the paffages well clofed up, they will be fo effectually fuffocated as to rife no more. The young brood of the nefts, will furnifh an excellent entertainment for poultry, or for fifh, if thrown into the ponds. The tops of their nefts are often within half a foot of the furface, but fometimes not within a foot or foot and a half.

672. Or a hole may be made juft over the top of their nefts, and a large quantity of water poured therein fufficient to drown them: Boiling water will quickly and effectually deftroy them, either in the ground, or among thatch, or in hollow trees. In fituations where the other methods cannot fo conveniently be purfued, fmoke and the fumes of brimftone may be introduced, in order to diflodge or fmother them.

673. Hornets hang their nefts to the eves, rafters, beams of barns, out-houfes, or in hollow trees. They are of a globular form, the external part of which, like that of the wafp's nefts, is compofed of the fibres of wood, and much refembles courfe greyifh paper. As they are

more

more formidable and dangerous than Wasps, so their numbers are proportionably smaller. The best way to effect their destruction is to take a bag large enough to slip over their nest, the mouth of which should have a running string, whereby it may easily be drawn close together.

674. On a rainy day or night, gently draw the bag over the nest so as to take the whole in, and immediately draw the strings tight, so that the nest and hornets altogether be fast included in the bag, which should be directly immersed in water, and remain an hour or more; after which it may safely be taken out, the nest pulled to pieces, and the hornets brushed off and buried; but the cakes that have brood in them, as well as those of Wasps, if given to your poultry, will prove a delicious feast.

675. The next enemy to our industrious Bees, is a large moth called the Wax-Moth, as the maggots proceeding from it devour the wax for their sustenance. The mother of these insects, is extremely attentive to discover every crevice, chasm, or hole about a hive, especially about the skirts, as a proper nests for her eggs. Should she not prove successful about the externals of the hive, she will watch an opportunity of slipping within, and of doing it there. The eggs soon become a large, white, and voracious maggot, which spins over itself a defence, and annoys the Bees. The maggots continually increase and consume the combs, until at length they pos-

sess

fefs the principal part of the hive, and the poor Bees perifh with famine, or are obliged to feparate and feek new habitations. Old ftraw hives are very fubject to the depreda-tions of thefe infects, having fuch inviting harbour for them. Boxes are not fo fubject to be infefted with them as hives, efpecially if the crevices and joinings be carefully ftop-ped up with any kind of cement : but neither boxes nor hives in the double method are li-able to fuffer much from thefe deftroyers ; for being fo often fhifted, they have not length of time, even if they get in, to prove very formidable. Which is another proof of the advantages of our changing open method.

676. However it is very proper, as a great prefervative from vermin, that all hives and boxes in the fpring and autumn be now and then lifted up, the edges rubbed and the floors cleanfed ; or, if the floors be moveable, exchanged for frefh dry ones. The beft time to do it is early in the morning ; when the Bees are chilled and drowfy, it may be done fo nimbly as to be finifhed before they have recovered themfelves enough to moleft you. This is particularly needful in the fpring, as foon as the Bees feem brifk : as dur-ing the winter there will be a collection of crumbs of wax, dead Bees, that perhaps have died of age, and other filth ; which, if not removed, will annoy the Bees and hinder their work.

677. Wood-lice are alfo great deftroyers of Bees. Bee-ftands, cots or houfes, that are

made

made of old decayed wood, harbour and encourage their breed. Old timber or old
hedges, near the hives have the fame bad tendency. During the cold of the winter and
fpring they will breed in the combs and confume the honey. They fhould be often fought
for and killed.

678. Earwigs are nightly plunderers; they
can enter by a very narrow chafm; and conceal themfelves in a very fmall fpace. They
fteal in at night, drag out Bee after Bee,
fucking out their vitals, and leave nothing but
their fkins, as fo many fcalps, emblems of
their butchery; thus gradually diminifhing
the Stock, while the Apiator is oftentimes
ignorantly wondering at the caufe. When
the fhells of Bees are perceived about
a Stock, it fhews the pernicious bufinefs is
begun. Search for the nefts of the ear-wigs,
and kill them. Clofe every crevice that may
have given them admittance: the edges of the
hives and floors, and every part of the ftands or
houfe muft be brufhed and made very clean.
Let no ftraw, rags, or cloth remain about the
hives, for thefe infects prefently conceal themfelves and fettle therein: and continue to
fearch for them every day, fo long as any
mangled Bees are found about the hive.

679. The hives and houfes fhould likewife be
often brufhed, and kept particularly free from
fpiders webs. This requires to be done almoft
every day during the fummer; or many of the
Bees will be intangled in thefe fatal nets, and
become victims to thefe folitary devourers.

680. Snails

680. Snails and Slugs fhould often be fearched for, and taken away; and nothing left about the hives to conceal them.

681. Cleanlinefs is an article of confequence in the prefervation of Bees, as may be feen by the many enemies with which they are encompaffed. Their increafe and profperity therefore, may rationally be expected to be in proportion to the care taken of them.

Riches feldom flow into the lap of indolence; but the hand of induftry fhall be rewarded with plenty.

CHAPTER XIX.

Of their WARS *and* ROBBERIES, *and Directions how to terminate or prevent them.*

682. AMAZING! can fuch epithets be applicable to the induftrious Bees? Yes, it cannot be concealed, that in fome particulars, they but too much refemble the *rational fpecies.* But which are moft to blame? Let the philofopher and the divine determine. I am only a champion for the Bees, and hope to exculpate them.

In their own habitations, and among their own communities, as well as when at their labours, Bees are as pacific as a monk in his cell : but if pinched with hunger, at a time when no provifion is to be got by *honeſt induſtry*, they become defperate and furious: " Hunger, (according to the old proverb) " will break through ftone walls :" The Bees, thus fituated, will turn robbers rather than die. But among the rulers of mankind can this neceffity be pleaded for the deluge of blood fo frequently fpilt? Alas! no!

683. Bees are never poor through want of provident care, or through indolence, on their own part ; but frequently from a long continuance of inclement weather, or from fwarming too *late*, or through an infufficiency of numbers. When by fome or all of thefe caufes, they have been prevented from re-plenifhing their hives in time, they confult upon furnifhing themfelves in an expeditious manner, by befieging and plundering the caftles of fome of the neighbourhood.

684. Being determined upon the point, fcouts are fent out to obtain intelligence, and others as fpies, who if poffible are to get in undifcovered, and to make the proper obfervations of the force, ftrength, and treafure of the Stock to be attacked. At firft the fpies are very timorous, trying to pitch here and there, and fometimes fettling at the doorway to make obfervations, and then are upon the wing again. The invaded Bees at the fame inftant, if they are ftrong in force, will

endeavour

endeavour to feize and difpatch them for their infolence; from which time a ftrong guard will always be kept at the entrance.

685. But if a few have been fo fuccefsful as to get admittance, and tafte the fweets with impunity, the next day they will form a regular attack in full force. In confequence of which, a moft fatal fcene of war and flaughter will enfue. All is fury and tumult: kill or be killed is the dreadful alternative. Thoufands on both fides prefently lie dead or dying; nor does night put an end to the conflict. Day after day, the bloody conteft is renewed, both within the hive and without. For the invaders will never give out if they have once penetrated fo far as to open the fealed combs. In this cafe nothing but fury, defolation and death is to be feen' throughout the whole domain. ·One only circumftance excepted; which is, the death of the Queen of the invaded Stock. This the enemy knows, and therefore to make fhort work, the boldeft of them endeavour to rufh, upon her as foon as poffible; in this attempt great numbers fall victims to their rafhnefs; but whenever any of them reach. her, fhe is inftantly flain. A truce is now immediately founded by both armies, and hoftilities fuddenly ccafe, an alliance is made, and the vanquifhed Bees affift in tranfporting their own treafure to the caftle of their invaders.

686. Sometimes however, the Queen, and a few of her fubjects, efcape; leaving her city and treafure in the poffeffion of the conquerors.

querors. Sad reverſe of fortune! bereaved
of every thing! what expedient can ſave
them? famine or fighting is the deplored
alternative. The laſt, as the leſſer evil, is
preferred. They become in their turn, a
ſet of lawleſs rovers. Seeking therefore another Bee-garden, they endeavour to re-
taliate their cruel treatment on ſome of theſe:
and in the attempt will ſurely die or conquer.

687. Will the ſenate decree a civic crown,
to him who ſhall point out the method of
terminating theſe ruinous wars and ſaving a
Queen.

688. Crown or no crown, we will **try**
our ſkill. Whenever ſtrange Bees are ſeen,
trying to ſlide into a hive, the door-way muſt
be contracted to half an inch, as a narrow paſſage can be eaſily defended by a few againſt
a great number. This is beſt done by ſlips
of tin or tea-lead perforated with holes; and
having a paſſage cut out at the bottom of
half an inch in length, and faſtened to the
hive by a nail at each end: or, by a piece
of elder ſlit and the pith taken out; two of
theſe are to be placed in the door-way, the
reſt plaiſtered up with clay or cow dung.
Then thruſt a twig into the hive, to rouſe
the anger of the Bees, to make them keep
guard. But if notwithſtanding this, the next
day more ſtrangers appear, ſtop the hive
quite up, leaving only ſome air-holes.

689. By theſe means, both the true and
falſe Bees will be kept out 'till evening, when
those

endeavour to feize and difpatch them for
their infolence; from which time a ftrong
guard will always be kept at the entrance.

685. But if a few have been fo fuccefsful
as to get admittance, and tafte the fweets
with impunity, the next day they will form
a regular attack in full force. In confequence
of which, a moft fatal fcene of war and
flaughter will enfue. All is fury and tumult:
kill or be killed is the dreadful alternative.
Thoufands on both fides prefently lie dead
or dying; nor does night put an end to the
conflict. Day after day, the bloody conteft is renewed, both within the hive and
without. For the invaders will never give
out if they have once penetrated fo far as to
open the fealed combs. In this cafe nothing
but fury, defolation and death is to be feen
throughout the whole domain. One only
circumftance excepted; which is, the death
of the Queen of the invaded Stock. This the
enemy knows, and therefore to make fhort
work, the boldeft of them endeavour to rufh
upon her as foon as poffible; in this attempt great numbers fall victims to their
rafhnefs; but whenever any of them reach
her, fhe is inftantly flain. A truce is now
immediately founded by both armies, and hoftilities fuddenly ccafe, an alliance is made, and
the vanquifhed Bees affift in tranfporting their
own treafure to the caftle of their invaders.

686. Sometimes however, the Queen, and
a few of her fubjects, efcape; leaving her
city and treafure in the poffeffion of the conquerors.

querors. Sad reverfe of fortune! bereaved
of every thing! what expedient can fave
them? famine or fighting is the deplored
alternative. The laft, as the leffer evil, is
preferred. They become in their turn, a
fet of lawlefs rovers. Seeking therefore another Bee-garden, they endeavour to re-
taliate their cruel treatment on fome of thefe:
and in the attempt will furely die or conquer.

687. Will the fenate decree a civic crown,
to him who fhall point out the method of
terminating thefe ruinous wars and faving a
Queen.

688. Crown or no crown, we will try
our fkill. Whenever ftrange Bees are feen,
trying to flide into a hive, the door-way muft
be contracted to half an inch, as a narrow paffage can be eafily defended by a few againft
a great number. This is beft done by flips
of tin or tea-lead perforated with holes; and
having a paffage cut out at the bottom of
half an inch in length, and faftened to the
hive by a nail at each end: or, by a piece
of elder flit and the pith taken out; two of
thefe are to be placed in the door-way, the
reft plaiftered up with clay or cow dung.
Then thruft a twig into the hive, to roufe
the anger of the Bees, to make them keep
guard. But if notwithftanding this, the next
day more ftrangers appear, ftop the hive
quite up, leaving only fome air-holes.

689. By thefe means, both the true and
falfe Bees will be kept out 'till evening, when

thofe

thofe of all the other Stocks are gone to reft: at which times the falfe Bees that are without will return home; then unftopping the hive, if any falfe be within, they will alfo iffue out and depart, and your own Bees that were kept waiting without will enter.

690. Feel the weight of your hive, and if in good condition and fufficiently ftocked with Bees, you may. venture to let it ftand a fiege the next day, provided the door-way of it be ftopped very early the next morning, fome time before any Bees are yet abroad. In confequence of this, the enemy Bees, as faft as they come and are attempting to enter, may be knocked down with a piece of thin board, or the like, and killed, by a perfon appointed on purpofe: this is to be continued without intermiffion, fo long as any of them appear. In about four, five, or fix hours, according to the number, the whole will be deftroyed. After waiting an hour longer, and no more are perceived to come, your own Bees may be let out. This confinement will make your own Bees furious againft any future affault.

691. But fhould a Stock be affaulted, and the fight begun before you are apprized of it, immediately ftop the door-way up; and at night, if you find it poor and weak, unite it to fome other Stock (380), taking care to preferve the brood (588); for being fo much weakened, it will hardly turn to any account in ftanding, or will moft likely fall-a prey to fome other invaders.

When

When a Stock is hefet day after day, it is a fign that the robbers have tafted deep of the nectar; in this cafe it will be beft to take it, if light, and to drive the Bees and unite them to another hive. But if weighty, let it ftand, and kill the robbers. If they are not killed all in one day, two or three days may be taken, keeping the Bees ftopped up all the while. But it will be beft to finifh them if poffible in one day, left in revenge for their difappointment they fhould fall upon fome of your other Stocks. A good method to prevent it, is to irritate all your other Stocks by thrufting a twig into each of their hives.

692. When a Stock has been affaulted, but prefently becomes quiet, and great crouds are obferved going in and out, it denotes the death of the Queen. If this Stock be not immediately ftopped up, all the honey will be carried away. In the evening unftop it, and about an hour afterwards, the Bees will have all quitted it, and what honey they have left will be at your fervice.

693. An attack by robbers may be eafily known by the number of dead Bees on the ground before the hive, as alfo by the crumbs of wax about the entrance of the hive, and by the Bees therein being in an uproar and confufion. Thefe battles of the Bees are more or lefs violent in proportion to the number of Bees invading or invaded, if the Stock be weak, and the robbers numerous, victory foon follows the firft affault.

694. If

694. If a Stock happen to be without a Queen, it makes but a feeble refiftance, or oftener none at all, which is alfo the cafe when late in the feafon, and the weather cold: For this occafions the bottom of the hive to be left vacant and without a guard at fuch times an half inch door-way will be fully fufficient.

695. As foon as robbers begin to fhew their evil defigns in a Bee-garden, the Bees of all your good Stocks will conftantly keep guard at the door-ways. Thefe are known to be *fuch,* by the unufual number of Bees *there,* at that feafon of the year; and by their being withdrawn as the intruders difappear. One year my Bees were obliged thus to defend their ports for near three weeks; now and then having flight fkirmifhes with the enemy; fometimes one Stock and fometimes another: but the robbers finding them all too well provided, and their reception rather too warm, retreated to a neighbour's Apiary, where they fucceeded to the ruin of two weak Stocks.

696. Thefe invaders, I afterwards underderftood, were a large Swarm of another neighbour's that did not rife until the latter end of July; and the remainder of the feafon proving very unfavourable, ftern famine drove them to thefe daring extremities.

697. It is fingular that Bees feldom or ever rob any Stocks of their own Apiary; unlefs there happen to be no weaker Stocks in the neighbourhood. Strong Stocks are very feldom

dom attacked; which is one reaſon, among many others, for keeping none but what are ſo.

698. The robbing-time is ſooner or later, according as the ſpring or ſummer is more or leſs favourable; but it is generally twice a year, ſpring and fall. In the ſpring it is not much, compared to that in the fall of the leaf. If in the ſpring the weather prove warm, the Bees are thereby invited out; but, unable to procure honey from the flowers, and their own ſtock being exhauſted, they are induced to become invaders of others property. The ſpring robbing is over the beginning of April, ſometimes early in March, according as the flowers are more or leſs fit for furniſhing ſubſiſtence.

699. But the moſt dangerous time is the latter end of July, and moſt part of Auguſt; nay, I have known ſome ſo late as the 3d of September. The Bees are moſt deſperate in autumn, knowing they can then have no other reſource. As ſoon as ever honey-gathering fails, robbing begins. Every day great attention muſt be paid to your Stocks, that the invaſion may be ſeen before much damage is done.

700. When Swarms have been plentiful, but late, and the weather indifferent, it will be a dangerous autumn; and will require a very watchful eye to be kept over the Apiary. Whenever one Stock is heſet, put your others in a proper poſture of defence, by contracting the entrances: this may prevent their being

U   put

put to the trial. A fmall force will defend a narrow pafs againft the power of a great army. However, difcretion muft be ufed in narrowing the door-ways, which muft be done only in proportion to the number of Bees at work, that they may not be too much crowded in their paffing in and out.

701. When a hive of any force begins to be affaulted, the Bees become very irritable and quarrelfome ; they will then fting the Apiator, though familiar with, and fond of him at other times.

702. A weak Stock that is in danger, had better be united to another weak Stock (if you have fuch a one) that has honey enough for both : by this means they will form a competent Stock to withftand the enemy, to refift the feverity of the winter's cold, and the fcantinefs of an auftere fpring,

C H A P,

CHAPTER XX.

On the great Mortality of BEES *in Winter and Spring ; the cause investigated, and how to prevent it : also the manner of feeding them to the best advantage.*

703. THE articles of this chapter are of great importance, as some hundred Stocks are lost every year, through ignorance or inattention to these points. Nor as yet, hath the practice been reduced to any degree of certainty, or well adapted to public use ; writers having differed greatly upon a subject which, in appearance, seems of no difficulty. However it is hoped, the experiments I have tried will enable me to remove all the difficulties.

704. It must be considered, that Bees are capable of resisting cold only to a certain degree. That which reduces them to a lethargic, or torpid state, is salutary; for thereby becoming motionless, perspiration, and circulation of the fluids, are stopped, and the consequent dissipation prevented; in this state any fresh supply of sustenance is unnecessary. But the warm air of the spring, dissolving their coagulated fluids, restores them again to activity and to the impulse of hunger.

705. But should they be exposed to such a degree of cold, as to coagulate their fluids

beyond

beyond the influence of heat to reftore, they are in a hopelefs ftate, and cannot be revivified.

706. But here occurs the grand difficulty; viz. that of knowing what degree of cold will keep Bees in the beneficial torpid ftate, without injuring them. It muft be allowed that this is far from being a fixed point, and not eafily to be afcertained. But though it is not prudent to walk too near a precipice, efpecially with a giddy head, yet we may fafely approach it at fome yards diftance. We hope, therefore, to fhew in the fequel, that any common capacity, may readily avoid each dangerous extreme, without being either a philofopher or a conjurer. Nor is there any neceffity for a thermometer* to regulate to a nicety this part of ruftic œconomy.

707. Though a Bee, fingle and at *reft,* be not able to refift a degree of cold much milder than that which congeals water, and will die in a temperament mild enough for moft other infects of our climate; yet by *motion* it can acquire fuch a heat as will enable it to refift an air that has made me quake on going into it from a warm room.

708. It is well known that exercife will preferve the human body in a genial comfortable glow of warmth, though in an air fo cold as otherwife would prove nearly fatal. The Bees experience a fimilar influence from motion.   709. When

---

* *Natural Hiftory of Bees,* p. 408.

. 709. When they are collected into a compact body, as is their ufual manner in their
hives, though then motionlefs, they retain,
by their numbers, a very confiderable heat,
and which increafes many degrees foon after,
and in proportion to any motion commenced.
To elucidate my meaning, let me compare a
hive to a barn, on entering which fingly, in a
cold winter's day, our bodies will be chilled,
and we fhall feel ourfelves very uncomfortable;
but fhould it be foon filled with people we
fhould prefently become not only warm but
even hot.

710. Though from the difference of fituations, difpofitions of places, and qualities
of hives, we cannot form one certain rule,
yet this we may fafely infer, that the greater
quantity of Bees there is in a hive, the lefs
danger they will be in of fuffering by cold.
For which reafon, while a populous Stock
will remain healthy, a poor one fhall be
perifhing. One hive fhall be thrown into a
ufeful lethargy by the fame cold weather,
which would fcarcely diminifh the heat of
another. And whilft the Bees in one hive,
fhall be confuming their provifions, thofe
in another fhall be expiring with cold.

711. From hence appears the neceffity of
a moderately fized hive (viz. half a bufhel)
for their winter refidence, for if too fmall
they will, in our *common* winters, be too
crouded and too warm : or if the hive be
over large, they will not be numerous enough
to keep up the falutary ftandard of health

U 3   fufficient

fufficient to counteract a cold, damp, and
noxious air. Many have been the inventions
of ingenious gentlemen to preferve Bees in
this healthy medium. It may be ufeful to give
a few remarks upon thofe of moft note.

712. And firft of placing Stocks in ice-
houfes. The impracticability of this method
with refpect to general ufe needs, fcarcely to
be pointed out to any one; it is fufficiently
obvious at the very firft view. None but the
opulent poffefs any; and it is by no means
probable, that any nobleman or gentleman in
the kingdom will permit the farmers and
cottagers to depofit their Bee Stocks in
their ice-houfes. The benefit arifing from
it alfo, would not repay the trouble, even
upon the fuppofition of a more certain prefervation; which yet is very doubtful: for
unlefs the Bees of each Stock were very
numerous, the icy coldnefs would certainly congeal their fluids beyond the limits
of a future diffolubility.

713. The next method, and which feems
more feafible*, is that of furrounding the
hives every way, with dry earth or fand, between hurdles, or in cafks, with a little trunk
to extend beyond the earth as a paffage for
the Bees: a pan of honey, properly covered
being firft placed underneath the hives.

714. To this it may be objected, that a
good Stock by this treatment will be kept
too

---

* *Natural Hiftory of Bees.*

too warm; fo much fo indeed, that unlefs
the winter prove very fevere, the Bees will
not be in a torpid ftate during any part of
it, and confequently confume a large quantity
of honey : which had they ftood expofed to
the weather, would have been faved. On
the contrary, fhould the winter be attended
with a cold, damp, and foggy air, both the
good and the bad Stocks will be in danger
from the abforbing power of the earth, which
fucks in like a fponge fuch noxious damps,
and thus the hives will be filled with putrid
exhalations, together with the confined and putrid perfpiration of the Bees themfelves. This
may be feen, though in a much lefs degree,
on the infide of the windows of box hives in
fuch weather. Under fuch circumftances how
is it poffible for the Bees to be otherwife than
weak and fickly? And indeed this will be
found to be the cafe ; the poor infects are
afflicted with the flux, and being too weak
to go abroad to empty themfelves they foil
each other as they hang, and alfo the floor ;
by thefe means the vicious quality of the confined air being increafed, the whole com-
munity at length becomes infected ; and the
Bees perifh by the very means that were intended for their prefervation : fome of the
more vigorous lighting upon the floor, become immediately fo chilled, and fo befineared
with the clammy excrement that, not being
able to rife, they prefently expire. Upon the
whole, this appears too hazardous for public
ufe, to fay nothing of the trouble and expence.

U 4 715. But

715. But further, suppofing they are hereby kept fo *warm* and dry as to obviate thefe inconveniences, will they not fuffer equally by over feeding? And will they not alfo confume more fupplied honey, during the winter and fpring, than the profits arifing from them will counter-balance, fhould they profper?

716. Another method has been propofed of fhutting Stocks up in a dark, cold out-houfe, from the middle of September to the middle of April,* as an improvement upon Reameaur's method of inclofing them in cafks (713).

717. This no doubt is much more prac-ticable: but from many experiments I tried this way, I perceived not the leaft fuperior advantage; and more frequently the contrary. To which I will add that the keeping them en-tirely fhut up, and inactive for feven months, is by no means what is wanted: Three months, at moft will fuffice for their indolence. But to take four months more of their breeding time, when they generally are anxious to repair their winter lofs, by raifing a young and fturdy brood againft the harveft of honey, feems a very prepofterous fcheme of management. The author was certainly too precipitate in pub-lifhing a method founded upon a fingle ex-periment, and that not in his favour; for he allows, that if his mode fhould be eligible, the degree of care neceffary in conducting it,

can

---

* *Article* 15*th, of De Re Ruftica.*

can fcarcely be expeded from fervants and
gardeners, who have many other things
to attend to; and I add much lefs can it
be expeded from farmers and cottagers;
befides, this gentleman did not confider, that
the Queen often begins to breed the beginning
of February, (if the Bees have liberty to
fetch in farina); and during this month, and
the fucceeding one of March, there is generally
a prodigious increafe of young. It is commonly believed that a Bee is twenty days
in hatching, and that the maggots are fed
with frefh farina, without which they perifh.
Therefore if the Bees be confined until the
middle of April, it will be twenty days before a fingle Bee is bred, which brings it to
the 5th of May, and confequently there muft
be a lofs of more than three months brood,
that is to fay, of a complete Swarm : for
many Swarms rife in April, and even at the
beginning of it, in favourable feafons. Whereas by the fhutting-up method, the Swarms
muft be very late, and frequently there will
be none at all. Nor can the three months
lofs of time be ever regained, fo as to render
fuch a Stock equal to one that has got fo
many thoufands of young vigorous Bees ready
to colled the honey as foon as it appears;
while they themfelves are chiefly employed
in rearing brood; and have but few labourers
to fpare for other work.

718. Befides, however fuch Stocks may
be confined, yet whenever the air is warm,
it will pervade their hives, and roufe the Bees

to

to action. They will then, by their difcon‑
tented notes, fhew how impatient they are of
the conftraint; and how eager to tafte the
fweets of the frefh air, to empty themfelves
abroad, and to renew their labours at the
time appointed by nature herfelf.

719. From what has been now offered,
the inference feems to be, that bad confe‑
quences muft arife from fhutting up Bees
indifcriminately. Perhaps, however, in ex‑
traordinary frofty weather, or deep fnows, it
may be of fervice to ftop up the door-ways of
hives, as they ftand; leaving only a fmall air‑
hole, and taking care that they be all opened
again as foon as the froft breaks.

720. Having tried a great number of ex‑
periments to afcertain the beft method of
prefervation, it appears to me that a good
Stock, viz. one well filled with honey and
numerous in Bees, in a found hive, and co‑
vered with a pan, hackel, or the like, will
ftand our ufual winters, without any detri‑
ment, and be more healthy, than by any
other treatment. But when the froft is un‑
commonly fevere, a fack, bag, or pea-halm,
thrown over them, during its continuance,
is all the additional attention neceffary.

721. The recital of fome obfervations will
illuftrate this more diftinctly. In the hard
froft, and deep fnow, of january 1776, the
barometer was between twenty-nine and thirty
degrees; and the thermometer from fifteen to
twenty-eight; fome days it was at the loweft
numbers; and the weather was more in‑
tenfely

tenſely cold than in 1740. During this froſt
two of my box Stocks, having no additional
covering, periſhed. Two weak Stocks, in ſtraw
hives on ſtands, ſuffered the ſame fate; theſe
had no covering except a plumb baſket.
All my other Stocks being rich, ſurvived
the ſeverity of the winter and flouriſhed
abundantly.

722. It is worth notice, that one of the
boxes that failed, had, notwithſtanding, plenty.
of Bees and of ſealed honey; and, what is
ſtill more extraordinary, the honey was liquid
and tranſparent, at the termination of the
froſt, when I took it. Upon examination I
found that the top of this box had warped,
and thereby let in too much cold air.

723. In confirmation that ſevere froſt will
not injure Bees, we appeal to Siberia and
Ruſſia; where the winters are many degrees
colder than any we have; where the hives
are formed of the bark of trees, which are
not ſo warm as our ſtraw hives; and alſo,
where Bees inhabit hollow trees, as with us;
and yet, notwithſtanding all theſe ſeeming impediments, are known to thrive; but whether,
equally with ours, hive for hive, remains to
be yet aſcertained.

724. Froſt is undoubtedly beneficial to the
Bees as well as to the owner, while only ſo
ſevere as to keep them motionleſs during the
winter; for in this caſe moſt part of their
honey will be ſaved; as they will not be
capable of feeding, 'till near the return of the
flowery ſweets furniſhing a freſh ſupply. Early

Swarms are likewife caufed by this fituation.
But the inftability of our climate, and the
frequent and often fudden tranfitions from
one extreme to another, prove more fatal to
the delicate conftitutions of the Bees than
a feries of any one kind of weather whatever.
Valetudinarians among us too frequently
fuffer from the fame caufe.

725. In contraft to the foregoing obfervation; the fpring of the fucceeding year viz.
1777, was too cold for the Bees to collect
any farina; I did not obferve them to carry
any in until the 16th of March, and then
but little, and thus it continued until the latter
end of April. This prevented the ufual increafe of brood. Nor indeed was the fummer
more propitious for the collection of honey.
In the beginning of May feveral weak Stocks
died, and the weather permitted little or no
forraging till the 26th of May, 'till which time
my Bees all partook of a general feeding, or
common table (760). Moft part of June was
cold, the 21ft of which a weak Stock died.
So that I was obliged to renew the feeding,
and continue it until July: the laft day of
which was fo cold, wet, and windy, as to
require fires being made in the parlours.
And yet, on that day, a neighbour's Swarm
rofe. The whole fummer proved fo unfavourable that none of my Stocks got a
fourth part of what would be neceffary for
their winter ftore. To complete the mif-
fortune, the enfuing autumn and winter
were alfo very unkindly, being replete with

damp

damp foggy air : this, as all the Stocks were
very poor, and fcanty of numbers, affected the
weakeft very feverely, caufing a fatal purging,
which deftroyed many of them before I
could find a remedy. The following fucceeded to my wifhes, and is the more valuable, as it is within the reach of the meaneft
cottager.

726. Incorporate two or three weak Stocks
into one (409, 629), joining them to that
which has the moft honey. This operation
fhould be performed in a warm room, if the
feafon be very cold.

727. The ftock-hive is then to be fet upon a
very clean and dry floor, on which coal-afhes
(or, where thefe cannot be procured, wood-
afhes will perhaps do) are to be laid about
an inch thick, and over thefe clean dry ftraw.
This management keeps the hive fufficiently
dry and warm at the bottom, and when the
Bees happen to dung, it paffes among the
ftraw, fo as not to foil or chill them when
they fall down, or alight. At the fame time
the hives muft be well covered with facks,
cloths, pea-haulms, or the like, fo as to keep
the whole hive moderately warm : but a fmall
opening is to be left for their paffing out,
whenever the mildnefs of the air or their occafions invite them. As the ftraw will keep
the edges of the hives hollow from the floor,
where pans are not ufed to cover them, in
lieu thereof bricks or large ftones muft be
laid on the tops, fufficient to keep the hives
clofe down to the floors.

728. By

728. By this fimple and eafy management I preferved all the reft of my Stocks, and they requited me by their future profperous labour. Flannels or woollen cloths laid on the floors of the hives, were found of no fervice. The ftraw and the afhes feem the beft antidote to the pernicious effects of cold foggy air, which I take to be the only *one* that is dangerous to Bees; preferve them from this and keep your hives full, and the froft will bite in vain.

729. Boxes are not near fo warm as ftraw-hives, therefore in hard weather they fhould have a bag or ftraw laid over them. But a medium muft be obferved, not to keep them fo warm, as to be in motion.

730. There is no fort of danger in permitting the Bees to fally out as they like. They are the beft judges of the degree of cold they can bear. The only danger is when the ground is covered with fnow, and at the fame time a fmiling fun invites them out to tafte its benign influence; but no fooner are the unfortunate Bees out, than they behold the face of nature intirely changed, they are confufed and confounded, they fall, and are immediately chilled to death by the fnow. The remedy is to fhade the door-ways from the rays of the fun, during this weather; or ftop them up, leaving only air-holes until the fnow is entirely gone.

731. When Bees have fallen to the bottom of the hive, and feem motionlefs or dead, it is a fign the Stock wants more warmth: in this

cafe,

cafe it will perish, unlefs immediately removed into a warm-room, and placed near
the fire until the Bees begin to revive, then
ftop up the door-way. fo that none can come
out, and at night put them on a prepared floor
(726) and cover them up warm.

732. Mr. Wildman directs that to preferve
the Bees in one of his boxes, which has windows in three of the fides, the glafs is to be
taken out in October, and pieces of blotting-
paper, or foft flannel, placed in lieu thereof,
This appears to me a troublefome and needlefs bufinefs; for my boxes, with like panes
of glafs, ftood in my Bee-houfe (which is
not very clofe) during a froft that was fevere enough to freeze water in the houfe,
and yet received no harm: though nothing
was done but covering the box with a bag:
neither is it neceffary to have any flips of wood
placed againft the glafs to prevent the Bees
from fixing their combs thereto. The glafs
will bear the preffure of the combs without
fuch affiftance: which will alfo prevent that
perfect infpection for which the windows
were chiefly intended. Perhaps Mr. Wildman trufted to theory, and did not try a box
without thofe precautions. Hence it is that the
world is peftered with theoretic deductions,
unfupported by practical demonftrations.

733. It is very uncertain whether a weak
Stock can be preferved by all the pains, expence, and care you can beftow; for it is an
hundred to one, but that it will be labour loft;
fuppofing it fucceeds, the produce of fuch
a feeble

a feeble Stock the next fummer, either as to fwarming or honey, will not be equal to the expence and attendance; nor adequate to what they would have furnifhed, if they had been united to a good Stock. It muft be folly to prefer a hazardous chance to an apparent certainty; for which reafon it has been directed (627) to keep no weak Stocks, but to incorporate them in the autumn.

734. Bees in weak Stocks may not unaptly be compared to a young trader, who from the ill-judged pride or parfimony of a parent is placed with a fmall capital, in a bufinefs that required a large one; but the means being difproportionate to the end, a bankruptcy is inevitable; notwithftanding the moft affiduous and conftant exertion of fkill, induftry, temperance, and frugality.

735. We come now to the article of *Feeding*; which in fome inftances is abfolutely neceffary; for it may fometimes happen that a fummer (fuch as was that of 1777) fhall prove fo very unfavourable as to furnifh little or no honey; confequently *no* Stock can have a fufficiency for the winter.

736. This is a trying cafe, for being both weak and poor, they demand our utmoft care they will require to be kept warm, and to be conftantly, though moderately fed. Where there are feveral poor Stocks, this will be very troublefome, and uncertain in the event; for if the feeding happens to be neglected but two or three days, it is moft likely that they will all perifh, (752).

737. But

737. But by uniting feveral of thefe together (even at that feafon) this attendance is greatly leffened; and the Bees being alfo fufficiently numerous to keep up a comfortable warmth, they can defcend without danger, to partake of the daily bounty beftowed upon them, and thereby efcape thofe two formidable enemies, cold and hunger.

738. The mode and matter with which they are to be fed, require a careful difcuffion, as errors in thefe have done much mifchief. Bees have been fed, with one or more of the following articles, according as whim, fuperftition, or fancy has directed; falt, bean-flour, fweet-wort, treacle, beergrounds, dead birds, toaft and honey, fruit, fugar, honey, and farina, with many others that I fuppofe have not come to my knowledge. Out of this farrago I fhall only remark upon honey, farina, and fugar; the reft I confider either as ufelefs or pernicious.

739. Several late authors have fuppofed honey the only and beft food for Bees. This Monfieur Reaumur difputes, from the inftances of Stocks dying, tho' furrounded with combs of honey; from whence he draws the conclufion, that honey alone is too lax a diet unlefs affifted by farina, which he characterizes as the *true bee-bread.* I apprehend the objections are as great againft the farina as the honey; for if farina be abfolutely *neceffary,* how is it that more Bees die in fpring, when plenty of frefh farina may be procured, than at any other feafon of the year? Many of

X   my

my Stocks have often failed, although they had a fufficiency both of *honey* and *farina*.

740. Befides, I have often fupplied poor Stocks with double the quantity of honey to what any of my other Stocks had in their hives, and yet they perifhed in the fpring.*

741. As honey ferved rather to increafe the malady than cure it, I next tried fugar, both of different forts, and mixed with water and with ale, boiled and unboiled: but all was found ineffectual, though the Bees at the fame time were properly fecured from cold. I then concluded the error muft arife from too great a profufion in the fupply of the food; taking the hint from the

---

* *Perhaps the following experiment, as being new, may not be unpleafing to the reader. To fupply the poor Bees (as I then thought) in the beft manner, I hung combs of honey to the bars of an empty hive by bits of very narrow tape: at firft I was anxious left they fhould gnaw the tapes afunder, before they had repaired and fixed the combs; and thereby let them tumble down to the bottom and crufh many to death: however, they agreeably deceived me; for they firft faftened the combs in their ufual manner, and then gnawed the tapes afunder, and drew them out of their hives, ten or twelve of them at a tape, like failors pulling at a rope. This experiment I repeated feveral times, with always the fame refult. Here it might be afked, how came the Bees by this fagacity? muft they not have reafoned upon the cafe, and that fuch a fingular one as neither they nor their predeceffors had ever feen before. Was it inftinct? or was it not rather the effect of thought? How infinitely diver- fified may this thinking fomething be! from the loweft de- gree of animation to that of a Newton; and from a Newton, by imperceptible gradations, to that of angels and archangels, even to infinite incomprehenfibility! But this is a point of too much fublimity for mortals to reach.*

the experiments in which the Bees died,
though furnifh'ed with combs enough to fupport two populous Stocks.

742. An experiment of Reaumur's, feems
to fix this point beyond difpute. " Some
" Bees were placed in a hive without
" leaving them any honey-combs, or even
" the liberty of feeking their food abroad.
" To compenfate for this they were fup-
" plied with pure honey. At firft they were
" fed *fparingly,* which kept them alive a-
" bove three weeks: however, I was after-
" wards too bounteous; they eating *fo much,*
" that they foon had *purgings*; they wetted
" one another; and fome days after, they all
" died; and were as wet on this occafion as
" as if they had been dipped in water thick-
" ened with honey."

743. From thefe inftances, we may conclude Bees are like fome creatures of a more
noble fpecies, who, not contented with a temperate enjoyment of abundance, feed to excefs, and thereby lay a fure foundation for
numberlefs difeafes, often terminating in an
untimely and painful death.

744. Thus the Bees, allured by a fudden
and too large fupply at once, and obtained
without either labour or pains, gorge themfelves fo as to bring on a fatal laxity; the very
difeafe your care and kindnefs intended to prevent. It is probable, however, that the purging
does not always arife folely from excefs, but
fometimes from a previous weaknefs, attended
with a retention of the perfpirable matter,

X 2 ccafioned

occafioned by a damp cold air. The Bees, incapable of difengaging themfelves from each other, are under the neceffity of emptying themfelves as they hang cluftered together, thereby foiling thofe beneath; the whole clufter at length becomes infected; the floor is bedewed with the excrement, which befmears thofe that fall on it; and at the fame time the air of the hive is rendered more noxious; which haftens the deftruction of the whole.

745. For the cure, Reaumur directs a comb of crude honey (by which he means farina) to be given to the fick Bees; but this I have found by experience to be of no real benefit. Rufden recommends falt and honey; but fo far from liking a compofition of this fort, they will be difpleafed with the offer. It has been afferted, that Bees will eat falt, and that they thrive beft near the fea. It may be fo, but not becaufe they fuck the falt water; it is not uncommon to afcribe effects to wrong caufes. I have often tried them with falt, and with falt-water; but inftead of pleafing, it manifeftly offended them. The only effectual method of cure is to take away the caufe; to keep none but populous hives; and, if there be occafion, to feed them, though but fparingly.

746. Whenever a number of Bees are feen dead at the bottom of the hive, it is a fign that their fituation is either too cold, too damp, or that they are famifhing (772). Tho' fometimes Bees may be found upon the floor, that have died merely of old age; for

as they enter the stage of life at different periods of the spring and summer, they will
depart from it also in all the various seasons
of the year. Nor hath the brightest genius,
by the deepest researches, yet discovered a spe-
cific to change the decrepitude of age into the
blooming vigour of youth and beauty. It is
divine temperance alone that is able to procure a happy longevity, though it cannot
communicate immortality.

747. Bees may be fed either with honey
or sugar. The last answers full as well, if
not better, than honey. I generally feed
with sugar, as being much cheaper here than
honey. But in some counties it may often
happen, that honey is not so valuable as
sugar, consequently the former is to be preferred.

748. Honey, after it has been some time
taken out of the combs, becomes grainy and
hard; and is then not digestible by the
Bees, unless reduced to the same liquid state
as when taken from the hives. This may be
done by putting a quarter of a pint of *mild* ale
to a pound and an half of honey, and mixing
it well together; this will be of a similar con-
sistence with hive honey, and will not grow
seedy again. Warder directs water, (perhaps
the Doctor was a water drinker) but I know
by frequent trial, that ale is more agreeable to
the Bees; not that they will be tipsey with
it, but it acts on them as a cordial, gives them
more vigour, they thrive upon it, and look
plump and shining.

X 3   749. If

749. If fugar be ufed, it fhould be of the coarfeft and dampeft kind; that which feels fandy or grainy is improper, and for the fame reafon as grainy honey. For as the Bees receive their food by licking it with their tongues, as dogs lap, and not by fucking or grinding, therefore when fuch fugar is given them, the hard grains are left until a moift air diffolves them. The fugar muft therefore be damped with a little ale, not boiled, nor with fo much as to make it run. Sometimes, however, in the early part of the fpring, the Bees of a Stock are weak and fickly; they then require more of the cordial quality of the ale, and cannot feed on the fugar unlefs made as liquid as the honey; (I fpeak from experience) but as the fpring advances they grow ftronger, and require it to be thicker.

750. The fediment of treacle cafks, or the grounds of beer, will give the Bees a loofenefs, fo will fweet-wort, if given in great quantities and often; but a little, when you brew, will be an acceptable change.

751. That *ale and fugar* will preferve Bees, feems evident from an experiment made in May, 1773. The greater part of that month had been wet and cold, after a long feafon of moderate froft and funny days. At that time there was plenty of borage, apple, and other bloffoms; yet two of my Stocks, that were full of Bees, were near perifhing of famine; fome hundreds lay on the ground before the hive, living, but too much chilled to rife. They were taken up, and carried to a proper diftance

diſtance from the fire, where they preſently revived. I then fed them with ſugar and ale, and returned them to the Stocks, which were conſtantly fed with the ſame, though but ſparingly, until honey-gathering commenced; and they afterwards amply recompenced me for my aſſiſtance.

752. I have at other times treated Stocks in the ſame manner. But what aſcertains the propriety of this meaſure, beyond a poſſibility of doubt is, that having only neglected to feed them three or four days . they have periſhed. Doubtleſs, this is attended with ſome trouble; ſo is feeding poultry and pigs: let the farmer's wife refrain from it three or four days, and ſee how fat they will be.

753. The manner of furniſhing the food becomes our next conſideration. Warder condemns the country dames for what he thinks a very deſtructive manner of feeding. But I have tried both his method and theirs, and found my Bees died when fed as he directs, while the good women preſerved theirs by their uſual means.

754. But to be more particular: the ſetting plates of honey under hives is attended with many inconveniences. Lifting the hive up, in order to ſet the plate under, and afterwards to take it away, greatly irritates the Bees; and each time the Apiator will be ſlung, as alſo ſome of the Bees cruſhed under the plate, and under the edge of the hives. Alſo as the combs in general extend down to, and are faſtened to the floor, there is con-

X 4 ſequently.

fequently no room for the plate to ftand
under without damaging the combs, or preventing the hive from fetting clofe to the
floor. Befides which, the method of laying
a paper with holes in it over the plate of
honey, is certainly an improper one, as the
paper will be apt to flip afide, or wrinkle up,
fo that the Bees will get under, and numbers
of them be fmothered in the honey. Old
combs fet under, is a preferable method to
the above, but is not free from fome of thefe
objections.

755. Mr. Wildman contrived a circular
little box, with a mouth to it, to enter a
little way into the door-way of the hive. I
diflike it, as being too expenfive; as ftanding
expofed to the cold out of the hive; as the
honey is to be covered with paper, which
makes it liable to the foregoing objections:
and laftly, as the Bees are obliged to leave
the warm hive to feed in the box.

756. I have tried perforated tin tubes, let
into the top of the hives, and into the fides;
tin trunks, and a variety of other contrivances, but find none equal to the fimple,
eafy, and cheap method of kexes: thefe are
troughs made of the joints of any plant that is
pithy or hollow; thofe of elder are the beft of
all for this purpofe. Select thofe joints that are
longeft, and not more than one year's growth;
take the rind or bark off, as alfo the upper
part, 'till the joint is fhallow enough to flide in
at the door-ways of the hives, leaving about
two inches at one end uncut, as a handle, and
at the other end a little of the pith, to prevent
the

the fugar or honey from fliding out into the hive. Make the under part a little flat, that it may reft fteady, and not be liable to turn afide, which it will be apt to do if left in its natural roundnefs, and thereby the hive floor will be foiled with the fugar, to the detriment of the Bees.

757. As thefe little troughs are but narrow, the Bees will ftand on the edges, and feed out of them, equally as fafe as at their combs; and as their length is fix, feven, or eight inches, their food is introduced into the warm part of the hive. By thefe means they are not too much chilled by any degree of coldnefs in the air that makes it neceffary for them to feed. For in a very cold ftate of the atmofphere they are torpid, and take no food at all (704).

758. One of thefe troughs, or kexes, full, is enough, in general, to fupply any Stock twenty-four hours. They fhould be placed in the hive every evening, and changed the next. Such Stocks as do not nearly confume the quantity, fhould have lefs given them at a time, that there may be no danger of their overcharging themfelves (741).

759. This method of feeding is only neceffary when the weather is not mild enough for the Bees to come out of their hives to feed; or when you want to fupply only a particular hive or hives; or, if feeding become neceffary before the Wafps are gone. But be fure never to place the food at the entrance of the hive; for, if there be any poor Stocks in the neighbourhood,

bourhood, they will be allured to partake of it with your own Bees, and thus occasion the death of many every day by their quarrels. This may be called *Separate Feeding*.

760. But to shorten the trouble, when the weather is sufficiently mild, either in autumn or spring, as occasion may be, and the Bees seem active, all the Stocks may be fed at once; which is called *Public Feeding*. This is best done by procuring a piece of some compact wood, as ash, oak, &c. about eight inches long, four wide, and an inch thick at least; let this be made full of circular holes by an auger, or rather a center bit, each hole to be half an inch in diameter, and a quarter of an inch distant from each other, and as deep as the wood will admit, but so as to hold water. If there be any inconvenience in getting the holes made, the board may have grooves cut out, of half an inch in width, leaving wood enough at each end to stop the sugar from running out; or, if cut quite through it must be stopped with putty.

761. These instruments, (which I shall call feeders, especially the first kind of them, as in some degree, resembling honey-combs) the Bees will cordially feed out of without danger of besmearing themselves, which they generally do when platters or plates are set, however well regulated; and without occasioning any dangerous quarrels among them; for though they will not stab each other, yet they will sometimes box and bite, and tumble one another about among their food, so as to

destroy

deſtroy many lives, when they cannot get
readily at it.   The ſugar or honey may be
made thinner for theſe public feedings than
for the private, ſo thin indeed as to pour thro'
a tea-pot, which will be the moſt convenient
inſtrument to fill the holes with.

762. Theſe feeders ſhould be ſet upon a
ſtand of ſome ſort, about the middle of the
Apiary, and placed under an old hive, pan,
or the like, leaving an ample vacancy for
their entrance at the bottom ; for if not pro-
tected from the wet, a ſudden ſhower may
prove deſtructive to many hundred Bees.
One of theſe feeders, filled, is ſufficient for
twelve Stocks for a day's ſupply.

763. There is no preciſely determining the
quantity of honey or ſugar neceſſary to ſupport a Stock through the winter and ſpring.
The numbers are ſo different in different
Stocks, and the weather ſo various, that one
year may require double that of another,
Sixteen pounds of ſugar and one quart of ale
ſuſtained twelve of my poor Stocks through
the autumn and until the ſucceeding May ;
at which time they deſerted the ſugar, and
began to provide for themſelves.

764. By this method of feeding the whole
expence of feeding twelve poor Stocks thro'
a very dreary ſeaſon, amounted only to five
ſhillings and eight-pence, whereas ſix, eight,
or ten pounds of honey have been given to
ſingle Stocks, upon another plan, and yet ſuch
Stocks periſhed.

765. In

765. In the spring all Stocks should be examined, by poising them between your hands, whether they be light or no. This should be done as soon as they begin to breed, for afterwards, the additional weight of the brood and farina, will induce you to think they are rich in honey, when at the same time, they may have little or none in their hives, and may perish for mere want, *seemingly* in the midst of plenty. But by examining them early, you will be certain to distinguish such as will want your help, 'till honey pasture comes in, from those that do not.

766. If any of your neighbours keep Bees, their Stocks will partake of the public treat, equally with your own. In such a case, and when your Stocks are poor, and *must* be fed, the separate feeding is to be preferred, except when the air is too cold for any strange Bees to come so far from home. You may easily see, by the flight of the Bees, whether any come from the surrounding quarters.

767. Public feeding will be extremely dangerous to your Apiary, if used before the time of robbing be over, as it will intice the robbers to assault some of your Stocks.

768. There is no danger of your own Bees coming out to feed in too cold weather; mine have publicly fed in December without damage; though in other years May and June have proved so unfavourable, that none would venture out, though at short allowance, and greatly pressed with hunger; but I have known that when they have been out, and

fed

fed for two or three hours, yet upon feeling
the air too chilly, they have returned, though
in the middle of the day, and the fun fhining
out.

769. Where a good price is made of honey,
feeding in autumn and fpring will always be
advantageous, although your Stocks be well
furnifhed; for the more fugar and ale they
confume, fo much the greater will be the faving of the Stock honey; they will fwarm the
fooner, and the fooner fill an additional hive:
or fhould the inclement feafon continue longer
than ufual, your Stocks will be in fecurity
and plenty while thofe of your neighbours
are ftarving. Here then is a management
doubly advantageous.

770. The continuance of feeding, muft
however be regulated by the commencement
of honey gathering; for although the Bees
will in general negleƈt the fugar as foon as
their favourite flowers appear, yet they will
not always, but fometimes carry in both
honey and fugar, and thereby debafe the
quality of the comb honey. As foon therefore as they feem to *flight* the fugar, the feeding muft be difcontinued.

771. Whenever it is obferved in the fpring
that the Bees of any hives do not fly out as
others do, fuch may be concluded to be famifhing, or on the point of dying: turn up
the hive, and if they do not ftir, remove
them to the houfe fire; as foon as they begin to crawl give them a kex of liquid food,
and ftop the paffage fo that none may come
out;

out; at night fet them in their place again, cover them warm, and continue to feed them every day, as long as neceffary: but, if on turning them up they appear lively, and have honey, but have ceafed from working, it is a fign they have loft their Queen, and therefore muft be united to fome other Stock (376), or you will have neither honey nor Bees left.

772. The Queen's death is often occafioned by age, difeafe, or fome accident. If at this time the Stock be numerous and rich, the Bees will defert the hive, and take their treafure with them (636): but if *they* fhould not, other Bees or vermin will, unlefs the Apiator be fharp-fighted en ough to prevent them.

773. When Bees fly in an idle manner about their hive in the fpring, when thofe of the other Stocks do not, it is fign of poverty, and they will require fuccour 'till the honey feafon commences (765, 752). At any time if you fee the wax crumbled on the hive floors, or about the door-way, it is a token the Bees are in fome diftrefs; turn the hive up, if very light, and without honey, but the floor dry, and the Bees lively, it denotes famine; the Bees however may be faved by proper feeding or uniting.

774. When Bees are motionlefs, merely through hunger, heat will not reftore them; but, when the hive is turned up, if fome fugar or a fmall quantity of liquid honey be dropped among them it will recover great part of them.

775. When

775· Whenever many of your Bees are obferved to fly about the door, with a lamenting tone, in fpring or autumn, it is to acquaint the Apiator that they are in diftrefs, and want his charitable affiftance: by infpecting the Stocks, and by the unufual number at fome of the door-ways, you may know which Stock wants fuccour : this muft be immediate, for the next day may be too late.

776. As foon as there is plenty of farina in early fpring, and mild weather to favour the collection of it, the Bees will breed apace. Having thus a continual increafe of many mouths, if there be not plenty of honey in ftore, or if the feafon continue for a length of time propitious for breeding, but unfavourable for honey-gathering, the Stocks, efpecially the poor ones, will be more in danger than at any other time : hence it is that fuch numbers of Stocks perifh in May. The prevention is a cautious and timely feeding. Hunger, which increafes the fiercenefs of many ferocious creatures, has a contrary effect on the Bees, caufing them to be very tame, fo that a hive may then be turned up without their offering to fting.

777. The way to avoid having poor Stocks is to be fo moderate in their number, that they ftarve not each other, through the want of pafture to fupply them all (566). By thefe means, though lefs in fhew, you will have more in fubftance, and be always a fuccefsful and profperous Apiator; without being or fearing either a witch or a conjuror.

778. If

778. If Stocks at any time be removed from one part of an Apiary to another, the ſtand or door-way from whence they are taken, muſt be diſguiſed by a mat, cloth, or the like, or the Bees will waſte much time, and many be loſt, by returning to the ſame ſtand again.

779. The ſlits or openings that are made to admit the ſliders in the tops of the hives and box, ſhould always be ſtopped up by ſmall wedges of wood or of tea lead, to keep out the moth and other inſects; unleſs in hot weather, when they may be open to let in the air, to keep the hives from being too hot.

CHAPTER XXI.

How to Extract the HONEY *and* WAX *from the* COMBS; *with ſeveral new Methods of doing it.*

780. THE combs ſhould be taken out of the hives as ſoon as poſſible, and the honey drained from them while yet warm, as it will then run more freely. To further this intention, the hives ſhould be brought into a warm room, if the air be cool,

but

but where no Bees can enter: for otherwife the fmell of the honey will attract multitudes to their deftruction; and likewife greatly interrupt the operation.

781. In my open top hives and boxes, that have but one fpleet, a notch muft be cut in the edges of the combs, that the fpleet may be taken out without damaging any other part of the combs; for which purpofe one end of the fpleet muft be cut through, clofe to the fide of the hive, and it may then be eafily drawn out. The combs are then to be loofened from the fides of the hive, by being cut through at their edges by a long thin knife; then lifting up the body of the hive, all the combs will be left ftanding upon the barred top; from which they may be feparated by a knife, fo as to come away whole. This advantage alone in my hives will more than compenfate for the extra expence.

782. If there be any Bees upon the combs, when taken out, they fhould be brufhed, or rather blown off, and if befmeared with honey, wafhed in two or three waters made a little warm; being then laid on a fieve, and placed in the fun-fhine, or before a fire, they will revive again, and fly to their refpective homes.

783. Thofe parts of the combs that are empty fhould be cut off firft, and thofe that are black and drofly, laid by themfelves; as muft alfo thofe that have farina; but if any have brood, great care fhould be taken not to crufh them, as they muft be put into an

Y empty

empty hive (588), and placed over any Stock that moſt wants ſtrengthening.

784. Then thoſe parts of the combs that contain virgin honey (830) are to be cut out, and drained by themſelves; -for there are ſcarcely any hives but what have ſome portion of virgin combs in them.

785. Great care muſt be taken that no maggots, or the juice of them, or any of the farina be ſqueezed out among the honey, for both communicate a bad flavour and quality to it; therefore a little honey had better be loſt; or thoſe parts which cannot be ſeparated without foulneſs, be returned again for the Bees to feed on; by which in the end no loſs will be ſuſtained.

786. It is uſual to lay the combs on ſieves for the honey to drain through; but the honey is too long in paſſing through them, and thereby the moſt volatile and fragrant parts are exhaled.

787. A better apparatus is a frame of wires adapted to the ſize of your pans, each wire about one inch diſtant from another; through theſe the honey will ſeparate much ſooner. Lay the combs thereon, cut through the cells about the middle and turn them; in three or four hours the honey will be run out; then cutting through the upper parts as they lay, turn them alſo downward, and the whole will be ſoon finiſhed. Large *tin* dripping-pans are to be preferred for this purpoſe, as iron pans have generally ſome ruſt on them, and earthen-

ware

ware abforbs or fucks in a great deal of the honey, which *tin* does not.

788. As feveral fmall portions of the combs will fall between the wires along with the the honey, a bag muft be provided of a conical form, that is, wide at top, and tapering to a point at bottom ; it is to be made of fine flannel, or fuch canvas or cloth as the dairy people ftrain their milk through. This is to be hung between two chairs, or to the ceiling, and a jar, or other proper veffel fet underneath to receive the honey as it runs through. The honey is to be poured out of the draining pans into thefe bags, whereby it will be entirely freed from every particle of wax, much more fo than if paffed through hair fieves in the common way. Care muft be taken that the bags be not hung fo near the fire as to melt the wax, for that will fpoil both ; but a moderate degree of heat will greatly forward the operation ; and the honey will be the better the lefs time it is expofed to the duft and the air.

789. In large Apiaries, where perhaps fifty or a hundred Stocks are taken up at once, the prefs is by fome ufed, without any previous drainings ; which in the common way, would be a very tedious procefs, for fuch quantities. With fubmiffion, however, I fhould imagine, that if a number of large tin pans, with fticks only laid acrofs them, were ufed, the fuperior goodnefs of the honey would amply repay the firft coft of the pans ; and the procefs would be accomplifhed in a very

Y 2   moderate

moderate time. By the prefs all the honey
is made alike impure ; which gives too much
room for the odious character of fophiftication,
though perhaps the accufation of a want of
neatnefs might be more applicable. If equal
delicacy were obferved in the extraction of
honey as in the management of the diary, it
would fully pay for the trouble ; and perhaps
introduce honey once more to general accep-
tance.

790. The firft running from virgin combs
only fhould be referved by itfelf, as being
of the firft quality ; provided cuftomers
can be found to give a proportionable
price. The next in value is that which drains
from the other combs indifcriminately: and.
a third fort is produced from the combs
when fqueezed or preffed through the bags.
This fort will be foul, and fit only for cattle,
or fome external ufe.

800. But where mead is made, it will
hardly be worth while to prefs the combs ;
as they may be thrown into water for that
purpofe directly ; or the combs, after preffing, may be placed, a few at a time, in the
Apiary, in *dry* pans, and the Bees will take
care that not a particle of the honey fhall be
loft. If a quantity of the combs be given
them at once, they will fuffocate each other
among them. For the fame reafon the draining
pans muft be ftrewed over with ftraw, or herbs,
&c. before they are given to them ; otherwife,
in their eagernefs they will befmear themfelves
all over. Thefe pans, &c. fhould be fet under

der fome fhelter, left a fudden fhower wafh the honey away and drown the Bees. If they are fet out in a rainy day, it will prevent the neighbouring Bees from partaking with your own.

801. The pots or veffels of honey fhould remain a few days to fettle before they are clofely covered for fale; for if they contain any fmall particles of wax, thefe will rife to the top, and are to be fkimmed off. The good combs are to be kept apart from the bad; as they are intended to be melted feparately (807).

802. The ufual method of feparating the wax from the droffy part of the combs is to *boil* them in a proportionable large quantity of water; which is to be frequently ftirred to prevent the wax from burning: when it has boiled fufficiently to have thoroughly melted the combs, it is to be put into *hair* bags, fuch as bottoms of fieves are made of, and then preffed by fome convenient inftrument fo long as any wax paffes thro': the droffy part that remains may be re-boiled in frefh water, and re-preffed, whereby more wax will be obtained.

A veffel of cold water is to be fo placed as to receive the wax as it comes from the prefs or bag, to cool the wax the fooner, and to prevent its fticking. The wax is then to be melted a fecond time, and preffed through bags made of cream cloths; after which it is to be melted a third time, and paffed through bags made of ftill finer cloth. Laftly, it is to be melted again, without any water, and poured into pans wider at top than at bottom, fo that

Y 3 the

the wax when cold, may be turned out without difficulty : and not only so, but the smaller the bottom of the cake is, the drofs will be more collected, and confequently the lefs wafte made in fcraping it off. This tedious method might be greatly fhortened by firft boiling the combs in water, with each quart of which half an ounce of aqua-fortis has been previoufly mixed. After being boiled, the wax will be within two or three inches of the top, intermixed with farina; but a confiderable quantity of drofs will be at the bottom. If the whole of this mafs be fuffered to ftand until quite cold, the drofs at the bottom may be cut off; and the remainder being fo much more free from impurities, the wax will be far more eafily extricated.

803. When the wax is in the mould, if there be any froth, blow it to one fide and fkim it off. The moulds or veffels it is poured into fhould be firft wetted with cold water, to prevent the cakes flicking to them. The moulds are to be kept in a warm room until cold, otherwife the cakes of wax will crack in the middle. If they happen to flick in turning out, warming the veffels a little will loofen them fo as to come out with eafe.

It fhould be obferved, that the combs ought not to be fqueezed when put into the water ; as they will melt the fooner, and the farina, and other impurities be more readily feparated.

I would propofe a bag made of flannel of a moderate thicknefs, as far preferable for
ftraining

ftraining the wax through than either linen
or canvas. It fhould be hung during the
procefs as near the fire as poffible without
burning. A hoop fhould be faftened at the
top of the bag to keep it properly extended, fo
as to receive the wax with the greater facility. Before the wax is put into the bag, it
fhould be well and brifkly boiled, and that for
fome time; otherwife the wax will not be
fufficiently difengaged from the drofs, farina,
and fkins of the maggots; with the two laft
it is fo intimately united, as to be very difficult to feparate. A veffel of *cold* water is to
be placed under the bag, to receive the wax
as it drops. The firft running will be good,
but as the flannel thickens, by the wax adhering to it, it will come through ftill more pure;
and though from foul combs, will be equal
to any of the wax from the virgin combs.

804. When the pores of the bag become
fo choaked with wax as to prevent its paffing through, return the remaining grofs
matter into the boiling water again, and as
much as can be fcraped off the bag infide and
out. To fhorten the procefs it will be proper to have a kettle of water boiling by
the fide of the other to recruit its wafte,
and to boil the bag in, to clear it of the
ftill adhering wax and drofs; which will
otherwife prevent any more wax paffing
through it; and this muft be repeated as often as it becomes clogged. In the fame manner fieves or bags of any other materials muft
be treated.

Y 4   805. The

805. The feparated wax muft have all the water fqueezed from it before it is melted to be put into the moulds: for the water will make the wax liable to crumble.

806. Some ftrain their wax through hair fieves; but thefe are foon clogged up, and then but little wax will pafs, confequently there will be a diminution of the profic. Where Apiaries are very large, a prefs is generally ufed to feparate the wax; and in fome places it is done between hot irons.

807. A greater quantity of wax will be procured if the virgin and other yellow combs that have no farina or brood in them, be melted by themfelves: for the fewer impurities there be, the fooner the wax will run from it; whereas if entangled with a large quantity of drofs, the prefs having lefs power over it. the more difficult and tedious the feparation will be. Upon the whole, whichever of thefe methods be taken, it is a very troublefome bufinefs, confumes much firing, a quantity of wax is wafted in the operation, and the drofly matter, which is thrown away, contains a confiderable portion of wax.

808. Many and great were my endeavours to obviate thefe difficulties, which have puzzled me ever fince I kept Bees; at laft I hit upon the following *proceffes*; which I give to the public as the moft perfect that have hitherto come to my knowledge. But it will be neceffary, by way of introduction, to make fome difcriminating obfervations on *combs*. If we carefully feparate the hard dark coloured or

black

black cells from each other, either full or
empty, they will uniformly be found to confift
of a film or very fine fkin, inftead of a *partition
of wax.* For *Supreme Wifdom* has induced the
Bees with fuch œconomic fagacity, that as
foon as a maggot has quitted its fkin, they cement or hang it up againft the waxen fides of
the cell; and very likely feveral of them
fucceffively, until they become fufficiently
ftrong to form a partition of themfelves;
the wax is then *taken away* and applied either
to form new or to cover other cells: for the
Bees in many inftances are found to be extremely faving of their wax.

809. But in order the more certainly
to afcertain this opinion, I boiled fome of
thefe combs, which were entirely empty,
but not the leaft trace of any wax was
found. The experiment was repeated with
the fame kind of combs filled with farina, and
the refult was exactly fimilar. To corrobo-
rate this fact ftill more, if feveral of thefe fkins
or films be twifted together, and lighted, they
will burn like a candle, as many other fubftances of this kind will do; though not containing the leaft particle of wax; whereas, if
we prefs together feveral of the fineft virgin
cells, and hold them to a candle, they will
melt but not flame. To which we may add,
that thefe fkin partitions do not manifeft any
waxen property, either to the eye or the touch:
much lefs has farina any fuch quality when
tried by fire. From hence it may be concluded,
that we may as well attempt to extract wax
from

from a pasteboard, as from such kind of
combs. Therefore, that so very large a quantity of drossy matter may not prevent a more
perfect purification of real waxen combs,
they should be previously separated by the
hand, and thrown on the fire, to make the
pot boil, as the best use they can be put
to; which will much shorten both the
trouble, time, and the expence of fuel usually
bestowed upon this useless rubbish. People
therefore need no longer wonder that the
combs from old stock hives yield little or no
wax; for if any be obtained, it is what covered the honey cells. This also shews the
great advantage of a frequent change of hives
for the acquisition of double or treble the
quantity of wax, than can be procured by
the old way.

Process the First.

For extracting Marketable WAX *without
Pressing.*

810. Take a tin cullender, all the holes of
which are *round*; the handles must also be off,
instead of which fix across it a strong wire or
iron bail, or a tin one like those of watering-
pots; and if soldered on the inside, it will
be most convenient. The cullender in size
must be adapted to that of the pot or kettle
you intend to use; but to go within side of
it, as close to the sides as possible. Set the
pot on the fire, with about three or four
inches depth of water therein, in which is to
be mixed single *aqua-fortis*, in the proportion
of half an ounce for each quart of water. In
this

this put as many wax combs as will conveniently boil when melted. As soon as they begin to melt, they fhould be frequently ftirred until all be thoroughly melted; let it then boil without ftirring, that the wax may rife clear. It fhould be made to boil very brifkly, during the whole procefs. As foon as the yellow froth rifes, put in the cullender or fieve, and prefs it down in · the liquor, until it be about half full; but great care muft be taken that none of the liquor rife over the edge of the cullender, as that will foul what is therein, and fpoil the operation. With a wooden, or what is better, a tin ladle, firft dipped in cold water, lightly fkim off the wax as it rifes upon the furface, and put it into a narrow bottomed pan (previoufly rinfed in cold water) fet as near as can be to the pot on the fire, and continue fkimming the wax off as long as any rifes, deprefling the cullender in proportion as the liquor finks.

811. Inftead of a cullender a bair fieve may be fubftituted; but where a perfon keeps fix or eight Stocks of Bees, it will be moft profitable and convenient to have a tin veffel made on purpofe to fit a due proportioned kettle or pot, the fides of which fhould be quite ftraight, fo that when the *tin feparater* flides down, there may be no vacancy for the farina to rife up between. The holes in this tin feparater fhould be as numerous and fmall as poffible in the bottom, and about two inches up the fides; the bottom fhould be quite flat,

without

without a rim, like that of a quart tin pot,
that it may prefs the dregs the clofer down,
when near the bottom.

812. When the liquor in the pan is nearly
cold, the wax is to be taken out, and what
drofs adheres to it fcraped off. The wax is
then to be re-boiled in a fmall quantity of
water, and about a fourth part as much
aqua-fortis as before to a quart ; as foon as
it boils take it off, and let it ftand until cold.
The wax will concrete at top, and the remaining drofs being again fcraped off, may
be further purified with other combs.

813. This procefs will not only extract the
wax more completely than any of the methods
generally ufed, but it is alfo much lefs troublefome, and in every other refpect more eligible;
for the aqua-fortis may be got for a penny an
ounce, confequently that trifling charge is
much over-balanced by the other fuperior
advantages. As aqua-fortis procured from
different places may not always be of equal
ftrength, a confequent variation will be found
in the procefs. The operator muft therefore
add or fubftract in conformity. Some practice is neceffary to form a judgment, or to
conduct this or any other operation fkilfully.
Double aqua-fortis will not anfwer the purpofe, either in this or any of the following
procefles, nearly fo well as the fingle, and
the wax produced will be of a pale dingy
colour.

814. A lefs expenfive method, though not
fo eligible, is to put the combs loofely into

a canvas, or rather a fine hair bag, tied up clofe at the end, and put into a kettle with a due proportion of aqua-fortis and water; a leaden or iron weight is to be laid on the bag to keep it down to the bottom. It muft be made to boil fo as to throw up the froth brifkly, which is to be taken off as (810): a thick board with a handle in the middle is then to be put in, to prefs out what wax may be ftill adhering. It is afterwards to be treated as (812). It fhould be carefully obferved that in thefe procefles of fkimming off the froth, what rifes of a clear yellow fhould be referved by itfelf, as often requiring no further purification. The more forcible the froth is thrown up, the purer it will be; and the operation the fooner finifhed: by this bag-method, full as much wax, if not more, may be obtained, as by any of the ufual modes.

Procefs the Second.

815. *To extract Marketable* WAX *from the* COMBS *by a fingle Operation, without either ftraining or preffing.*

816. Take an earthen veffel, much narrower at the bottom than at the top; put therein a quart of water, and one ounce of fingle *aqua-fortis,* or the like proportion for larger or lefler quantities: ftir them well together, and then put in fo many good wax
combs

combs as, when melted, will reach within a
a finger's length of the top of the pan; set it
on a clear but strong fire, and as soon as it
begins to melt, stir it about, and so continue
until it boils, and even longer, if the combs
be not all thoroughly melted; remove it then
from the fire, and let it stand until it be
cold.

817. The wax will be in a cake at the top,
and the impurities underneath it: there will
be two sorts of impurities; the lowest will
be almost entirely drofs; this is to be taken
off by itself, and is of no value; the next
will be a layer of drofs, but with some wax
intermixed; this also is to be taken off, (so as
to leave the cake pure and referved by itself;
as also any foulnefs that may be on the top;
both which may be refined along with more
combs the next boiling.

818. Old combs that have wax in them, or
other refufe that has been prefled, but yet retain a confiderable portion of wax, may be thus
treated, and will yield as fine yellow wax as
the beft combs; provided the combs or refufe
have been previoufly prefled down, and kept
in a clofe tub or veffel in a houfe for five or
fix weeks: which will occafion the *impurities*
to ferment and rot, (the *wax* will *not*) and
thereby difengage the parts, and difpofe them
more aptly for feparation.

Procefs

Proceſs the Third.

To extraƈt WAX *from the* COMBS *by a ſingle operation, in a greater degree of purity, and without ſtraining, preſſing, or the uſe of a menſtruum.*

820. Take the ſame kind of veſſel as is uſed in Proceſs the ſecond, put into it about a quarter of a pint of water, to keep the wax from burning; then put in ſo many entire *empty* virgin combs, or at leaſt ſuch as are of a good yellow, as the veſſel will conveniently hold; ſet the pan over a briſk but clear fire; as ſoon as the combs begin to melt, keep it *ſtirring* until it boils; then *ceaſe,* and a clear yellow froth will riſe on the ſide or middle. This is to be ſkilfully taken off as faſt as it riſes, and put into a pan previouſly ſet cloſe by. The fire muſt be ſo managed as to keep the froth riſing up, but not ſo fierce as to make it boil over. If it riſe too faſt, remove the pan to a leſs hot part, or damp the fire a little. The combs, when firſt melted, ſhould only be ſufficient to riſe within three inches of the top of the pan, to prevent the neceſſary riſing froth from running over; when the froth riſes a little foul, return it out of the ladle into the pan again, and draw the foul ſcum aſide from the part where the froth riſes, or the whole will be ſpoiled: when no more clear froth will riſe, take the pan off, and turn the remainder out into a veſſel of cold water. It may be afterwards further purified
along

along with other combs, by the fecond Procefs. A fhallow tin ladle will be moft convenient for this bufinefs; but for want of that
a bafting-ladle with the top taken off, will
do very well.

821. The pan that has the purified wax
is to remain near the fire undifturbed, and
with a cloth over it, until it is cold; it will
then turn out a cake of fine wax (if it has
been managed judicioufly) and free from drofs.

822. This Procefs may be very ferviceable
as preparatory to forming *white* wax; and for
feveral other nice purpofes, where great purity
is required; and in fact is the readieft and
cheapeft method of extraction of any; but is
reftricted only to fine combs.

Procefs the Fourth.

To render Wax *mifcible with Water.*

823. In a quart of water diffolve one ounce
of pearl or pot afh; add combs as in Procefs
the fecond, and boil them until melted : the
whole will then appear of a milky colour, the
wax and water being incorporated, and when
cold will refemble cream. To reftore the
wax re-boil it with three times the weight of
aqua-fortis as there was of afhes; hereby the
wax will be extricated from the water, and
refume its ufual ftate, only of a paler colour
than common. I give this Procefs as one
that I happened on in the courfe of my experiments, not knowing but it might convey
fome ufeful *hint,* or prove of real fervice.

824. Doubt-

824. Doubtlefs fome ingenious perfons, who keep confiderable Apiaries, may add to the above improvements ; which are but new to myfelf, and confequently not likely to be fo perfect as time and experience may render them.

825. Combs fhould never be kept long before they are melted, for, though they be covered in a clofe box, the Wax-Moth will find a place to depofit its eggs in, and the young maggots will gain an entrance to the deftruction of the combs ; after which, turning to perfect moths, they will prove very hurtful to your Apiary.

826. A hive of combs yields but a fmall portion of wax, compared with the quantity of honey. A hive of three pecks well filled, and of not more than two years ftanding, may afford twenty-five pounds of honey, and not above two pounds of wax. Stocks, taken one with another, in the common way of management, do not upon an average afford above one pound of wax each.

C H A P T E R XXII.

Characteriftic and Medical Obfervations on Honey.

827. IT has been already obferved, that the perfection of honey arifes from the fuperior quality of the flowers from which it is gathered (514) and alfo from the degree

Z

of

of care and cleanlinefs in its feparation from
the combs. The former is regulated by the
fituation of the Apiary for pafturage, and by
the weather; for however plentiful the beft
of honey-flowers may be, if the weather
prove too cold, too wet, or too dry, when
they are in bloom, they can yield no honey;
or what amounts to the fame, the Bees cannot fly out to procure it; but the weather
perhaps proving more favourable afterwards,
when the beft flowers are gone, and a more
inferior fort are blowing, the Bees in this
cafe are neceffitated to collect from them. If
a furloin of beef cannot be had, we muft take
up with a leg. Hence it is, that in fome
years, no fine honey is produced. And on
thefe principles it may be fuppofed, that even
in the fame year, different Apiaries may produce honey of very different qualities, though
the pafturage be equal, the difference arifing
from the weather being favourable to one
fituation, and not to another.

828. The honey that is generally fold in
the London fhops, is too haftily condemned,
as being fophifticated with flour. To afcertain this point, I mixed with a fmall
quantity of my fineft honey, fome flour, in
different proportions; by none of which was
it altered to the appearance of London
honey. Therefore the difference muft be
afcribed to the nature of the places from
which it is ufually brought; that is to fay, the
heath countries. Thefe indeed produce a
great abundance, but, from the nature of the
flowers,

flowers, the honey is but indifferent (507, 560) ; to this muſt be added, the groſs method of extracting the honey from the combs by means of a preſs; which ſufficiently accounts for its too common coarſeneſs and foulneſs.

829. To explain this more diſtinctly, it muſt be remarked, that in Stocks which ſtand more than two years, the combs become black, and the cells foul, by the quantity of brood ſucceſſively depoſited in them. Not only ſo, but when a hive is taken up, there is frequently ſome brood or maggots in parts of the combs; as alſo farina, both new and ſtale. The taſte of the maggots is like that of ruſty bacon ; and that of the farina, a nauſeous bitter. If any of theſe therefore, through careleſsneſs, be preſſed out along with the natural impurities of the combs, and intimately incorporated with the honey, it is no wonder, that this becomes diſagreeable to the ſight and taſte, and even unwhóleſome ; nor that in general, it is difeſteemed and neglected.

830. It is a prevailing opinion among country people, that all *ſwarm honey is virgin*. This proceeds from a ſuppoſition that a Swarm conſiſts intirely of young Bees, and therefore their honey muſt be the heſt. But in neither caſe is this true. A Swarm conſiſts both of old and young, equally with a Stock : but even admitting they were all young Bees, what difference can there be in the ſelection of the flowers between the old and the young ? If there be any, however, it muſt be in

Z 2 favour

favour of the old Bees as more knowing and moie fkilful than the others. The truth is, none are virgin combs that have had brood or farina in the cells, whether it be in a Swarm or Stock. Now a Swarm breeds through the fummer equally with a Stock, confequently great part of their combs, efpecially the central ones, are filled with brood, as well as thofe of the Stock. So that in both, it is only a part or portion of the combs, that contains true virgin honey; if by *that name* be meant honey of the *greateft purity*. The grand point therefore is, when the combs are taken, to feparate the virgin parts from the other with the greateft care and nicenefs poffible.

831. By managing Bees in the ftory method, the advantage in this refpect is very great, as whole hives or boxes may be taken filled with *intire virgin* honey and wax: but which is always impracticable by the common hives and management, and in general by the collateral method.

832. It muft be confidered, however, that honey may be really virgin, and yet but bad honey in its quality. For, as before noticed, honey as collected by the Bees, in the firft inftance, is good, bad, or indifferent, according to the nature of the flowers from which it is gathered. And therefore a purchafer may be fupplied with intire virgin honey, and yet be greatly difappointed. For inftance, honey gathered from heath, and depofited in new virgin cells, will be true virgin honey:

but

but as heath affords only that of a bad quality, the nature of the place where it is
lodged cannot improve it.

833. As fine virgin honey is procured in
much fmaller quanties than any other, the
price ought moft certainly to be larger in
proportion. Thofe who will not give a good
price muft expect to have an inferior fort im-
pofed upon them inftead of the beft. But
as few buyers are competent judges they are
apt to think the demand exorbitant. If
the feller be of tried honefty, and the buyer
not avaricious, a confidence may be placed
without danger of impofition.

834. Foreign honey is much extolled as
being far fuperior to any produced in England.
This in a great meafure may be true, but
not intirely; the wild thyme and rofemary of
Narbonne in France; of Minorca; of
Mount Hymettus, in Greece; of Hybla, in
Italy, may be injured, while in bloom, by
fhowery weather; and this opportunity being
loft, the reft of their flowers will yield no better honey than our own country affords. Befides, as they have fuch prodigious quantities,
it is very probable that the Apiators of thofe
countries are not more cleanly or more
careful in the extraction of it from the combs
than the farmers dames of our own ifland.
Shall old England's peafantry fubmit the palm
of cleanlinefs to thofe of France or Spain,
or any fouthern climate whatever?

835. It is poffible to have as fine honey in
England as the foreign, in any and every year,

Z 3

by

by having a large garden planted with a great quantity of aromatic flowers. It may farther be remarked, that the foreign honey muſt greatly vary in its quality, in different years, according as the weather has been more or leſs favourable. The different apiaries alſo, as with us, owing to diverſity of ſituation, and of management, cannot be ſuppoſed to produce honey always equally fine. Therefore, let us not be carried away by the "whiſtling of a name", but let our ſenſes of ſmell and taſte come in for a ſhare in the judgment.

836. Honey when expoſed long to the air, grows hard, rough, and ſeedy: to prevent which the Bees ſeal or cover the cells of honey with wax; as in this ſtate it is to them quite indigeſtible. Not that all honey is alike in this reſpect; ſome years afford it of a more liquid nature than others; and difference of ſituations often has the ſame effect. If honey be kept in a warm place, it will ferment, and turn acid.

837. New honey is better than old, as it is continually loſing ſome of its fragrancy, unleſs very cloſely confined by a bladder. That which is collected in the ſpring and ſummer is ſuperior to that of the autumn; the clear than the yellow. That which has a kind of acid ſweet than that which is wholly ſo. The beſt is light coloured, fragrant, and ſomething aromatic, partaking of the nature of the flowers it was gathered from. The colour depends on that of the different juices which

which yield it. Thus the honey collected from trees is higher coloured than that from flowers; and that from the bloſſoms of heath, darker coloured than what is gathered from any other flower.

838. For medical purpoſes honey is directed to be clarified. This is performed by ſetting a baſon, containing the honey in a veſſel of hot water, over a clear fire without ſmoke, and taking off the ſcum as it riſes. If the honey be foul, this method will free it from the groſſer impurities, but not from the lighter heterogeneous matters with which it is uſually mixed, ſuch as duſt and farinaceous ſubſtances; nor from the juice of the maggots, with which it oftentimes is blended. Neither has a vapour bath force enough to effect this, nor even a violent boiling of the honey in a naked veſſel. On the contrary, if the honey be really *virgin*, nothing will be thrown upon the ſurface by boiling, except froth; and inſtead of being improved by this management it will be robbed of its moſt eſſential excellence; viz. its aromatic fragrance, and be debaſed to a ſugary flavour.

839. If honey be bought for virgin; it will be eaſy to diſcover whether it be really ſo or not, by clarifying a ſmall portion of it. One exception, however, muſt be made, viz. that ſmall portions of wax, notwithſtanding all the care that can be taken, will paſs through the hair-cloths with the honey in draining. This however generally riſes upon

the

the ſurface, after the pots have ſtood a few days, and is eaſily taken off.

840. Perhaps the beſt way to purify honey is to incloſe it in a bladder, and put it into hot water, until it be juſt fluid, and then to paſs it through a thick flannel bag of a conical or funnel ſhape. The bladder will confine the volatile parts, and the reſt of the operation being quickly performed, little detriment will be ſuffered. But care muſt be taken that it be not kept in the water until it is ſo warm as to melt the particles of wax that may be intangled in the honey. As honey partakes both of an acid and ſaline nature, the veſſels in which it is kept, ought not to be (as is uſually the caſe) glazed with lead; as is that called Delf, the cream coloured ſtone ware, and all the common earthen ware.

841. It is well known, that acids and ſaline ſubſtances will diſſolve a portion of of lead, if they be any conſiderable time in contact with it. This ſaturnine impregnation often proves highly prejudicial, eſpecially to delicate conſtitutions; while the real cauſe of the complaint is not ſo much as ſuſpected. For this reaſon, honey ſhould always be kept in white or brown ſtone pots or jars: which being glazed with ſalt, are as free from any noxious quality as the porcelain from China.

842. In a medical view, the fineſt honey, concentrates the eſſence of the moſt ſalutary flowers; " *and is the moſt exalted of· all*
Balſams

Balfams whatever". But like them it is heating, in what manner foever it be taken; whether as food or phyfic. It fuits chiefly cold and phlegmatic habits; old men; or thofe who by ficknefs or other caufes abound in grofs vifcid humours. But to perfons of a bilious or hectic † conftitution it generally proves inflammatory.

843. It is ufeful as a detergent ‡ and aperitive,§ powerfully diffolving the too fluggifh juices, and promoting the expectoration of tough phlegm. A continued ufe of it as an article of diet, has been found of fingular fervice in the gravel and ftone.

844. Where honey proves griping or purgative, the boiling of it will moderate thefe effects, by diminifhing its tendency to fermentation. However falutary honey in general may be, yet there is a peculiarity in fome conftitutions which renders the leaft quantity of it highly difagreeable, occafioning exceffive ficknefs and vomiting, and fevere griping, nay in fome perfons, the effects produced by its ufe refemble thofe occafioned by poifon.‖ A doubt arifes with refpect to thefe cafes, whether the noxious quality, might not rather proceed, from fome heterogeneous particles or impurities, incorporated with the honey, than from *pure* honey itfelf. In this branch of phyfics, as well as in many others, accurate

---

* *Dr. Leake's Medical Inftructions.*
† *Hot or feverifh.*   ‡ *Cleanfing.*   § *Opening.*
‖ *This Medical character of honey is taken from authors of the firft eminence.*

accurate and repeated experiments are wanted in order to afcertain the truth.

845. If domeſtic wines, were made with honey inſtead of ſugar, they would be more ſimilar to foreign wines: they would be of a more delicate flavour; of a more cordial quality, and ſet lighter upon the ſtomach. Though honey, when made into Mead, or in any other form, has proved diſagreeable to many, yet when made along with fruit, into wine, it has proved to the ſame perſons both agreeable and exhilerating.

To make MEAD, *equal to foreign Wines.*

846. To every gallon of water, put three pounds of the fineſt honey: boil it as long as any impurities riſe; which are to be carefully ſkimmed off. It will ferment of itſelf, but ſome chooſe to haſten it with a little yeaſt, putting therein half of a lemon peel, pared thin. When it is fermented ſufficiently, put it into your veſſel, and the peel with it: leave a ſmall vent, as long as there ſeems any degree of fermentation; then add to it half a pound more of honey for every gallon of liquor; and immediately bung it down cloſe. Let it ſtand ſix months and then bottle it off for uſe. If intended to be kept ſeveral years, three pounds and a half of honey muſt be at firſt put to a gallon of water.

847. As the intention of boiling is only to ſeparate the impurities, and to induce a perfect union of the honey and water. It is ſelf-evident a ſhort boiling will fully an-

ſwer

fwer every purpofe. This fhould be carefully noticed; becaufe the longer the liquor
is boiled, the lefs will it be difpofed afterwards to ferment kindly; in confequence of
which, inftead of being of a vinous quality,
it will have a difagreeable lufcious fweetnefs;
and not that fine racy flavour, of which it is
capable equal to foreign wine.

848. This intention is alfo fruftrated by
the injudicious though common practice of
making the liquor fo ftrong of the honey as
to bear an egg : this renders it a mere ftum,
and prevents ts undergoing that complete
and *regular* fermentation, which is neceffary
to the production of a perfect, uniform
vinous liquor.

849. The expreffed juices of fruits, and
all fugary vegetables, have naturally a fpon-
taneous tendency to ferment into a vinous
liquor, without the addition of a ferment.
Therefore the quantity of yeaft neceffary to
fet the liquor to work is but very trifling, and,
if done in warm weather, perhaps it will
fucceed beft without any. If the yeaft be
not perfectly good and free from any ill
flavour, it will be impoffible to produce a
perfect and effectual fermentation; and whatever ill flavour the yeaft is charged with will
be communicated to the whole body of the
liquor. For which reafon it is, that the
lemon peel is directed not to be put to the
liquor, until the fermentation is begun. For
then a very fmall quantity of any flavourable
ingredient will communicate its flavour to a
large

large cafk of liquor; whereas, if put to it before or after the fermentation, it will be imperceptible.

. 850. It requires a circumfpect attention to mark the progrefs of the fermentation, that it exceed not the limits of the *vinous*, by running into that of the *acetous*. This is a knowledge acquired only by practical obfervation made on the liquor, during its progrefs, and by frequently tafting of it; for as foon as it has acquired the vinous flavour the progrefs of the fermentation muft be ftopped, or it will foon turn to the acetous, and therefore at the vinous point the liquor muft be tunned up. By this means the heat is leffened, and the progrefs gradually ftopped, the heavier particles condenfe and fubfide, while the lighter, by the frequent filling of the cafk are thrown out at the bung-hole, and leave the liquor compleatly purged of all matter which might hereafter endanger a pernicious fret, or turbidnefs. On the contrary, if the liquor happens to be checked in the working, fo as not to attain the due degree of fermentation, the motion being loft, the *fæces* or *dregs* will not fubfide, nor will the liquor afterwards become fine or lively. While the liquor is fermenting, the veffel fhould have fuch a covering as barely to allow for the efcape of the air let loofe by the operation.

. 851. The principles of fermentation are of too extenfive a nature to be inlarged further upon in a work like this; what has been delivered

livered will I hope prove of fome ufe, not only in the making of Mead, but of all domeſtick wines; as alfo in brewing. People in general having a very confufed and imperfect idea of conducting a procefs which requires great nicety and ſkill.

CHAPTER XXIII.

How to find BEES *in* WOODS, *and to ſecure them in a* HIVE.

852. THE heſt time to look for them is in the ſpring, when the fallows, and other plants that afford plenty of farina, are in bloom. If many Bees be ſeen collecting from thefe bloſſoms, or frequently vifiting any fprings or ponds, it indicates that their habitations are not far off; and if no perfons keep any pretty near, it may fafely be concluded, that they are wild Bees, and not private property.

853. In order to difcover from whence they come, diſſolve fome red or yellow oker, or any other colouring fubſtance, in water, and dipping fome fprigs or grafs in this folution, ſprinkle the Bees with it as they alight. Wheat flour alfo or any other coloured powder may be ſhook or puffed over them, fo as to mark them for further examination. For, by obferving whether their returns be fooner or later, or whether they aſſemble in greater or fmaller numbers, the diſtance of their reſidence

fidence may be gueffed with tolerable accuracy. If they return foon, it is probable you may trace them home without much trouble: But if not, take the joint of a large reed, or of elder, force a part of the pith out at one end, put a little honey, or ale and fugar, into it, and ftop that end with a cork or paper; then cut a fmall flit over where the honey lies, that the fmell of it may attract the Bees. The pith of the other end is alfo to be taken out, fo as to leave a fmall partition between the two hollows; this end is to be left open. Place this joint near their haunts, and they will foon be allured to enter into the hollow: when about half a dozen are in ftop the open end with your finger. Soon afterwards let one of the Bees out, purfue it as long as it is in fight, then letting another fly, if it continues the fame courfe follow that alfo: but if any of them take a different route, let another fly, and fo proceed until you find feveral take the fame courfe, and thereby lead you to their abode.

854. If this fhould happen to be in a hollow tree, &c. (324) and it is defireable to diflodge them, it may be done, as directed (298). Fumigation will oblige them to quit their habitation and treafure. At firft iffuing out they will be in a great rage, therefore the operator, as well as the bye-ftanders, muft be upon their guard, or they will fmart for it. The fmoaking a fhort pipe of tobacco will keep them from the face, or any thing held in the hand that emits a great fmoke, will keep them at a proper diftance. If they are taken e rly

enough

enough in the honey feafon to replenifh a
hive, it will only be neceffary to place therein fuch combs, or part of combs, as have
brood in them, faftening them in with fpleets
in the beft manner you can.

855. But if done too late in the feafon for
the Bees to furnifh a new habitation with a
fufficiency of winter ftore, the combs muft
be taken out of the tree, as whole as poffible,
and placed in an empty hive in the moft judicious manner, and fimilar to what the Bees
themfelves do. Then putting in the Bees,
they will foon fecure and repair them to the
greateft advantage.

856. Great care however muft be taken
that the Queen be not killed in the operation.
When this happens it may be known by the
Bees not working out the next day as others
do. In fuch a cafe a fpare Queen or royal cell
muft be given them, or they muft be united
to another Stock; taking the honey yourfelf
in reward for your trouble.

At the latter end of a fummer, and when it is
not intended to preferve the Bees, but only to
take the honey, the procefs may be fhortened;
for by only making a fufficient opening in
the tree, then drumming and making a great
noife about it, to terrify the Bees, (having
on the fafe-guard 73) you may take out
the combs feverally, brufh the Bees off, and
lay the combs in a proper veffel. In all
thefe operations it is neceffary that the perfon
who operates fhould be well defended.

857. If a hive, the infide of which has
been rubbed with fugar and ale, or rather a
hive

hive with some empty combs in it, be set, during the swarming season, where wild Bees resort, it will probably intice a Swarm to settle therein.

858. Thus have I faithfully finished, to the best of my abilities, the account of the most eligible methods of conducting the various operations relating to these wonderful insects. Wonderful in their nature, properties, and super-eminently useful above all others; affording not only food and medicine, but also a very valuable article to the mechanic and manufacturer; and supplying the absence of the solar light by the splendor and elegance of its illuminations in the habitations of the noble and the opulent. The silk-worm indeed may in some measure vie with the Bees, as adorning by its labour the persons and habitations of the beautiful, the wealthy, and the great. But with respect to the other tribes, our insects are unrivalled in all.

859. Therefore, while we contemplate the *Divine Wisdom* in a display so wonderful and beneficial, let us not forget the *moral* instruction naturally deducible from it: for with the greatest propriety, may be inscribed on every Apiary, *Behold the School of Sobriety, Industry, and Oeconomy !*

F I N I S.

THE

INDEX.

Note. *The Figures refer to the Paragraphs, not to the Pages.*

A.

ADditional Hive, some seasons will not afford, 530; none from Stocks the same summer, 577; in spring, 625; when to supply, 615; hives of combs to be preserved for, 630; when not to be added, 632.

Age of Bees, 35; they die of, 746.

Air, cold and damp, very fatal to Bees, 714; to preserve from, 726; putrid, from filth on the floors, 744.

Ale and Sugar, Bees are fond of, 747; useful to sprinkle them with, 370, 381; best to feed with, 747.

Amellus of Virgil, a remark on, 529.

Antients, ignorant how to captivate the Queen, 348.

A a *Apiary*

B.

A a 2   joice

in

D. *Dav-*

D.

Feeding

of comb to be fixed therein, 434; in a pyramidal form, 448; in a hoop or circle, 449; afcending ranges deftructive to the Bees, 450; requiring a great number to perform it, 450; one range ufeful, 452; glaffes on purpofe, 453; others more proper, 453; how to fet on a box or hive, 455; pieces of combs to be fixed in the glaffes, 460; how to take off, 444, 451; precautions and directions as to the quantity of honey that may be taken by the glaffes, 461; parts of full combs being put herein, the Bees will eat the honey out, 461; not to be fet on a Stock that is intended to Swarm, 462; in fcarce feafons glaffes cannot be fupplied, 463; inferior veffels may ferve inftead of glaffes, 462; this method is fuperior to boxes contrived for the purpofe, 465; glaffes not fo agreeable to the Bees as hives or boxes, 490; moft eligible for drawing the fineft honey, 514.

Goofeberries, the only fruit Bees will feed on, 540.

Green-houfe plant, not of general utility, 526.

Guard, generally kept by Bees againft robbing Bees, 695.

Gunpowder, to ftupify Bees with, 409; and Wafps; 671.

H.

Hackels, not fo eligible as pans to cover Stocks, 156.

I.

C c   *Increafe*

K.

L.

Moth,

Q.   Queen

Q.

by driving, 405, 411; takes the air,
386; caught by ftupefaction, 389, and
following; more eligible than driving,
409; how to diftinguifh her, 416; often
eludes the fearch, 416; makes excur-
fions, 417, and following; a royal cell
will induce the Bees to work, 422; to
obtain a fpare one, 422; method to view
a royal nuptial, 423; a token of her
death, 499, 772; depofits eggs in an upper hive, 587, 588; Bees on fome occafions defert her, 607; may be killed
in feparating hives, 613; of a Stock dying,
636; how known, 636, and follow-
ing; the Bees defert their hive thereon, 636, and following; but not always,
639; as do Swarms, 640; in greateft
danger, when attacked by robbers, 685;
when killed, how to manage the hive,
692.

R.

S.

Safe-guard

Safe-guard againſt Bees, how made, 73; fot
the face, 76.

Saws, uſed in ſeparation, 126, 59*, 598.

Sea, Bees ſuppoſed to thrive beſt near, 745.

Seaſons unfavourable, to provide againſt, 647,
726.

Separation, (ſee alſo *Taking*) contrivances to
obviate the difficulty of, 123; by a tin
plate and ſaws, 592; by ſaws alone, 599;
by a thin board and cloth, 600; by a
board with a wire meſh, 602; at night,
without inſtruments, 605; not quite complete without force, 607; of under hives,
609; by day-light improper, 611; of
collateral boxes, 612; Queen may be
killed in, 613; laying out afterwards,
how to manage, 610; after ſeparation
to know if the upper one is a Swarm,
398, 401.

Settling of a Swarm upon a perſon, how to
manage 334, and following.

Signs of ſwarming, 250; Bees often riſe without any, 253, 278, and following; of the
petition of a Princeſs to ſwarm, 255;
ſigns not to be depended upon, 263.

Situation, of an Apiary, 72; compariſon of
good and bad, 504, and following; good,
507; White's remarks on, 560.

Sliders, the ſuperiority of, 196; a deſcription
of, 130; the ready means of ſetting glaſſes
over hives, 197.

Slits, that receive the ſliders, to be ſtopped,
779; ſmall, in hives, the inconvenience
of, 163, 711.

Smelling,

D d 2 plained,

tation prepared, 261; an empty hive
fometimes will allure, 261; to know if
efcaped, 262; none but good to be kept,
264, 266; eftimate of the weight, number, and meafure, 264, 265; directions for
hiving, 269, and following; the young
Queen fometimes drops, 274; reafons why
they are often too foon or too late, 275;
conftant *watching* the only fecurity againft
lofing of, 278; fwarming hours, 279; to
prevent 281; to provoke, 282; divided
in hiving, 291; after having rofe, 292;
not ftaying in a hive 293; tinkling ufeful
293; ftorms terrify them, 295; to make
them fettle, 294, and following, 298; the
means to ftop a Swarm that is rifing, 300;
to prevent Swarms intermixing, 301; a
certain token of a Swarm's going to rife,
302; falfe tokens, 302; to prevent its
re-entering the mother Stock, 303; will
return if without a Queen, 303; its appearance when fettled, 304; will fometimes
fettle of themfelves, 305; an enticement to
caufe them to fettle, 305; fhould be hived
foon, 306; how to hive them from a
bough, 309; by means of a cloth, 307,
308, 311; to remain 'till evening, 311;
when not, 311; how to manage when
too large, 312; when untowardly fettled,
303, and following: in high trees, 314;
to diflodge and make them fettle more
conveniently, 315; in a hedge, 317, 318;
round the body of a tree, 316, 319;
brufhing

U. *Uniting,*

U.

W.

ERRATA.

Page 39, line 7, for *of,* read *or*; l. 8, for *fig.* 6, read *fig.* 8, *b*; laſt l. after *fig.* 8, add *c*; p. 47, l. 20, after *fig.* 7 add *c, c, c*; p. 48, l. 5, for *braided* read *bradded*; p. 60. l. 17 for *and,* read *at*; ibid. l. 4, from the bottom, after *diſunion* add, *until the glue is perfectly dry*; p. 62, l. 12, after *to be* read *partially ſtopped up, leaving a free paſſage to the grooves, otherwiſe,* &c. p. 64, for ſection 187, read 157; p. 65, l. 7, for *Goddy* read *Geddy*; p. 111, l. 6, from the bottom, for *Stock* read *Swarm*; p. 168, l. 16, for *riſing* read *reſting*; ibid. l. 3, from the bottom, for *in ſliders* read *ſliders in*; p. 169, l. 12, for *burt* read *bunt*; p. 183, l. 10, from the bottom, for *on* read *no*; p. 192, laſt l. for *glaſſes* read *board*; p. 197, l. 3, for *is adapted* read *was intended*; p. 219, l. 9, after *Sallows* add a*; ibid. l. 10, from the bottom, for *Garden Fennel* read *Garden Teazel*; p. 221, l. 3, from the bottom, after *ſprouts,* add *if permitted to flower*; p. 229, l. 5, for *a quarter of,* read *half*; p. 263, l. 19, after *not* add *that.*

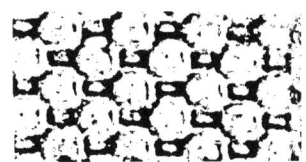

Advertiſement.

*** GENTLEMEN who do not reſide too far from London, may be furniſhed by the Author with a pair of ſtraw hives, or of boxes and ſliders, of his conſtruction, as ſtandards for others to be made by: for the inferior workmen, eſpecially in country places, are often very deficient in making them of the requiſite exactneſs without a pattern.

The hives, or boxes, to be paid for on delivery, at the *Four Swans Inn, Biſhopſgate-Street*.

N. B. Eight or ten days previous notice is requeſted.

WS - #0007 - 311220 - C0 - 229/152/22 [24] - CB - 9780331326642